FROM CRUSADES TO CONSTITUTION

THE ISLAMIC INFLUENCE IN WESTERN IDEALS

DR. MOHAMED KARIM

From Crusades to Constitution

The Islamic Influence in Western Ideals

Dr Mohamed Karim

ISBN: 9798878689311

Preface

In the Shadows of History: Zionism, Islam, and the Western World

In "From Crusades to Constitution: The Islamic Influence in Western Ideals," we embark on a historical voyage, one that not only traverses the well-trodden paths of Western civilization but also ventures into the less explored alleys and hidden corners where overlooked influences and connections lie. This book is an odyssey of discovery, challenging conventional narratives and bringing to light the intricate interplay between various forces that have shaped our world. Among these forces, a critical thread that weaves through the narrative is the birth and evolution of Zionism, a movement often discussed in modern contexts but seldom explored in its historical interconnectedness with the Islamic world and its impact on Western ideologies.

The journey of this book is rooted in a critical, investigative approach, unafraid to delve into controversy or provoke thought. We aim to uncover hidden facts, untold events, overlooked statistics, and the names of individuals and entities whose roles have been either forgotten or understated in the mainstream recounting of history. Our exploration is not just a correction of historical oversights; it's an awakening call, challenging readers to rethink established knowledge and perceptions.

As we navigate through the tumultuous period of the Crusades, we will not only see them as religious wars but also as pivotal points of cultural, economic, and ideological exchange, where the seeds of Zionism, alongside other movements, began to take root. We will explore the Renaissance, not solely as a European awakening but as a period heavily influenced by Islamic scholarship and thought, and where early Zionist ideas subtly began to form and influence the Western world.

Our narrative will traverse through the corridors of power in the Ottoman Empire and the courts of European monarchies, revealing a complex web of diplomacy, rivalry, and mutual influence, where the undercurrents of Zionism began to emerge. The rise of Protestantism with Martin Luther and John Calvin will be examined not just as a religious revolution but also in the context of how these religious upheavals paralleled, contrasted, and sometimes intersected with both Islamic principles and the nascent ideas of Zionism.

The exploration of the New World by the Spanish and Portuguese will be reevaluated as an endeavor deeply intertwined with their experiences and interactions with the Muslim world and the early Zionist thoughts. This book will also scrutinize the foundations of American ideology, searching for traces of both Islamic and Zionist influence in the very fabric of what is often considered a purely Western creation – the United States Constitution.

Moreover, this journey will draw parallels between the evolution of Zionism and the formation of the United States, highlighting similarities in their ideological underpinnings and historical trajectories. As we explore these themes, the book will shed light on the complex relationship between Zionism, Islam, and the Western world, revealing a more nuanced, interconnected, and, perhaps, controversial history.

"From Crusades to Constitution" is more than a historical account; it is a challenge to the mainstream narratives, an invitation to view our shared global history through a lens that acknowledges the significant role of Islamic and Zionist influences in the formation of Western civilization. This book is a call for a deeper understanding and a reevaluation of our past, to better comprehend the present and envision the future.

Chapter 1: The Crusades: Europe's Clash with Islam

Section 1: Historical Background of the Crusades

Introduction to the Crusades

The Crusades, often portrayed as a series of holy wars waged by Christian Europe against the Islamic powers of the Near East, form a complex tapestry of religious fervor, political intrigue, and economic ambition. This section peels back the layers of these epoch-defining events, uncovering the intricate web of circumstances that led to their inception.

The Spark of Religious Zeal

Rooted in a deep-seated religious zeal, the Crusades were propelled by the Christian call to reclaim the Holy Land from Muslim rule. This fervor was not just an expression of devout faith but also a response to the expanding influence of the Islamic world, which was perceived as a direct threat to Christendom. The declaration of the Crusades by Pope Urban II at the Council of Clermont in 1095 was as much a unifying call for the fragmented Christian kingdoms of Europe as it was a declaration of religious war.

Economic and Social Undercurrents

Beneath the religious veneer, the Crusades were fueled by economic motivations. The control of trade routes to the East, rich with spices and silk, was a significant lure for European monarchs and nobles. Moreover, the Crusades offered a solution to internal strife within Europe: diverting the aggression of warring feudal lords and restless knights towards a common external enemy.

The Impact of Earlier Islamic Conquests

To fully understand the genesis of the Crusades, one must consider the backdrop of earlier Islamic conquests. The rapid expansion of Islamic empires, starting in the 7th century, had reshaped the geopolitical landscape of the Mediterranean and beyond. The fall of key Christian territories, such as Jerusalem in 638 and later the Byzantine loss of Anatolia, had a profound psychological impact on the Christian world.

Interplay of Politics and Religion

The decision to embark on the Crusades was not merely a spiritual endeavor; it was deeply entwined with the political ambitions of European leaders. The promise of land, wealth, and titles in the East was a tantalizing prospect for European nobility. Simultaneously, the Byzantine Empire, under threat from Seljuk Turks, saw in the Crusades an opportunity to regain lost territories and reassert its dominance.

Setting the Stage for the First Crusade

As the first Crusade was called, a wave of religious and knightly fervor swept across Europe. This section sets the stage for the unprecedented mobilization of forces that would march towards the Holy Land, not fully aware of the lasting impact their actions would have on the course of history, and the intricate interplay of religious beliefs, political ambitions, and economic motivations that underpinned their journey.

Section 2: European Motivations and Goals

Diverse Motivations Behind the Crusades

The motivations driving the Crusades were as varied as the participants themselves. While religious fervor was the rallying cry, the underlying reasons encompassed a spectrum of personal, political, and economic ambitions.

Religious Zeal and the Quest for Salvation

At the heart of the Crusader's journey lay a deeply ingrained religious belief. The promise of salvation and the remission of sins for those who took up the cross were powerful motivators. This spiritual incentive, often emphasized by the clergy, tapped into the medieval Christian psyche, intertwining religious duty with the allure of heavenly reward.

Political Ambitions and the Quest for Power

Kings, princes, and nobles saw the Crusades as a pathway to expand their power and influence. For younger sons of nobility, who stood to inherit little or nothing under the laws of primogeniture, the Crusades offered a chance to acquire land and titles. For monarchs, they provided a means to assert their dominance, both at home and abroad.

Economic Gain and Adventure

The lure of the East, with its wealth and resources, was a significant draw. Many Crusaders were motivated by the prospects of acquiring riches, land, and trade opportunities. Alongside these tangible gains, the Crusades also promised adventure and a break from the monotony of feudal life, attracting not only knights and nobles but also merchants, adventurers, and those seeking a new beginning.

A Response to Islamic Expansion

It is critical to note that the Crusades were also, in part, a reaction to the centuries of Islamic expansion which had seen vast swathes of Christian lands fall under Muslim rule. The loss of these territories, especially Jerusalem, was a bitter pill for Christendom, fueling a desire for retaking lost ground.

Unification Under the Papal Banner

For the Papacy, the Crusades offered an opportunity to unify the fragmented Christian world under its leadership. It was a chance for the Pope to assert spiritual authority, not just over the Eastern Orthodox Church but also over the warring Christian kingdoms of Europe.

The First Crusade: A Mosaic of Motives

As the First Crusade commenced, it brought together a diverse array of individuals, each driven by their own unique set of motivations. From devout peasants stirred by religious zeal to ambitious nobles seeking glory and riches, the Crusader armies were a microcosm of medieval European society, united under the banner of the cross but driven by a complex web of personal, political, and economic goals.

Section 3: Key Battles and Turning Points

Pivotal Conflicts of the Crusades

The Crusades were marked by numerous battles and sieges, each with its own significance and impact on the course of history. This section examines some of the most crucial conflicts and turning points that defined this era.

The Siege of Jerusalem (1099)

The First Crusade culminated in the Siege of Jerusalem, a brutal and pivotal event that led to the capture of the city by the Crusaders. The siege was characterized by intense combat and concluded with the mass slaughter of the city's Muslim and Jewish inhabitants, an act that left an indelible scar and set a precedent for religious brutality in the conflicts to come.

The Battle of Hattin (1187)

The Battle of Hattin was a turning point in the Crusader-Muslim conflicts. Led by the charismatic Muslim leader Saladin, the Islamic forces decisively defeated the Crusaders, leading to the recapture of Jerusalem. This battle not only demonstrated Saladin's military prowess but also his chivalry, as he treated his captives with respect, contrasting sharply with the earlier conduct of the Crusaders in Jerusalem.

The Siege of Acre (1189-1191)

The Siege of Acre, part of the Third Crusade, was one of the longest and bloodiest sieges of the Crusades. It ended in a costly victory for the Crusaders and marked the beginning of the struggle for the Holy Land's coastal cities, pivotal for maintaining supply lines and military reinforcements from Europe.

The Fourth Crusade and the Sack of Constantinople (1204)

In a dramatic deviation from its original goal, the Fourth Crusade ended with the Crusaders sacking Constantinople, the capital of the Christian Byzantine Empire. This event was a significant betrayal and profoundly weakened Christendom, both militarily and morally, while also deepening the rift between the Roman Catholic and Eastern Orthodox Churches.

The Battle of Ain Jalut (1260)

Although not a battle involving Crusaders directly, the Battle of Ain Jalut, where the Mamluks of Egypt defeated the Mongols, had significant implications for the Crusades. It marked the first substantial defeat of the Mongols and ensured that the Muslim Near East would not fall into Mongol hands, thereby indirectly impacting the Crusader states.

Impact and Legacy of These Conflicts

Each of these battles and sieges was not just a military engagement but also a moment that shaped the cultural, religious, and political landscape of the era. They left a legacy of heroism, tragedy, and a complex interplay of faith and power that resonates through history to the present day.

This section provides an overview of key military engagements during the Crusades,

Section 4: Impact on European Mindset

Shaping the European Consciousness

The Crusades had a profound and lasting impact on the European mindset, influencing not just contemporaneous views but also shaping European identity and perceptions for centuries.

The Crusader Mentality

The experience of the Crusades fostered a distinct 'Crusader mentality' characterized by a mix of religious fervor, martial valor, and a sense of superiority over non-Christian cultures. This mentality permeated European society, from the noble knights who led the charge to the common folk who supported these endeavors either in spirit or in person.

Perceptions of Islam and the East

The Crusades significantly shaped European perceptions of Islam and Eastern societies. Muslims were often depicted as the antithesis of Christian virtues, a viewpoint that was sometimes more reflective of European anxieties and prejudices than the reality of Islamic culture and civilization. This simplistic binary narrative overlooked the complexities and nuances of the Muslim world, contributing to long-standing misconceptions and stereotypes.

Impact on Religious Tolerance

The brutality and intolerance exhibited during the Crusades had a lasting impact on European attitudes towards religious diversity. This period marked a turning point where religious coexistence, particularly in regions like the Iberian Peninsula and the Eastern Mediterranean, gave way to increasing sectarianism and strife.

The Legacy of the Military Orders

The Crusades saw the rise of military orders like the Knights Templar and the Knights Hospitaller. These organizations, with their unique blend of monasticism and militarism, left a lasting legacy in European society. They influenced not only military tactics and organization but also banking, trade, and cultural patronage.

Crusades and the Feudal System

The mobilization for the Crusades had significant social and economic repercussions on the feudal system. Participation in the Crusades was costly, leading many nobles to sell or mortgage their lands, thus gradually shifting the feudal power dynamics. Additionally, the absence of many lords during the Crusades led to changes in local governance and increased the power of the monarchy in some regions.

Intellectual and Cultural Exchange

Despite the often-hostile nature of the Crusades, they facilitated a significant exchange of knowledge and culture between the Islamic world and Europe. This exchange influenced European art, architecture, science, and learning, setting the stage for the Renaissance.

Section 5: Lessons Learned and Missed Opportunities

A Dual Legacy of Enlightenment and Entrenchment

The Crusades, a series of conflicts spanning centuries, left behind a legacy of both enlightenment and missed opportunities. This section examines the lessons learned and those that were overlooked, offering insights into how history's course might have changed under different circumstances.

Lessons in Military Strategy and Technology

The Crusades served as a crucible for military innovation and strategy. Europeans were exposed to advanced Islamic military techniques, including siege warfare and naval tactics, which they later adapted and adopted. This period also saw the introduction of new technologies, such as the crossbow and improved ship designs, which would significantly impact European warfare.

Diplomatic Engagements and Missed Peace Opportunities

There were moments during the Crusades where diplomacy took precedence over warfare. These instances, however, were often short-lived, overshadowed by the overarching goal of conquest. The failure to seize these opportunities for lasting peace and mutual understanding between Christian and Muslim powers was a missed opportunity with long-lasting repercussions.

Economic Lessons: Trade and Commerce

The Crusades opened up new trade routes and introduced Europeans to a variety of goods from the East, leading to an increased appetite for spices, silk, and other luxuries. This exposure would later drive the Age of Exploration. However, the heavy cost of financing crusading expeditions also led to economic strain in many European states, illustrating the double-edged nature of such ventures.

Cultural Exchange and Intellectual Enrichment

While the Crusades are often remembered for their violence and intolerance, they also facilitated a considerable exchange of ideas and culture. Europeans came into contact with the rich intellectual and artistic traditions of the Islamic world, leading to a transfer of knowledge in areas such as medicine, mathematics, and philosophy. This cultural osmosis laid the groundwork for the Renaissance but was often underappreciated at the time.

Religious Intolerance and the Seeds of Conflict

One of the most enduring lessons of the Crusades was the deep entrenchment of religious intolerance. The campaigns cemented an 'us versus them' mentality that would fuel religious conflicts for centuries. The failure to foster religious tolerance and understanding during and after the Crusades represents a significant missed opportunity for early interfaith harmony.

The Crusades as a Historical Mirror

The Crusades act as a mirror reflecting the complexities of human nature — our capacity for both great achievements and profound shortsightedness. By examining the lessons learned and those that were missed, we gain a deeper understanding of the multifaceted nature of this historical period and its enduring impact on the world.

Section 6: Trade and Cultural Exchanges

The Unintended Consequences of Conflict

While the Crusades are often remembered for their religious and military aspects, one of their most enduring legacies was the facilitation of trade and cultural exchanges between Europe and the Islamic world. This section delves into how these interactions, born out of conflict, shaped the economic and cultural landscapes of both regions.

The Revival of European Trade

The Crusades opened up the East to European traders, leading to a revival of trade in the Mediterranean and beyond. Cities like Venice and Genoa became bustling centers of commerce, trading in spices, silk, and other exotic goods from the Islamic world. This trade had a profound impact on the European economy, stimulating growth and leading to the development of new financial practices.

Cultural Exchange: Art, Architecture, and Learning

Cultural exchange was an inevitable consequence of the Crusades. Europeans encountered advanced Islamic art, architecture, and learning, which left a lasting impression. The influence of Islamic architecture and art can be seen in the Gothic style that emerged in Europe, while translated Islamic texts on subjects like mathematics, astronomy, and medicine played a crucial role in European scientific advancements.

Transmission of Knowledge

The Crusades facilitated the transfer of knowledge from the Islamic world to Europe. European scholars gained access to ancient Greek texts that had been preserved and expanded upon by Muslim scholars. This transfer of knowledge was pivotal in igniting the European Renaissance, challenging existing dogmas, and fostering new ways of thinking.

The Spice Trade and European Cuisine

The spice trade, a lucrative aspect of Crusader commerce, had a significant impact on European cuisine. Spices such as pepper, cinnamon, and nutmeg, previously rare and expensive, became more commonplace, leading to a transformation in European culinary tastes.

Linguistic and Literary Influences

The interaction between Crusaders and the Islamic world also led to linguistic exchanges. The introduction of new words into European languages, many of Arabic origin, reflects the deep cultural interplay of this period. Furthermore, the narratives of the Crusades, both in Europe and the Islamic world, enriched the literary traditions of both cultures, contributing to a rich legacy of epic poetry, chronicles, and travelogues.

A Complex Web of Influence

The trade and cultural exchanges resulting from the Crusades were complex and multifaceted. They were not just a byproduct of conflict but a testament to the interconnectedness of civilizations. These exchanges played a crucial role in shaping the intellectual and cultural landscapes of both Europe and the Islamic world, demonstrating how, even in times of conflict, the exchange of goods, ideas, and culture can have far-reaching and transformative effects.

Section 7: The Role of the Church

The Church as a Driving Force

The role of the Church in the Crusades was pivotal, acting as both a spiritual guide and a political entity. This section examines how the Church influenced the course of the Crusades and the broader implications of its involvement.

Papal Authority and the Call to Arms

The Crusades were initiated by Papal decree, demonstrating the immense power and influence of the Church in medieval Europe. Pope Urban II's call for the First Crusade at the Council of Clermont in 1095 was a masterstroke of religious rhetoric, framing the campaign as a holy war to reclaim the Holy Land, offering salvation and indulgences to those who joined.

Spiritual Justification for War

The Church played a crucial role in providing the spiritual justification for the Crusades. By framing them as a religious duty, the Church effectively mobilized a wide cross-section of European society, from nobles to peasants. The concept of fighting for God's will was a powerful motivator that transcended traditional feudal loyalties.

The Church's Diplomatic Role

The Church also acted as a diplomatic entity, negotiating alliances, organizing logistics, and sometimes mediating disputes among the Crusading leaders. This role showcased the Church's ability to operate as a political power, influencing the strategies and outcomes of the Crusades.

Management of Crusader States

In the Crusader states established in the Holy Land, the Church played a significant administrative role. It was involved in governing these territories, managing relations with local populations, and overseeing the spiritual welfare of the Crusader kingdoms.

Impact on Church Doctrine and Policy

The Crusades had a significant impact on Church doctrine and policy. The concept of a holy war, initially controversial, became more accepted within Christian theology due to the

Crusades. Additionally, the Church's involvement in these military campaigns helped to solidify its position as a central authority in both spiritual and temporal matters.

Long-Term Effects on the Church's Power

While the Crusades initially bolstered the Church's power and prestige, they also exposed its limitations. Failures and setbacks, especially in the later Crusades, led to increased criticism and diminished the Church's moral authority in some quarters. The loss of Jerusalem and the eventual failure of the Crusader states dealt a blow to the Church's claim of divinely sanctioned success.

Section 8: Muslim Perspective and Response

Understanding the Other Side of the Story

The Crusades, often viewed through a European lens, were also a pivotal chapter in Islamic history. This section explores the Muslim perspective on the Crusades, their response, and the broader implications for the Islamic world.

Initial Muslim Reactions to the Crusades

The first wave of Crusaders took many in the Muslim world by surprise. Initially, there was a lack of unified response, partly due to the fragmented nature of the Muslim Near East, with various local rulers and dynasties vying for power. The Crusades were initially seen as just another in a long line of conflicts, not fully realizing the scale or the religious fervor driving the Europeans.

Rise of Muslim Leaders and Unification

The Crusades eventually led to a greater sense of unity among Muslim rulers, particularly under the leadership of figures like Saladin (Salah al-Din Yusuf ibn Ayyub). Saladin's successful recapture of Jerusalem and his ability to unite different Muslim factions under a common cause was a turning point, showcasing a more organized and effective response to the Crusades.

Jihad: The Islamic Counter-Crusade

In response to the Crusades, the concept of Jihad, or holy struggle, gained prominence in the Islamic world. It was used not only as a call to arms to defend Muslim lands but also as a rallying cry for unity and resilience against the Crusader invasions.

Diplomacy and Coexistence

Despite the overarching conflict, there were periods of diplomacy and coexistence between Muslim rulers and the Crusader states. Trade and political agreements were not uncommon, indicating a level of pragmatism and mutual benefit, even in times of religious and ideological opposition.

Cultural and Intellectual Resilience

The Islamic world, though facing military challenges, continued to flourish culturally and intellectually during the Crusades. Centers of learning like Baghdad, Damascus, and Cairo remained hubs of scholarship, contributing to advancements in science, medicine, and philosophy.

The Crusades' Impact on Islamic Identity

The Crusades had a lasting impact on Islamic identity and consciousness. They are remembered as a period of both challenge and resilience, contributing to a narrative of resistance and survival in the face of external aggression. This period also reinforced the importance of Jerusalem and other holy sites in the Islamic tradition.

Legacy and Historical Memory

In the Islamic world, the memory of the Crusades is interwoven with historical narratives of resistance against foreign invasion. The Crusades are often cited as an early example of Western intervention in the Middle East, shaping perceptions and attitudes towards the West that persist in some forms to this day.

Section 9: Legacy of the Crusades

The Enduring Echoes of a Bygone Era

The Crusades, spanning nearly two centuries, left an indelible mark on both the Western and Islamic worlds. This section delves into the multifaceted legacy of these conflicts, exploring how they shaped subsequent history and continue to resonate in the modern world.

Shaping Modern European Identity

The Crusades played a crucial role in the formation of a European identity. The concept of a united Christendom, though never fully realized, was a powerful idea that transcended national boundaries. The tales of valor and piety from the Crusades entered European folklore, literature, and art, becoming an integral part of the cultural heritage.

Influencing International Law and Warfare

The nature and conduct of the Crusades had a significant impact on the development of international law and the rules of warfare. While the Crusades were marked by brutality and disregard for non-combatants, they also sparked early discussions about the ethics of war, treatment of prisoners, and protection of holy sites, laying groundwork for future international humanitarian principles.

Economic Impact and the Growth of Trade

The Crusades facilitated the growth of long-distance trade, leading to economic development in various parts of Europe. The demand for Eastern goods spurred exploration and the eventual search for alternative trade routes, culminating in the Age of Discovery.

Impact on Architecture and Urban Development

The return of Crusaders to Europe brought new architectural styles and innovations, influenced by Islamic architecture encountered in the East. This exchange led to significant developments in European architecture, visible in the Gothic style of cathedrals and fortifications.

Perpetuating Religious and Cultural Misunderstandings

One of the more troubling legacies of the Crusades is the perpetuation of religious and cultural misunderstandings. The simplistic portrayal of Muslims as the 'infidel enemy' in Crusader rhetoric contributed to long-standing stereotypes and prejudices, affecting interfaith relations for centuries.

The Crusades in Islamic Historical Memory

In the Islamic world, the Crusades are remembered as a period of resistance against foreign invasion. This historical memory has influenced Islamic perspectives on Western interventions and relations, contributing to a narrative of defense against external threats.

Modern Relevance and Misappropriation

In contemporary times, the Crusades are sometimes invoked in political and religious rhetoric, often misappropriated or simplified to suit modern agendas. The complexity and nuances of these historical events are frequently overshadowed by their use as symbols in contemporary conflicts and discussions.

Section 10: Setting the Stage for Exploration

The Crusades as a Precursor to the Age of Exploration

The final section of this chapter examines how the Crusades set the stage for the subsequent Age of Exploration, marking the beginning of a new era in European history.

Introduction to Global Connectivity

The Crusades were among the first events in European history that created a sense of global connectivity. The need to reach the Holy Land sparked interest in long-distance travel and navigation, planting seeds for the later European ventures across the oceans.

Exposure to New Cultures and Geographies

The interaction with the Islamic world during the Crusades exposed Europeans to different cultures, languages, and knowledge systems. This exposure broadened European horizons, making them more receptive to the idea of exploring and engaging with distant lands and peoples.

Technological Advances and Nautical Skills

The challenges of mounting and sustaining long crusading campaigns led to advancements in shipbuilding, navigation, and military technology. These advancements were crucial in equipping European explorers with the tools and skills necessary for oceanic exploration.

Demand for Eastern Goods and Alternative Trade Routes

The Crusades intensified European demand for Eastern goods like spices, silk, and precious metals. As the overland routes controlled by Muslim powers were difficult and expensive, there was a growing interest in finding sea routes to Asia, which later fueled expeditions by explorers like Vasco da Gama and Christopher Columbus.

Economic Motivations: From Pilgrimage to Profit

While the Crusades began primarily as religious pilgrimages, they gradually took on more economic motivations. This shift from religious to economic objectives was a precursor to the Age of Exploration, where the quest for trade and new territories became primary drivers.

The Crusader States and Early Colonialism

The establishment and governance of Crusader states in the Near East provided Europeans with early experience in overseas administration and colonization. These experiences offered lessons (both positive and negative) in dealing with foreign cultures and managing distant territories.

A Changed Perspective on the World

The Crusades fundamentally changed the European perspective of the world. They broke down the insular mindset of medieval Europe, igniting a curiosity and ambition that would drive the Age of Exploration. This period marked the beginning of Europe's long and often tumultuous engagement with the wider world, setting the stage for the global interactions that would define the modern era.

Chapter 2: Ottoman Dominance and European Navigation

Section 1: The Ottoman Empire's Rise

The Emergence of a New Power

This section delves into the rise of the Ottoman Empire and how its expansion influenced European navigation and exploration strategies.

Origins and Early Expansion

The Ottoman Empire's origins in the late 13th and early 14th centuries marked the emergence of a new power in the Islamic world. From a small principality in Anatolia, the Ottomans rapidly expanded their territory, showcasing military prowess and strategic acumen.

Consolidation of Power

Key to the Ottoman rise was their consolidation of power in the region. Through a combination of military conquests, diplomatic maneuvering, and alliances, the Ottomans established themselves as a dominant force in the Near East, eventually taking Constantinople in 1453, a watershed moment in world history.

Impact on the Byzantine Empire

The Ottoman expansion directly impacted the Byzantine Empire, contributing to its decline and fall. The loss of Constantinople not only symbolized the end of the Byzantine era but also had profound implications for Europe, as it disrupted traditional trade routes and instilled a sense of urgency to find alternate paths to the East.

Control Over Land Trade Routes

As the Ottomans expanded, they gained control over key land trade routes, particularly those linking Europe to Asia. This control allowed them to monopolize the lucrative spice trade, prompting Europeans to seek new trade routes that bypassed Ottoman territories.

Military Strength and Naval Power

The Ottomans' military strength was not limited to land; they also developed a formidable naval force. This naval power enabled them to control major parts of the Mediterranean, further challenging European powers and impacting their maritime strategies.

Cultural and Administrative Sophistication

The Ottoman Empire was not just a military power; it also developed a sophisticated administrative system and embraced a rich cultural and artistic heritage. The empire became a melting pot of different cultures and religions, reflecting the diversity of its territories.

A Catalyst for European Exploration

The rise of the Ottoman Empire acted as a catalyst for European exploration. The need to find alternative routes to the East for trade purposes became more pressing in the face of Ottoman dominance. This urgency would eventually lead to the Age of Exploration, where European powers sought new paths to the riches of Asia, inadvertently leading to the discovery of the New World.

Section 2: Control Over Trade Routes

The Ottoman Monopoly on Eastern Commerce

This section examines how the Ottoman Empire's control over key trade routes affected European commerce, leading to significant shifts in global trade dynamics.

Strategic Geographic Position

The Ottoman Empire's strategic position at the crossroads of Europe and Asia granted it control over critical land routes, including the Silk Road. This control allowed the Ottomans to exert significant influence over the flow of goods, particularly luxury items like spices, silk, and precious stones, from East to Asia.

Impact on European Traders

European traders, particularly those from maritime republics like Venice and Genoa, had previously thrived on the trade with the East. The Ottoman ascendancy disrupted these traditional routes, imposing higher tariffs and, in some cases, outright monopolies, which significantly increased the cost and reduced the profitability of trade for European merchants.

Search for Sea Routes

In response to the Ottoman control of land routes, European powers, notably Spain and Portugal, began to invest in maritime exploration. Their goal was to discover sea routes to Asia that would bypass Ottoman-controlled territories, allowing direct access to the sources of coveted goods.

The Spice Trade as a Driving Force

The spice trade was particularly crucial in this era. Spices were highly valued in Europe for their use in cuisine, medicine, and preservation. The high demand and profitability of spices like pepper, cinnamon, and cloves motivated European explorers to embark on hazardous voyages in search of new trade routes.

Technological Advancements in Navigation

The necessity to find new routes spurred advancements in navigation and shipbuilding. Innovations such as the astrolabe, the magnetic compass, and the caravel made longer sea voyages feasible, setting the stage for the great explorations of the 15th and 16th centuries.

A Shift in Global Trade Dynamics

The Ottoman control of trade routes inadvertently catalyzed a shift in global trade dynamics. The European quest to bypass Ottoman territory not only led to the discovery of new lands but also to the eventual establishment of European colonial empires. This shift had profound and lasting impacts on the global economic and political landscape.

Section 3: The Quest for Alternative Routes

Europe's Navigational Pivot

In this section, we explore how the control of the traditional trade routes by the Ottoman Empire prompted European powers to seek alternative pathways to the riches of Asia, eventually influencing the discovery of the New World and laying the groundwork for ideas that would shape the United States Constitution.

The Age of Exploration Begins

Spanish and Portuguese Ventures: Spain and Portugal, located on the geographical periphery of Europe and thus less hindered by Ottoman control, led the charge in maritime exploration. Notable figures like Prince Henry the Navigator of Portugal played pivotal roles in this endeavor. Motivation for New Routes: The primary motivation was economic – to access the wealth of Asia by sea. However, these explorations also carried religious and strategic objectives, echoing the Crusader mentality of spreading Christianity and countering Islamic influence.

Technological Advancements and Maritime Skills

Navigational Tools and Shipbuilding: The necessity to navigate open oceans led to significant advancements in navigation and shipbuilding. The development of the caravel, along with innovations like the astrolabe and improved cartography, made transoceanic voyages feasible. Knowledge Exchange: This period saw a blend of knowledge from various cultures, including Islamic and Chinese navigational and maritime technologies, which were crucial in enabling these voyages.

Discovery of the New World

Columbus and Subsequent Explorers: Christopher Columbus's voyage in 1492, which was initially aimed at finding a westward route to Asia, led to the unexpected discovery of the Americas. This opened a new chapter in world history, leading to further explorations and the eventual colonization of the New World.

Impact on European Worldview

Expansion of Worldview: The discovery of new lands expanded the European worldview, challenging existing perceptions and knowledge. This period marked the beginning of a global consciousness in Europe.

From Exploration to Enlightenment

The Seed of Enlightenment: The Age of Exploration set the stage for the Enlightenment, a philosophical movement that emphasized reason, individualism, and a scientific approach to understanding the world. These principles would later influence the founding fathers of the United States.

Influence on American Constitutional Thought

Emerging Ideas of Governance and Rights: The encounter with diverse cultures and governance systems, along with the philosophical developments of the Enlightenment, contributed to a new understanding of governance, sovereignty, and individual rights. These ideas would find expression in the American Constitution, mirroring, in some ways, the complex interplay of religious, cultural, and political ideas inherited from the Crusades through the Age of Exploration.

Section 4: Economic Implications

The Shift in Global Economics

This section explores the economic implications of the Ottoman dominance over trade routes and how it catalyzed significant changes in global economic patterns, laying the groundwork for economic principles that would later influence American constitutional economics.

European Economic Transformation

From Feudal Economy to Global Trade: The need to find new trade routes contributed to the shift from a feudal, land-based economy to a mercantile, trade-oriented economy in Europe. This transformation was a precursor to the modern capitalist system.
Growth of Merchant Classes: The Age of Exploration led to the rise of powerful merchant classes in European societies. These merchants, who gained wealth and influence through trade, would later play a crucial role in promoting ideas of economic freedom and property rights.

Ottoman Influence on European Trade

Monopolies and Trade Control: The Ottoman control of land routes forced Europeans to seek maritime trade routes, inadvertently leading to the discovery of new continents and the opening of global trade networks.
Competition and Military Spending: The competition with the Ottoman Empire also led to increased military spending in Europe, spurring advancements in military technology and naval power.

The Birth of the Global Economy

Intercontinental Trade Networks: The European pursuit of alternative trade routes led to the establishment of intercontinental trade networks, integrating economies across continents and laying the foundation for the global economy.
Colonialism and Resource Exploitation: The discovery of new lands eventually led to colonization, with European powers exploiting the natural resources and labor of colonized regions, a practice that would have lasting economic and social repercussions.

Impact on American Economic Ideals

Foundations of American Economic Thought: The economic transformations in Europe influenced the economic philosophies of the American Founding Fathers. Concepts such as free trade, private property, and economic liberty were embedded in the foundations of the United States Constitution.
Reflections in the Constitution: The U.S. Constitution's provisions on commerce, taxation, and property rights can be traced back to these economic shifts. The framers sought to create an economic system that balanced regulation with freedom, influenced by their understanding of European economic evolution.

Section 5: Cultural and Knowledge Exchange

Bridging Civilizations Through Contact

This section examines the cultural and intellectual exchanges between the Ottoman Empire and Europe during the Age of Exploration and how these interactions contributed to the intellectual environment that influenced the formation of the United States Constitution.

Influence of Ottoman Culture on Europe

Artistic and Architectural Influences: The contact with the Ottoman Empire introduced Europeans to new artistic styles and architectural designs. The infusion of these elements can be seen in the Renaissance art and architecture, which blended Eastern and Western aesthetics.
Adoption of Exotic Goods: European tastes were transformed by the adoption of goods such as coffee and textiles, which became symbols of refinement and sophistication in European society.

Knowledge Exchange and Intellectual Growth

Transmission of Scientific Knowledge: The Ottomans, as custodians of Islamic and ancient Greek knowledge, played a crucial role in the transfer of scientific and philosophical texts to Europe. This knowledge exchange was instrumental in the Scientific Revolution and the Enlightenment.
Linguistic and Literary Impacts: The interaction with the Ottoman world enriched European languages, introducing new words and concepts. It also inspired a wealth of literature, from travelogues to fictional works, broadening the European literary canon.

The Enlightenment and Constitutional Thought

Philosophical Interchange: The Enlightenment, influenced by the influx of new ideas and knowledge from the Islamic world and other cultures encountered during exploration, fostered a climate of intellectual curiosity and skepticism about traditional authority, which influenced the philosophical underpinnings of the U.S. Constitution.
Ideas of Governance and Rights: Exposure to different cultures and governance systems broadened European perspectives on law, human rights, and statecraft. These ideas were reflected in the debates and writings of the American Founding Fathers.

The Role of Ottoman Diplomacy

Diplomatic Exchanges and Understanding: The diplomatic relations between European states and the Ottoman Empire provided a framework for international diplomacy and law. The complexities of these interactions contributed to a deeper understanding of foreign policy and international relations in Western thought.
Influence on American Diplomatic Traditions: The experiences of European powers in negotiating with the Ottomans influenced the development of diplomatic practices and principles in the United States, including concepts of sovereignty and international engagement.

Section 6: The Spice Trade and Its Lures

The Economic Engine Behind Exploration

This section explores the pivotal role of the spice trade in driving European exploration, its impact on global economic patterns, and how these economic shifts influenced the emerging economic theories that would later shape American constitutional thought.

The Allure of Eastern Spices

High Demand in Europe: Spices such as pepper, cloves, cinnamon, and nutmeg were in high demand in Europe for their culinary, medicinal, and preservative properties. Their rarity and the long, perilous journey they took from the East made them incredibly valuable.
Cultural and Social Significance: Beyond their practical uses, spices held cultural and social significance in Europe. They were symbols of wealth and status and played a role in the social rituals of the European elite.

Ottoman Control and European Response

Monopoly Over Land Routes: The Ottoman Empire's control over land routes to the East significantly increased the cost of spices in Europe, creating a strong economic incentive for Europeans to find alternative routes to the spice-rich lands of Asia.
Motivation for Maritime Exploration: The lucrative spice trade was a major driving force behind the Age of Exploration. European powers sought maritime routes to Asia to bypass Ottoman-controlled land routes, leading to significant maritime advancements.

Impact on Global Trade Networks

Establishment of New Trade Routes: The European quest for spices led to the establishment of new maritime trade routes, reshaping global trade networks. This shift had a profound impact on the economies of both Europe and the regions they explored and colonized.
Rise of Trading Companies: The spice trade gave rise to powerful European trading companies, such as the Dutch East India Company and the British East India Company. These companies played a significant role in the early global economy and colonial expansion.

Influences on American Economic Thought

Emerging Capitalist Principles: The spice trade and its economic implications contributed to the development of early capitalist principles in Europe. These principles, emphasizing trade, private enterprise, and market competition, influenced the economic ideas of the American Founding Fathers.
Constitutional Provisions on Trade and Commerce: The importance of trade in the Age of Exploration is reflected in the United States Constitution's provisions on commerce. The framers recognized the significance of trade in economic development and sought to create a framework that facilitated commerce and protected economic interests.

Section 7: The Economic Implications

Transforming the European Economic Landscape

This section explores the broader economic implications of the Ottoman dominance and European navigation efforts, focusing on how these developments influenced the economic landscape of Europe and subsequently impacted the economic philosophies that shaped early American governance.

Shift in Trade Dynamics

Decentralization of Trade: The Ottoman control over traditional land routes forced European powers to explore alternative sea routes, leading to a decentralization of trade. This shift reduced the dominance of traditional trade centers and gave rise to new economic powers in Europe.
Growth of Maritime Economies: Maritime nations like Portugal, Spain, the Netherlands, and England experienced significant economic growth as they established new trade routes and colonies. This growth marked a shift from land-based power to naval and trade power.

Emergence of Capitalism

Rise of Capitalist Practices: The need to finance expensive voyages and trade expeditions led to the development of joint-stock companies and the emergence of stock exchanges. These institutions were foundational in the development of modern capitalist economies.
Private Enterprise and Risk-Taking: The Age of Exploration fostered a culture of risk-taking and private enterprise. This entrepreneurial spirit would be a crucial influence on American economic thought, emphasizing the role of private initiative and risk in economic growth.

Globalization of Trade

Creation of Global Trade Networks: The European navigation efforts led to the creation of global trade networks, connecting continents and cultures. This early form of globalization had far-reaching economic and social implications, laying the groundwork for the interconnected global economy of today.
Impact on Indigenous Economies: The European expansion had significant impacts on indigenous economies around the world. The introduction of new goods, the exploitation of resources, and the integration into global trade networks fundamentally altered local economic structures.

Influence on American Economic Foundations

Adaptation of European Economic Practices: The economic practices developed during this era, such as banking, joint-stock companies, and international trade, were adapted and implemented in the American colonies. They influenced the economic systems and policies of the early United States.
Constitutional Provisions Reflecting Economic Shifts: The United States Constitution reflects the economic realities and philosophies of the time. Provisions regarding commerce, taxation, and property rights demonstrate the influence of European economic transformations initiated during the Age of Exploration.

Section 8: Cultural and Knowledge Exchange

The Interplay of Civilizations

This section delves into the rich cultural and intellectual exchanges between the Ottoman Empire, Europe, and the regions explored during the Age of Exploration, highlighting how these interactions contributed to the evolving cultural and intellectual landscape that influenced the formation of American constitutional ideas.

Influence of Ottoman and Islamic Culture on Europe

Artistic and Scholarly Influence: The contact with the Ottoman Empire and the broader Islamic world introduced Europeans to a range of artistic styles, scientific knowledge, and philosophical ideas. This exchange significantly influenced the European Renaissance, contributing to developments in art, science, and literature.
Adoption and Adaptation of Ideas: Europeans not only borrowed from Islamic culture but also adapted these ideas, creating a unique blend that reflected the intercultural dialogue of the era.

Expansion of Worldview through Exploration

Encounters with Diverse Cultures: European explorers encountered diverse cultures, customs, and governance systems in Africa, Asia, and the Americas. These encounters challenged existing European worldviews and broadened their understanding of human societies.
Transmission of New Knowledge: The information and experiences gathered during these explorations were transmitted back to Europe, where they influenced scientific, cultural, and philosophical thought.

Impact on Enlightenment Philosophy

Influencing Enlightenment Thinkers: The cultural and intellectual exchanges of this period played a crucial role in shaping the Enlightenment, a philosophical movement that emphasized reason, individual rights, and scientific inquiry. Enlightenment philosophy significantly influenced the American Founding Fathers.
Concepts of Governance and Liberty: Exposure to different systems of governance and ideas about liberty during these exchanges informed European political thought. These ideas were instrumental in shaping the political philosophies underlying the U.S. Constitution.

The Role of Ottoman Diplomacy and Interaction

Diplomatic Exchanges: The diplomatic relations between the Ottoman Empire and European powers provided insights into foreign policy and international law, contributing to the development of diplomatic practices that influenced early American diplomacy.
Understanding of Sovereignty and International Relations: Interactions with the Ottoman Empire, which had a sophisticated system of governance and law, helped shape European understanding of sovereignty and international relations, concepts that would be integral to the development of American constitutional governance.

Section 9: The Impact of Islamic Naval Power

Navigating New Waters: The Influence of Islamic Maritime Strength

This section explores how the naval power of the Islamic world, particularly the Ottoman Empire, influenced European maritime strategies and contributed to the advancements in naval technology that were crucial for European exploration and the eventual shaping of American naval and trade policies.

Ottoman Naval Dominance in the Mediterranean

Formidable Ottoman Fleet: The Ottoman Empire, under leaders like Suleiman the Magnificent, developed a powerful navy that dominated the Mediterranean. This presented a significant challenge to European powers, particularly to their ambitions in the region.
Mediterranean as a Battleground: Key naval battles in the Mediterranean, such as the Battle of Lepanto, showcased the might of the Ottoman fleet and its tactical innovations, prompting European powers to enhance their naval capabilities.

European Response and Naval Advancements

Naval Arms Race: The threat posed by the Ottoman navy acted as a catalyst for a naval arms race in Europe. This competition led to significant advancements in shipbuilding, armaments, and naval tactics.
Development of the Galleon: The European response included the development of the galleon, a large, multi-decked sailing ship that was faster and more heavily armed. These ships were instrumental in long-distance voyages and in establishing European presence overseas.

Influence on Global Exploration

Redefining Maritime Exploration: The advancements in naval technology not only allowed Europe to challenge Ottoman dominance but also enabled them to embark on transoceanic voyages. This period marked the beginning of an era of global exploration and eventual colonization.
Mapping and Navigational Skills: Encounters with Islamic naval power also led to improvements in mapping and navigational skills, essential for the success of long voyages. The blend of Islamic and European navigational knowledge was crucial in this development.

Implications for Early American Naval Power

Foundations of American Naval Tradition: The naval traditions and technologies developed during this time influenced the early American naval policies. The United States, in its formative years, looked to these European models to develop its own navy, crucial for protecting its interests and trade routes.
Constitutional Provisions on Naval Power: The U.S. Constitution's provisions regarding the establishment of a navy reflect the importance of naval power recognized during this era. The framers understood the significance of a strong navy in international relations and trade protection.

Section 10: Resource Exploitation and Trade Dynamics

The Economic Consequences of Exploration and Colonization

This section discusses how the European response to Ottoman dominance and the subsequent Age of Exploration led to the exploitation of resources in newly discovered lands, shaping the dynamics of global trade and influencing early American economic policies and practices.

The Drive for Resources

European Quest for Wealth: The search for alternate routes to Asia was not only about spices but also about finding new sources of wealth. This quest led to the exploitation of resources in the Americas, Africa, and Asia, fundamentally altering global trade dynamics.
Impact on Indigenous Populations: The arrival of Europeans in the New World and other regions led to significant consequences for indigenous populations, including displacement, forced labor, and the introduction of new diseases.

Colonial Trade Networks

Establishment of Colonial Economies: European powers established colonial economies in the territories they conquered. These economies were often based on the extraction of valuable resources like gold, silver, and agricultural products.
The Triangle Trade: A complex trade network developed, linking Europe, Africa, and the Americas. This included the transatlantic slave trade, which became a central element of the colonial economy and had lasting social and economic impacts.

Influence on Mercantilism

Development of Mercantilist Policies: The economic practices during this period contributed to the development of mercantilism, an economic theory that emphasized the accumulation of wealth, primarily through trade. Mercantilism influenced European economic policies and had a lasting impact on international economic relations.
Mercantilism in American Economic Thought: The mercantilist policies of the colonial powers, especially Britain, affected the economic development of the American colonies. This influence was evident in the early economic debates and policies of the United States.

Reflections in the U.S. Constitution

Constitutional Provisions on Trade and Economy: The U.S. Constitution reflects the complex trade dynamics and economic realities of the time. Provisions regarding commerce, taxation, and regulation of trade were influenced by the experiences of colonial exploitation and the mercantilist policies of European powers.
Foundations of American Economic Policy: The framers of the Constitution sought to create an economic system that balanced free trade with regulation, drawing on the lessons learned from the colonial experience and the evolving global economy.

Chapter 3: The Reconquista and the New World

Section 1: Background and Overview of the Reconquista

Setting the Stage for a New Era

This section provides an overview of the Reconquista, the centuries-long campaign to reclaim Iberian territories from Muslim rule, and how this pivotal period in European history set the stage for the exploration and colonization of the New World, influencing the cultural and political landscape that would eventually shape American ideals.

Origins of the Reconquista

Historical Context: The Reconquista began in the early 8th century following the Muslim conquest of the Iberian Peninsula. It was not a continuous effort but a series of campaigns by various Christian kingdoms aiming to reclaim lands controlled by Muslim states.

Religious and Cultural Significance: The Reconquista was deeply embedded in the religious and cultural identity of the Iberian Christian kingdoms. It was seen as a holy war, similar to the Crusades, with the aim of restoring Christian rule over lost territories.

Evolution of the Campaign

Fragmented Efforts to Unified Crusade: Initially, the Reconquista was characterized by fragmented efforts from individual Christian kingdoms. Over time, it evolved into a more unified crusade, especially following significant victories like the capture of Toledo in 1085.
Role of Religious Orders: Various religious and military orders played a crucial role in the Reconquista, mobilizing resources and fighters in the name of Christian conquest and consolidation.

The Fall of Granada and Its Aftermath

Completion of the Reconquista: The campaign culminated in 1492 with the fall of Granada, the last Muslim stronghold in Iberia. This event marked the end of 700 years of Muslim presence in the Iberian Peninsula.
Cultural and Demographic Shifts: The completion of the Reconquista led to significant cultural and demographic changes, including the forced conversion, expulsion, or persecution of Muslims and Jews, fundamentally altering the social fabric of Spain and Portugal.

Implications for Exploration and Colonization

Shift in Focus to Overseas Exploration: The end of the Reconquista coincided with the beginning of the Age of Exploration. The resources and energies that had been focused on the Reconquista were now redirected towards exploration and colonization.
Nationalistic and Religious Zeal in Exploration: The nationalistic and religious fervor that fueled the Reconquista also influenced the motivations for exploration. The Spanish and Portuguese explorers carried with them the desire to spread Christianity and gain glory for their kingdoms.

Influence on Western Civilization and American Ideals

Foundations for Western Expansion: The Reconquista laid the foundations for Western expansion, both in terms of military conquest and the spread of Christianity. These foundations influenced the ideological underpinnings of later European colonization in the Americas and the shaping of American civilization.

Section 2: Christian and Muslim Dynamics in Iberia

Exploring the Interplay of Cultures

This section delves into the complex interplay between Christian and Muslim cultures in Iberia during the Reconquista, exploring how this centuries-long interaction influenced the religious, cultural, and political landscapes of Spain and Portugal, and subsequently shaped their approaches to exploration and colonization.

Cultural Coexistence and Conflict

Convivencia: In certain periods of the Reconquista, there was a notable cultural coexistence, known as 'Convivencia', between Christians, Muslims, and Jews in Iberia. This period was marked by a relative tolerance and intellectual flourishing.
Conflict and Convergence: Despite moments of coexistence, the Reconquista was predominantly characterized by conflict. However, this prolonged interaction led to significant cultural and intellectual exchanges, influencing art, architecture, science, and philosophy.

Influence on Iberian Society

Shaping of Social and Cultural Norms: The presence and interaction with the Islamic world in Iberia influenced various aspects of Iberian society, including language, art, architecture, and knowledge systems.
Religious Impact: The conflict between Christianity and Islam during the Reconquista had a profound impact on religious attitudes in Iberia, often intensifying religious fervor and shaping the militant and missionary character of Spanish and Portuguese exploration.

Role of Religious Institutions

Church Influence in Politics and Society: The Church played a significant role in the Reconquista, not only as a religious but also as a political force, influencing the strategies of Christian kingdoms and shaping societal norms.
Formation of Religious Orders: The Reconquista saw the rise of religious military orders, such as the Order of Santiago and the Knights Templar, which played key roles in military campaigns and later in overseas exploration and colonization.

Legacy of Islamic Rule in Iberia

Architectural and Scientific Legacy: The Islamic rule in Iberia left a lasting architectural legacy, evident in landmarks such as the Alhambra in Granada. The period also contributed to the transmission of scientific and philosophical knowledge from the Muslim world to Europe.
Economic Systems and Administration: The Islamic influence extended to economic practices and administrative systems, some of which were adopted by the Christian rulers post-Reconquista.

Preparation for Overseas Expansion

Militaristic and Navigational Skills: The prolonged military campaigns against Muslim states in Iberia honed the militaristic and navigational skills of the Iberian kingdoms, which were instrumental in their subsequent overseas explorations.
Religious Motivation for Colonization: The Reconquista's religious zeal carried over into the Age of Exploration, where the spread of Christianity became a primary motive alongside economic and political goals in the colonization of the New World.

Section 3: The Fall of Granada and Its Aftermath

A Turning Point in Iberian History

This section examines the fall of Granada in 1492, the final stronghold of Muslim rule in Spain, and its profound aftermath, both within Iberia and in the broader context of European expansion and the eventual shaping of American ideals.

The Conquest of Granada

End of the Reconquista: The capture of Granada by the Catholic Monarchs, Ferdinand II of Aragon and Isabella I of Castile, marked the end of the 700-year-long Muslim presence in Iberia and the completion of the Reconquista.
Symbolic and Strategic Significance: Granada's fall was a significant victory for Christian Europe and a symbolic event that was celebrated as a triumph of Christianity over Islam.

Sociopolitical Changes in Spain

Centralization of Power: The conquest of Granada facilitated the further centralization of power in the hands of the Catholic Monarchs, paving the way for a unified Spain.

Religious Uniformity: The aftermath of the Reconquista saw efforts to establish religious uniformity in Spain, most notably through the expulsion of Jews (the Alhambra Decree) and later Muslims, and the establishment of the Spanish Inquisition.

Impact on Spanish Society and Culture

Cultural Integration and Loss: The end of Muslim rule led to significant cultural changes. While certain aspects of Islamic culture were integrated, much was lost or systematically erased in the quest for a homogenous Christian identity.
Economic and Demographic Shifts: The expulsion of Jews and Muslims had significant economic and demographic impacts, leading to a loss of a skilled workforce and altering the cultural landscape of Spain.

Repercussions on Exploration and Colonization

Redirecting Ambitions: With the Reconquista complete, Spain redirected its ambitions towards exploration. The same year Granada fell, Christopher Columbus received support from the Catholic Monarchs for his expedition, leading to the "discovery" of the Americas.
Spread of Christianity: The Reconquista's religious fervor influenced Spanish colonization efforts, with the spread of Christianity being a central objective in the New World, often mirroring the missionary zeal witnessed during the Reconquista.

Influences on American Colonial Policy

Legacy in American Colonialism: The practices and policies established during the Reconquista influenced Spain's approach to colonization in the Americas, which included religious conversion, cultural assimilation, and territorial expansion. These policies indirectly shaped the early colonial experiences in North America, impacting the development of what would become the United States.

Section 4: Financing and Motivation for Exploration

The Economic and Ideological Drivers of the Age of Exploration

In this section, we delve into how the culmination of the Reconquista influenced the financing and motivation for the subsequent European explorations, particularly the Spanish and Portuguese voyages, which played a pivotal role in shaping the geopolitical landscape of the New World and laid the groundwork for future American economic and political principles.

Transition from Reconquest to Exploration

Shift in Focus: Following the completion of the Reconquista, the Iberian kingdoms, with newfound unity and strength, shifted their focus from internal consolidation to external exploration and expansion.
Resource Allocation: The resources, both human and financial, that had been previously dedicated to the Reconquista were now available for ventures abroad. This reallocation was critical in propelling the early expeditions.

Economic Incentives for Exploration

Search for Wealth: The drive to find new trade routes and access untapped resources, especially in the East, was a primary economic motivation for exploration. The potential for wealth from these ventures attracted investment from both the monarchy and private entities.
Development of Financial Mechanisms: To fund these expeditions, innovative financial mechanisms were developed, including the formation of joint-stock companies and maritime insurance. These innovations were foundational in the development of modern financial systems.

Religious Motivation and Crusading Spirit

Continuation of the Crusading Ideal: The religious zeal of the Reconquista, with its goal of spreading Christianity, continued to influence the Spanish and Portuguese explorations. The notion of a crusade was transformed into a mission to evangelize new lands.
Papal Support and Influence: The Church, particularly through the Papal Bulls, played a significant role in motivating and legitimizing exploration. The religious sanctioning of these voyages gave them a sense of divine purpose.

National Prestige and Competition

Rivalry Among European Powers: The desire for national prestige and competition among European powers, especially following the Treaty of Tordesillas, was a significant motivator for exploration. This competition spurred rapid advancements in navigation and territorial claims.
Foundation for Colonial Expansion: The motivations and financing methods developed during this period laid the groundwork for European colonial expansion, which would have lasting effects on the global order and eventually influence the economic and political systems of the emerging United States.

Section 5: The Legacy of Iberian Rule in the Americas

Conquest and Colonization: Shaping a New World

This section examines the legacy of Iberian rule in the Americas following the Reconquista, highlighting how the ideologies, practices, and structures developed during this period influenced the colonization process and left an enduring mark on the cultural, social, and political fabric of the New World, which would later impact the development of American society and governance.

Patterns of Conquest and Governance

Model of Conquest: The methods of conquest employed by the Iberian powers in the Americas were influenced by their experiences during the Reconquista. These methods included military conquest, alliances with local powers, and the establishment of settlements.
Governance Structures: The administrative and governance structures set up in the Americas mirrored those in Iberia, with a focus on centralized control, the establishment of viceroys, and the integration of local elites into the colonial administration.

Cultural and Religious Imposition

Spread of Christianity: Just as the Reconquista was marked by a strong religious component, the Spanish and Portuguese colonization efforts were heavily focused on the conversion of indigenous populations to Christianity.
Cultural Syncretism: While the Iberian powers sought to impose their culture and religion, a process of cultural syncretism occurred, blending indigenous, African, and European elements, particularly in religion, language, and art.

Economic Exploitation and Social Systems

Extraction of Resources: The economic model in the colonies was primarily based on the extraction of resources, such as gold, silver, and agricultural products. This model was similar to the feudal systems and mercantile practices that had developed in Iberia.
Encomienda System: The encomienda system, a form of labor allocation and control, mirrored feudal practices in Iberia and had significant implications for the indigenous populations, leading to exploitation and decline.

Impact on Indigenous Populations

Demographic Changes: The arrival of the Iberians led to dramatic demographic changes, primarily due to disease, warfare, and exploitation. The indigenous populations faced significant declines, altering the demographic landscape of the Americas.
Resistance and Adaptation: Despite the overwhelming impact of colonization, indigenous populations exhibited resistance and adaptation, retaining and reshaping aspects of their cultures and societies.

Legacy in American History

Foundations for Future Colonies: The Iberian model of conquest and colonization set a precedent for future European colonization efforts, including those of the British and French in North America.
Influence on American Society and Governance: The legacy of Iberian rule in the Americas, with its complex interplay of cultural, economic, and social dynamics, indirectly influenced the development of societal structures and governance in what would become the United States.

Section 6: The Transfer of Military Tactics and Governance

From Iberian Battlefields to American Shores

This section delves into how the military tactics and governance strategies developed during the Reconquista were transferred to the New World, influencing the methods of conquest and colonial administration, which would later indirectly shape military and governance approaches in the emerging United States.

Adaptation of Military Tactics

Siege Warfare and Fortification: The techniques of siege warfare and fortification honed during the Reconquista were effectively adapted in the Americas, especially in the conquest of major indigenous settlements.
Use of Cavalry and Arms: The Iberian use of cavalry, which was crucial in the Reconquista, became a significant advantage in the Americas, as did the advanced European arms and armor.

Governance Models Transferred to the Colonies

Viceroyalty System: The administrative system of viceroys, a form of governance used in Iberia, was replicated in the Americas. This system allowed for centralized control while adapting to local conditions.
Legal and Judicial Frameworks: The legal systems developed in Iberia, including aspects of Islamic jurisprudence absorbed during the Reconquista, were introduced to the Americas, influencing colonial law and order.

Social and Economic Structures

Feudal-like Encomienda System: The encomienda system, reminiscent of feudal practices, was implemented in the colonies. This system granted Spanish conquerors control over indigenous labor and tribute, leading to exploitation and social stratification.
Mercantilist Policies: The mercantilist policies, focusing on the accumulation of wealth through trade and resource extraction, mirrored the economic motivations of the Reconquista and influenced colonial economic strategies.

Impact on Indigenous Warfare and Resistance

Indigenous Adaptation of European Tactics: Indigenous groups in the Americas often adapted European military tactics and technology in their resistance efforts against colonial forces.
Formation of Alliances: Just as alliances played a crucial role in the Reconquista, they became a critical aspect of colonial strategy, with European powers forming alliances with certain indigenous groups against others.

Influences on Early American Military and Governance

Military Traditions in the U.S.: The military traditions and strategies that developed during this period indirectly influenced the early American military ethos, including the emphasis on adaptability and alliance-building.
Governance and Legal Precedents: The governance structures and legal systems of the Spanish and Portuguese colonies provided a reference point for the emerging governance models in North America, influencing the development of legal and administrative systems in the United States.

Section 7: Religious Missionaries: Converting the New World

The Spiritual Conquest of the Americas

This section examines the role of religious missionaries in the New World following the Reconquista, exploring how their efforts to convert indigenous populations to Christianity paralleled the religious aspects of the Reconquista and how these missionary activities influenced cultural and social dynamics in the Americas, laying groundwork for aspects of American religious and cultural identity.

Continuation of the Missionary Zeal

Transfer of the Crusading Spirit: The religious fervor and missionary zeal that characterized the Reconquista were carried over to the Americas. Missionaries, mainly from Catholic orders, embarked on a spiritual conquest to convert indigenous populations.
Role of Religious Orders: Orders like the Franciscans, Dominicans, and Jesuits played pivotal roles in the missionary activities in the New World, establishing missions, churches, and schools.

Methods and Strategies of Conversion

Adaptation and Syncretism: Missionaries often adapted Christian teachings to local customs and beliefs, leading to a syncretic blend of Christian and indigenous religious practices.
Use of Indigenous Languages: Many missionaries learned local languages to effectively communicate Christian doctrines, contributing to linguistic studies and translations.

Impact on Indigenous Cultures

Cultural and Religious Transformation: The missionary efforts led to significant changes in the religious and cultural landscapes of indigenous societies. While conversion efforts were sometimes met with resistance, they also resulted in the widespread adoption of Christianity among indigenous populations.
Preservation and Loss of Indigenous Traditions: While missionaries documented indigenous cultures and languages, their efforts also contributed to the erosion and suppression of traditional beliefs and practices.

Influence on Colonial Society and Policies

Social Control and Moral Authority: The missionaries often held significant moral authority in colonial societies, influencing social norms, education, and governance.
Conflict and Cooperation with Colonial Authorities: While missionaries collaborated with colonial authorities in the pacification and control of indigenous populations, there were also instances of conflict, particularly when defending indigenous rights against colonial exploitation.

Legacy in American Religious and Cultural Landscape

Foundations for Religious Diversity: The missionary activities in the Spanish and Portuguese colonies contributed to the religious diversity in the Americas. This diversity, along with the concepts of religious mission and conversion, would later influence the religious landscape of the United States.
Influence on Education and Social Services: The missionary emphasis on education and social services laid early foundations for such institutions in the Americas, some of which influenced similar developments in North American colonies.

Section 8: Religious Tolerance and Persecution

Contrasting Ideals of Coexistence and Conflict

This section delves into the complex legacy of religious tolerance and persecution that emerged from the Reconquista, examining how these contrasting experiences influenced the Spanish and Portuguese colonial administrations in the New World, and subsequently impacted the development of religious freedom as a foundational concept in the United States.

From Coexistence to Persecution in Iberia

Era of Convivencia: The early period of the Reconquista and pre-Reconquista eras were marked by 'Convivencia', a relative coexistence among Christians, Muslims, and Jews in Iberia, leading to cultural and intellectual exchanges.
Shift to Intolerance: Over time, the Reconquista became more associated with religious intolerance, culminating in the expulsion of Jews (1492) and later Muslims (early 17th century) from Spain, and the establishment of the Spanish Inquisition, aimed at enforcing Catholic orthodoxy.

Impact on Colonial Policies

Replication of Religious Intolerance: The intolerance that characterized the later stages of the Reconquista was mirrored in the colonial policies in the New World, where conversion to Christianity was often pursued aggressively, sometimes accompanied by the suppression of indigenous religions.
Missionary Approaches: Despite the overarching theme of intolerance, some missionaries advocated for and practiced a degree of tolerance and understanding towards indigenous beliefs, leading to instances of cultural and religious syncretism.

Legacy of Religious Policies in the New World

Formation of Colonial Religious Identity: The religious policies in the colonies played a crucial role in shaping the religious identities of the colonial societies, with Catholicism becoming deeply entrenched in many parts of the Americas.
Resistance and Preservation of Indigenous Beliefs: Indigenous populations often resisted the imposition of Christianity, leading to a complex religious landscape where indigenous beliefs were maintained, albeit sometimes covertly or syncretically.

Influence on American Religious Freedom

Contrasting with British Colonies: The experience of religious intolerance in the Spanish and Portuguese colonies contrasted with certain British colonies in North America, where some were founded on principles of religious tolerance and freedom.
Shaping the Concept of Religious Liberty: These contrasting experiences contributed to the development of religious liberty as a key principle in American thought, eventually enshrined in the U.S. Constitution, reflecting a desire to avoid the religious conflicts and persecutions of European history.

Section 9: Economic Exploitation and Trade Dynamics

From Iberian Reconquest to American Colonization

This section explores the economic strategies and trade dynamics that evolved during and after the Reconquista and how these were replicated and modified in the Spanish and Portuguese colonies in the New World, ultimately influencing the economic foundations of the United States.

Economic Transformation in Post-Reconquista Iberia

Shift to Overseas Ventures: The completion of the Reconquista coincided with a shift in focus towards overseas exploration and colonization, driven by the search for new sources of wealth.
Economic Impact of Religious Expulsions: The expulsion of Jews and Muslims, who were integral to the Iberian economy, resulted in significant economic changes, leading to a greater emphasis on overseas wealth.

Colonial Economic Systems

Resource Extraction and Encomienda: Similar to the feudal systems in Europe, the Spanish and Portuguese established the encomienda system in the colonies, focused on extracting precious metals and agricultural products, often through the labor of indigenous people.
Mercantilism and Monopolistic Trade: The colonial economies were governed by mercantilist principles, with strict control over trade to benefit the home countries. This led to the development of monopolistic trading systems.

Impact on Global Trade

Creation of Global Trade Networks: The colonial endeavors greatly expanded global trade networks, connecting the Americas, Europe, Africa, and Asia. This global trade was pivotal in the development of the modern world economy.
Introduction of New Products and Exchange: The Columbian Exchange, involving the transfer of plants, animals, and diseases between the Old and New Worlds, profoundly impacted the economies and societies on both sides of the Atlantic.

Influence on American Economic Development

Foundations for American Economy: The economic practices and systems established in the Spanish and Portuguese colonies provided a model for economic development in the English colonies, which would become the United States.
Shaping Economic Ideals and Policies: The experiences of mercantilism and colonial exploitation influenced the economic thinking of the American Founding Fathers, who sought to create an economy based on free trade, individual enterprise, and resistance to monopolistic practices.

Section 10: The Persistence of Indigenous Cultures

Resilience and Adaptation in the Face of Colonization

This section examines the enduring strength and adaptability of indigenous cultures in the Americas despite the intense pressures of colonization following the Reconquista, exploring how these dynamics contributed to the rich cultural mosaic of the New World, which indirectly influenced the cultural and societal development of the United States.

Impact of Iberian Colonization on Indigenous Societies

Cultural Disruption and Assimilation: The arrival of the Spanish and Portuguese led to significant cultural disruptions for indigenous societies, with forced assimilation efforts, including religious conversion and the imposition of European social norms.

Resistance to Cultural Erasure: Despite these pressures, many indigenous groups resisted cultural erasure, maintaining and adapting their traditions, languages, and beliefs in the face of colonial domination.

Syncretism and Cultural Blending

Emergence of Syncretic Cultures: The interaction between European colonizers and indigenous populations led to the development of syncretic cultures, blending elements of indigenous, African, and European traditions, particularly in religion, art, and music.

Survival of Indigenous Practices: Many indigenous practices survived by intertwining with European customs, forming unique cultural expressions that persisted over generations.

Indigenous Contributions to Colonial Societies

Agricultural Knowledge and Practices: Indigenous knowledge of local agriculture and environment played a crucial role in the survival and development of colonial societies. Crops native to the Americas, like maize, potatoes, and tomatoes, were integrated into global food systems.

Influence on Colonial Economies: Indigenous labor and expertise were integral to the colonial economies, particularly in mining and agriculture.

Legacy in Modern American Societies

Influence on American Identity: The persistence and resilience of indigenous cultures contributed to the diverse cultural landscape of the Americas. This diversity is a key component of the identity of many American nations, including the United States.

Recognition and Resurgence: In modern times, there has been a growing recognition and resurgence of indigenous cultures, languages, and rights, reflecting a broader understanding of their importance in the historical and cultural fabric of the Americas.

Chapter 4: Protestant Reformation: A New Religious Landscape

Section 1: Martin Luther's 95 Theses and Its Impact

The Spark of Religious Reform

This section delves into the beginning of the Protestant Reformation, initiated by Martin Luther's 95 Theses, and examines how this pivotal religious movement reshaped the European religious landscape and indirectly influenced the founding principles of the United States.

Origins of Luther's Reformation

Context of the 95 Theses: Martin Luther's 95 Theses, posted in 1517, criticized the Roman Catholic Church's practices, particularly the sale of indulgences. This act is widely regarded as the start of the Protestant Reformation.

Luther's Call for Reform: Luther's writings called for a return to the Scriptures and criticized the authority of the Pope, setting off a chain of events that led to a significant religious upheaval in Europe.

Impact on European Christianity

Division of Christendom: Luther's challenge to the Catholic Church led to a profound division in Christendom, with the emergence of Protestant denominations that rejected the authority of the Papacy.

Spread of Reformation Ideas: The spread of Luther's ideas was facilitated by the printing press, leading to a rapid dissemination of Protestant thought across Europe.

Political and Social Repercussions

Empowerment of Secular Authorities: The Reformation weakened the power of the Catholic Church and empowered secular rulers, leading to significant political and social shifts, including wars and conflicts based on religious lines.
Cultural and Intellectual Changes: The emphasis on individual interpretation of the Scriptures contributed to cultural and intellectual changes, fostering a spirit of inquiry and challenging established authorities.

Influence on Exploration and Colonization

Religious Motivation in Exploration: The religious divisions in Europe influenced exploration and colonization, with Protestant nations seeking to spread their version of Christianity and escape religious persecution.
Colonial Religious Dynamics: The religious dynamics in Europe were mirrored in the colonies, where religious affiliation influenced settlement patterns, governance, and interactions with indigenous peoples.

Legacy in American Thought and Governance

Foundations for Religious Diversity and Freedom: The religious pluralism resulting from the Reformation set the stage for religious diversity in the American colonies. The experience of religious conflict and the value of individual belief influenced the founding principles of religious freedom in the United States.
Impact on American Ideals: The Reformation's emphasis on individual conscience and questioning of authority played a role in shaping American ideals of liberty, democracy, and individual rights.

Section 2: John Calvin's Teachings and Influence

The Expansion of Reformation Ideals

This section explores the significant contributions of John Calvin to the Protestant Reformation, examining how his teachings and the establishment of Calvinism further transformed the religious landscape of Europe and influenced the socio-political environment in the colonies that would become the United States.

Calvin's Theological Contributions

Development of Calvinism: John Calvin, a French theologian and reformer, played a pivotal role in the expansion of the Protestant movement. His theological work, particularly as articulated in his seminal work, "Institutes of the Christian Religion," laid the foundations for Calvinism.
Key Doctrines: Calvin's teachings emphasized the sovereignty of God, predestination, and the authority of Scripture. His doctrine of the 'elect' and the moral rectitude of believers had a profound influence on Protestant thought.

Spread of Calvinism

Influence Beyond Borders: Calvin's ideas quickly spread beyond France, taking root in various parts of Europe, including Switzerland, the Netherlands, Scotland, and parts of Germany. This spread contributed to the diversity of Protestantism.
Establishment of Reformed Churches: Calvin's influence led to the establishment of Reformed churches. His model of church governance, which emphasized a more democratic structure, contrasted with the hierarchical structure of the Catholic Church.

Impact on European Society and Politics

Socio-Political Shifts: Calvinism played a role in shaping the political and social landscapes of Europe. In some regions, it influenced the development of more democratic forms of governance and contributed to resistance against monarchial and papal authority.
Role in Conflicts: The spread of Calvinism, with its distinct doctrines and practices, contributed to religious and political conflicts, including civil wars and international wars, as Europe grappled with the challenges of religious plurality.

Calvinism in the New World

Influence on American Colonies: Calvinist beliefs were brought to the American colonies by groups such as the Puritans and the Dutch Reformed. These beliefs shaped the religious, cultural, and social fabric of several colonies, particularly in New England.
Ethical and Moral Underpinnings: Calvinist emphasis on morality, work ethic, and community governance influenced the societal norms and legislative frameworks in the colonies. This influence is evident in the development of laws, educational systems, and community structures.

Legacy in American Ideals and Governance

Foundations for American Values: The Calvinist emphasis on hard work, moral uprightness, and community responsibility contributed to what would later be identified as core American values. Influence on Constitutional Principles: Calvin's ideas on governance and the role of the governed in holding leaders accountable influenced the development of democratic principles and ideas of governance that would shape the U.S. Constitution.

Section 3: The Spread of Protestantism in Europe

The Fragmentation and Diversification of Christianity

This section explores the widespread impact of the Protestant Reformation across Europe, examining how the diversification of Christian practices and beliefs contributed to significant religious, cultural, and political shifts, and how these shifts influenced the social and ideological foundations of the American colonies.

Diverse Expressions of Protestantism

Regional Variations: The Reformation led to the emergence of various Protestant denominations, each with distinct practices and doctrines, such as Lutheranism in Germany, Calvinism in Switzerland, the Anglican Church in England, and Presbyterianism in Scotland.
Cultural and Political Factors: The adoption and adaptation of Protestantism in different regions were influenced by local cultural and political contexts, leading to a diverse religious landscape across Europe.

Societal and Political Repercussions

Challenging Established Authority: The spread of Protestantism significantly challenged the authority of the Catholic Church and the political power of the Papacy, leading to a reconfiguration of church-state relations in many European countries.
Religious Wars and Conflicts: The division between Protestant and Catholic territories led to a series of religious wars and conflicts, including the Thirty Years' War, which had devastating effects across the continent.

Influence on Governance and Thought

Emergence of Religious Tolerance: The religious fragmentation eventually contributed to the development of concepts of religious tolerance and freedom of conscience, as a pragmatic response to religious conflict.
Contribution to Democratic Ideals: The emphasis on individual interpretation of the Scriptures in Protestantism supported the development of ideas about personal liberty, which influenced emerging democratic ideals in Europe.

Protestantism in the American Colonies

Settlement and Religious Practice: Various Protestant groups sought refuge in the American colonies, seeking the freedom to practice their religion away from European persecution.
Shaping Colonial Societies: The religious beliefs of these settlers deeply influenced the social, cultural, and political development of the colonies. The Puritan work ethic, Quaker social justice principles, and Presbyterian communal governance are examples of such influences.

Legacy in American Development

Foundations for American Diversity: The diverse Protestant traditions in the colonies laid the groundwork for the religious pluralism that is a hallmark of American society.
Impact on American Political Philosophy: The Protestant emphasis on individualism, community governance, and resistance to centralized authority influenced the political philosophies underpinning the American Revolution and the formation of the U.S. Constitution.

Section 4: Protestantism vs. Catholicism: A New Divide

The Emergence of Deep Religious Schisms

This section examines the deepening divide between Protestantism and Catholicism during the Reformation, exploring how this religious schism influenced European politics, societal structures, and colonization efforts, and how these religious dynamics played a role in shaping the early American sociopolitical landscape.

Theological Differences and Conflicts

Core Disagreements: The fundamental theological disagreements between Protestant reformers and the Catholic Church centered around issues such as the authority of the Pope, the nature of salvation, and the role of religious traditions and rituals.

Polarization and Debate: These differences led to intense theological debates and polemics, contributing to a growing polarization between Protestant and Catholic communities across Europe.

Political Implications of the Divide

Religious Alignment and State Power: The religious divide often aligned with political power struggles, with monarchs and state leaders choosing sides based on both conviction and political expediency.
Wars and Alliances: The Protestant-Catholic divide was a significant factor in wars and political alliances during this period, reshaping the political map of Europe.

Impact on Society and Culture

Social Tensions and Persecutions: In regions divided between Protestant and Catholic populations, social tensions were common, sometimes leading to persecution and violence against religious minorities.
Cultural and Educational Developments: The divide also influenced cultural expressions and educational institutions, with each side establishing its schools, universities, and cultural norms.

Influence on Colonial Ventures

Religious Motivations in Colonization: The religious divide influenced the motivations and practices of European colonization. Protestant and Catholic powers sought to spread their respective versions of Christianity in the New World.
Settlement Patterns and Governance: The religious affiliations of different colonial powers led to distinct settlement patterns, governance models, and societal structures in their respective colonies.

Reformation's Influence on American Ideals

Religious Diversity and Conflict: The diverse religious settlements in the American colonies reflected the Protestant-Catholic divide in Europe, contributing to a landscape of religious plurality and sometimes conflict.
Foundations for Religious Freedom: The experience of religious strife and the desire for religious autonomy influenced the American colonies' push towards principles of religious freedom and separation of church and state, later enshrined in the U.S. Constitution.

Section 5: Religious Wars and Persecution

The Turbulent Consequences of Doctrinal Divides

This section delves into the period of religious wars and persecutions that ensued as a result of the deepening rifts between Protestantism and Catholicism, exploring how these conflicts reshaped European societies and influenced the migration patterns and governance structures of the American colonies.

Era of Religious Conflict in Europe

Major Conflicts: Significant religious wars, such as the German Peasants' War, the French Wars of Religion, and the Thirty Years' War, were fueled by the Protestant-Catholic divide. These conflicts devastated large areas of Europe, leading to significant loss of life and displacement of populations.
Persecutions and Martyrdoms: Both Protestant and Catholic authorities engaged in the persecution of those they deemed heretics. This era saw numerous martyrdoms and acts of violence against individuals and groups based on their religious beliefs.

Impact on European Societies

Social Disruption and Economic Impact: The religious wars caused widespread social disruption and had profound economic consequences, disrupting trade and agriculture, leading to famine and poverty in affected areas.
Political Realignments: The conflicts often resulted in political realignments, with territories and nations consolidating around religious identities. The Peace of Westphalia, which ended the Thirty Years' War, marked a significant shift towards the concept of national sovereignty.

Migration and Settlement in the New World

Escape from Persecution: The religious turmoil in Europe prompted many individuals and groups to seek refuge in the New World, where they could practice their faith freely. This migration significantly influenced the religious and cultural composition of the American colonies.
Formation of Religious Communities: In the Americas, religious refugees established communities that reflected their beliefs and practices. Examples include the Puritans in New England and the Quakers in Pennsylvania.

Influence on American Religious Landscape

Diversity and Tolerance: The variety of religious communities in the American colonies created a landscape of religious diversity. The experience of persecution in Europe contributed to a growing ethos of religious tolerance in the colonies.
Foundations for Religious Liberty: The legacy of religious wars and persecution in Europe was a critical factor in the development of the American principle of religious liberty, as the colonists sought to avoid the religious strife that had plagued Europe.

Section 6: The Role of Printing and Mass Communication

Spreading Ideas and Fueling Change

This section explores the crucial role of printing and mass communication in the spread of Reformation ideas, examining how these technological advancements facilitated a broader dissemination of religious and political thoughts, and how this ability to share and exchange ideas influenced the intellectual and cultural foundations of the American colonies.

The Printing Revolution

Gutenberg's Invention: The introduction of movable-type printing by Johannes Gutenberg in the mid-15th century revolutionized the dissemination of information. This technology allowed for the mass production of books, including the Bible, making them more accessible to a wider audience.
Amplification of Reformation Ideas: Printing played a critical role in the spread of Protestant Reformation ideas. Martin Luther's 95 Theses and subsequent writings were rapidly disseminated across Europe through printed materials, reaching a broad and diverse audience.

Impact on European Society

Increased Literacy and Education: The availability of printed materials contributed to an increase in literacy rates and a greater emphasis on education. This democratization of knowledge laid the groundwork for the Enlightenment and the development of critical thinking.
Formation of Public Opinion: Printing allowed for the formation of public opinion on a scale previously impossible. It enabled the spread of new ideas, criticism of established institutions, and the mobilization of public support for various causes.

Influence on Political and Religious Thought

Challenging Authority: The ability to spread ideas quickly and widely allowed reformers, thinkers, and political leaders to challenge the authority of the Church and secular rulers, fostering an environment of debate and dissent.
Diverse Religious Views: The proliferation of religious texts and interpretations promoted a diversity of religious views, contributing to the fragmentation of Christendom and the proliferation of various Protestant sects.

Legacy in the American Colonies

Transatlantic Exchange of Ideas: The printing press facilitated the transatlantic exchange of ideas, ensuring that European religious and political debates had an impact on the American colonies.
Foundation for American Free Press: The tradition of a free press, critical for the development of democratic societies, has its roots in the Reformation-era use of printing. This tradition was integral to the American struggle for independence and the formation of a democratic government.

Section 7: Protestant Ethics and the Spirit of Capitalism

The Intersection of Religion and Economy

This section examines how the Protestant Reformation, particularly through its ethical teachings, influenced the development of capitalism, and how these economic changes were reflected in the emerging economic systems and philosophies in the American colonies.

Max Weber's Thesis

Weber's Analysis: Sociologist Max Weber, in his seminal work "The Protestant Ethic and the Spirit of Capitalism," argued that the Protestant ethic, especially Calvinist beliefs about work and economic success, was a major force in the development of modern capitalism.
Religious Underpinnings of Economic Behavior: Weber suggested that the Protestant emphasis on hard work, discipline, and frugality contributed to a conducive environment for the growth of capitalism.

Influence of Protestantism on Economic Practices

Shaping Attitudes Towards Work and Wealth: Protestant teachings, which often viewed economic success as a sign of divine favor, influenced attitudes towards work and wealth. This led to a valorization of industriousness and entrepreneurialism.
Emergence of Modern Business Practices: The Protestant ethic fostered an environment where modern business practices could develop, including rational bookkeeping, efficient organization, and the pursuit of profit.

Impact on European Economies

Economic Transformation in Protestant Regions: Regions that embraced Protestantism often experienced significant economic transformations, with the emergence of a more robust and dynamic form of capitalism.
Contribution to Industrial Revolution: Some historians argue that the Protestant work ethic contributed to the conditions that led to the Industrial Revolution, particularly in Protestant-dominated countries like England.

Transference to the American Colonies

Economic Ethos in Early America: The Protestant ethic was brought to the American colonies by settlers, particularly the Puritans in New England, influencing the economic ethos of these communities.
Development of American Capitalism: The values of hard work, thrift, and efficiency were integral to the development of capitalism in the American colonies and later the United States. These values were reflected in the economic practices and policies of the early American states.

Legacy in American Economic Thought

Foundations for American Economic System: The Protestant ethic's influence on attitudes towards work and economic activity contributed to the foundations of the American economic system, emphasizing individual enterprise and a market-oriented economy.
Influence on American Values and Ideals: The principles derived from the Protestant ethic, such as self-reliance and industriousness, became embedded in American cultural values and ideals, shaping the American identity and approach to economic life.

Section 8: The Reformation and European Exploration

Religion as a Catalyst for Discovery and Expansion

This section examines how the Protestant Reformation influenced the motivations and dynamics of European exploration, particularly how religious factors intertwined with economic and political ambitions, shaping the European endeavors in the New World and their subsequent impact on the formation of American society and ideology.

Religious Motivation in Exploration

Escaping Persecution: For many Protestant groups in Europe, exploration and colonization offered an escape from religious persecution. This was a driving force behind some of the early settlements in North America, such as the Pilgrims in New England.
Spreading Protestantism: Alongside Catholic missions, there was a significant Protestant missionary movement. Nations like England and the Netherlands saw the New World as a fertile ground for spreading Protestantism, establishing a religious presence in their colonies.

Impact on Colonial Policies and Practices

Governance Influenced by Religious Beliefs: In colonies established by Protestant nations, governance structures and laws were often influenced by Protestant beliefs and values. This included a focus on moral conduct, communal responsibility, and a certain degree of self-governance.
Cultural and Social Dynamics: The religious beliefs of these settlers shaped the cultural and social dynamics of the colonies. For instance, the Puritan work ethic significantly influenced the development of societal norms in New England.

Competition and Conflict

Rivalries Between Protestant and Catholic Powers: The religious divide in Europe translated into rivalries in the New World. Protestant and Catholic powers often competed for territorial and spiritual dominance, influencing the geopolitical landscape of the Americas.
Conflict with Indigenous Religions: Both Protestant and Catholic colonizers often sought to convert indigenous populations, leading to conflicts and tensions with native religious practices and beliefs.

Influence on American Identity and Governance

Foundations for Religious Pluralism: The presence of various Protestant denominations in the colonies set the stage for religious pluralism, which would become a key feature of American society.
Impact on Democratic Principles: The emphasis on individual interpretation of scripture and the congregational form of church governance in many Protestant denominations influenced the development of democratic principles and ideas of self-governance in the American colonies.

Section 9: The Reformation and the Shaping of American Ideologies

Religious Roots of Political and Social Thought

In this section, we explore how the Protestant Reformation influenced the development of various ideologies in the American colonies, particularly focusing on how religious ideas contributed to emerging concepts of governance, individual rights, and societal organization that would later be central to American political identity and the U.S. Constitution.

Impact on Political Ideologies

Democratic Ideals: The Reformation's emphasis on individual conscience and direct access to scripture fostered democratic thinking. The idea that individuals could interpret religious texts themselves paralleled emerging ideas about political self-determination and governance.
Resistance to Authoritarianism: The Reformers' challenge to the authority of the Catholic Church and the monarchies aligned with it resonated with the American colonists' growing resistance to British rule. This resistance laid the groundwork for the American Revolution.

Social Contract Theory

Influence on Enlightenment Thinkers: The Reformation, by challenging established religious authority, influenced Enlightenment thinkers like John Locke, who developed the social contract theory. This theory, which posits that governments derive their authority from the consent of the governed, was a foundational element in American political thought.
Application in American Governance: Concepts of the social contract, individual rights, and the separation of powers were reflected in the U.S. Constitution and Federalist Papers.

Religious Freedom and Separation of Church and State

Diversity of Religious Beliefs: The variety of religious beliefs among the colonists, a result of the Reformation's fragmentation of Christendom, necessitated a degree of religious tolerance and eventually led to the idea of separating church and state.
First Amendment Principles: The experience of religious conflict and persecution in Europe and the diverse religious landscape in the colonies influenced the First Amendment's establishment of religious freedom and prohibition of a state church.

Economic Ethic and Capitalism

Protestant Work Ethic: The Protestant work ethic, emphasizing hard work, frugality, and diligence, influenced the economic practices and ethos of the colonies. This ethic aligned well with the emerging capitalist economy, contributing to the development of American economic systems.
Wealth and Morality: The Reformation's nuanced view of wealth and success, especially within Calvinism, impacted the American perspective on wealth, viewing economic success as a sign of moral virtue and God's favor.

Section 10: Modern Reflections on Interreligious Dynamics

The Lasting Impact of the Reformation on Contemporary Religious and Cultural Interactions

In this final section of Chapter 4, we explore how the enduring legacies of the Protestant Reformation continue to influence modern interreligious dynamics, cultural identities, and societal values, particularly in the context of the United States, where these historical religious shifts have had lasting impacts on national ethos and policy.

Continued Influence on Religious Pluralism

Diversity of Denominations: The Reformation's fragmentation of Christianity resulted in a multitude of denominations, a trait that is particularly pronounced in the United States. This diversity necessitates ongoing dialogue and understanding among different Christian traditions.
Challenges and Opportunities: The diversity of religious beliefs, while sometimes leading to conflict, also provides rich opportunities for interfaith dialogue and mutual understanding, contributing to the dynamic religious landscape of modern America.

Cultural and Ethical Implications

Shaping American Cultural Identity: The Protestant ethic, with its emphasis on industriousness and moral rectitude, continues to influence American cultural identity and societal values.
Ethical Frameworks and Public Life: The Reformation's impact on ethical frameworks has implications for contemporary debates on public policy, social justice, and moral reasoning in a pluralistic society.

Political and Legal Resonance

Foundations of Democratic Governance: The Reformation's influence on democratic ideals and individual rights continues to resonate in American political life, informing debates on governance, civil liberties, and the role of religion in public affairs.
Religious Freedom and the Law: The principle of religious freedom, deeply rooted in the Reformation's legacy, remains a central tenet of American law and public policy, shaping the nation's approach to religious diversity and state-church relations.

Interfaith Relations and Ecumenism

Dialogue and Reconciliation: The historical divisions and conflicts born out of the Reformation have given way to modern efforts at ecumenism – promoting unity and cooperation among different Christian traditions, as well as broader interfaith initiatives.
Global Perspective: The American experience of religious pluralism, influenced by the Reformation, contributes to the nation's approach to international religious issues, promoting tolerance, understanding, and respect for diverse religious beliefs and practices worldwide.

Legacy in Contemporary Society

Influence on Education and Thought: The Reformation's legacy in promoting critical thinking and questioning of authority can be seen in contemporary educational philosophies and intellectual discourse.
Adaptation in a Changing World: As societies continue to evolve, the Reformation's impact is reflected in the ongoing adaptation of religious institutions and beliefs to address new social, ethical, and environmental challenges.

Chapter 5: Islamic Finance and European Economy

Section 1: Islamic Principles of Finance

Foundations and Influences

This section explores the foundational principles of Islamic finance and how they contributed to the development of financial systems and practices in medieval Europe, laying the groundwork for modern economic structures.

Key Principles of Islamic Finance

Prohibition of Interest (Riba): A core principle of Islamic finance is the prohibition of riba, or usury, which is the charging of excessive or exploitative interest on loans.
Risk and Profit-Sharing: Islamic finance emphasizes risk-sharing in business ventures, where profits and losses are shared among partners, promoting equity and ethical investment.
Asset-Backed Financing: Financial transactions in Islamic finance are typically asset-backed, ensuring that they are tied to tangible economic activities and assets, as opposed to speculative ventures.

Early Islamic Banking and Commerce

Development of Financial Instruments: Islamic civilization developed various financial instruments for trade and investment, including Mudarabah (profit-sharing) and Murabaha (cost-plus financing).
Efficient Banking Systems: Islamic traders and financiers established sophisticated banking systems, including letters of credit (Sakk), which facilitated long-distance trade and commerce.

Influence on European Economic Practices

Transmission of Financial Knowledge: Through interactions in places like Al-Andalus (Islamic Spain), Sicily, and during the Crusades, Europeans were exposed to Islamic financial principles and practices.
Adaptation and Integration: Some Islamic financial concepts were adapted and integrated into European banking and commerce systems, influencing the development of European financial practices.

Section 2: Influence on European Banking and Commerce

Cross-Cultural Exchange and Economic Transformation

This section examines how Islamic principles of finance influenced the development of European banking and commerce, detailing the mechanisms of this influence and its lasting impact on the evolution of European economic systems.

Adoption of Islamic Financial Practices

Introduction of Credit Systems: Islamic finance's concept of credit and risk-sharing was influential in the development of European credit systems, which became fundamental to commercial transactions.
Cheque System (Sakk): The Islamic cheque system, known as 'Sakk', was an early form of the modern cheque. Its adoption facilitated trade across vast distances, a practice that European merchants and bankers soon adopted.

Influence on European Banking

Establishment of Banks: The concept of banking, as practiced in the Islamic world, was a precursor to the establishment of European banks. Islamic institutions that provided financial services, such as money changing and lending, served as models for early European banks.
Interest-Free Lending Models: Although Europe did not fully adopt the Islamic prohibition of interest, some aspects of Islamic interest-free lending influenced European financial practices, particularly in the form of charitable loans.

Development of Commerce and Trade

Trade Contracts and Partnerships: Islamic contract law, which governed trade and partnerships, introduced concepts such as Mudarabah (profit-sharing) to European merchants, influencing their trade practices.
Maritime Trade Laws: Islamic maritime trade laws impacted the development of similar laws in Europe. The principles of sharing profits and risks in maritime ventures were particularly influential.

Transmission of Knowledge and Skills

Financial Knowledge through Translation: Translation of Islamic financial texts into European languages during periods of cultural exchange, such as in Al-Andalus, played a crucial role in transmitting knowledge.
Training and Skills Development: Europeans learned sophisticated financial skills from their interactions with Islamic traders and scholars, enhancing their capabilities in banking and commerce.

Section 3: The Venetian Connection: Trade and Exchange

Bridging Islamic and European Economies

This section examines the crucial role played by the Venetian Republic in facilitating trade and exchange between the Islamic world and Europe, and how this interaction influenced European economic practices, contributing to the development of modern financial and trade systems.

Venice as a Commercial Hub

Strategic Location: Venice's strategic location made it a pivotal point for trade between the Islamic world and Europe. Its ports served as key terminals for goods from the East, including the Middle East and Asia.
Cultural and Economic Intermediary: Venice acted as a cultural and economic intermediary, adopting and adapting Islamic financial practices and integrating them into European commerce.

Trade Agreements and Networks

Bilateral Trade Agreements: The Venetians established extensive trade agreements with various Islamic states, facilitating the flow of goods such as spices, textiles, and precious metals.
Networks of Merchants and Diplomats: A network of Venetian merchants and diplomats across the Islamic world helped foster strong economic ties and cultural exchange.

Adoption of Islamic Financial Practices

Banking Innovations: Venetian merchants and financiers adopted Islamic banking practices, such as fund transfer systems and letters of credit, which were essential in managing long-distance trade.

Development of Accounting and Bookkeeping: Exposure to Islamic methods of bookkeeping and accounting led to the refinement of these practices in Venice, enhancing the efficiency and reliability of financial transactions.

Impact on European Economy

Introduction of New Products: The trade with the Islamic world introduced a variety of new products to Europe, significantly impacting European economies and consumption patterns.
Stimulation of Maritime Trade: The Venetian connection stimulated maritime trade in Europe, contributing to the Age of Exploration as European powers sought direct access to the sources of Eastern goods.

Legacy in Modern Economic Systems

Foundations for Global Trade: Venice's role in bridging Islamic and European economies laid early foundations for global trade networks, influencing the structure and dynamics of modern international trade.
Influence on Financial Institutions: The financial practices developed through Venetian-Islamic interactions contributed to the evolution of European banking institutions and financial systems.

Section 4: Development of Joint-Stock Companies

From Islamic Contracts to European Enterprise

This section explores how Islamic financial practices influenced the development of joint-stock companies in Europe, a pivotal innovation in the evolution of modern capitalism and global trade.

Islamic Foundations of Shared Investment

Mudarabah and Musharakah: Islamic finance introduced concepts like Mudarabah (profit-sharing) and Musharakah (joint venture), where capital and labor were pooled for a business venture, and profits and losses were shared. These principles laid the groundwork for collective investment models.
Risk Sharing in Trade Ventures: The Islamic approach to commerce emphasized risk sharing, an idea that was crucial to the development of joint ventures and collective funding of trade expeditions in Europe.

Adoption in European Commerce

Early Forms of Joint-Stock Companies: In Europe, the concept of pooling resources for trade ventures evolved into the early forms of joint-stock companies. These entities allowed investors to buy shares and thus share in the profits and losses of the venture.
Venetian and Genoese Adaptations: Venetian and Genoese traders were among the first in Europe to adopt these models, forming companies to fund their extensive trade networks, influenced by their interactions with the Islamic world.

Expansion and Legal Framework

Incorporation of Companies: The legal incorporation of joint-stock companies became more common, providing a framework for larger and more sustained business ventures. This development was crucial in the funding of exploration and colonization.
Governance Structures: The governance structures of these companies, including the concept of limited liability, were influenced by Islamic practices of business organization and contractual arrangements.

Impact on Global Trade

Facilitating Long-Distance Trade: Joint-stock companies were instrumental in financing long-distance trade ventures, including those to the Americas, Asia, and Africa.
Development of Capital Markets: These companies contributed to the development of capital markets in Europe, laying the foundation for modern financial systems and stock exchanges.

Legacy in Modern Economic Systems

Model for Modern Corporations: The joint-stock company model, with its roots in Islamic finance principles, evolved into the modern corporation, a fundamental component of today's global economy.
Influence on Economic Expansion: The ability to mobilize capital for large-scale ventures through joint-stock companies was a key factor in the economic expansion of European powers and the development of the global economic system.

Section 5: The Impact on Global Trade Networks

Islamic Finance as a Catalyst for International Commerce

This section discusses how the adoption and adaptation of Islamic financial practices by European powers significantly influenced the establishment and expansion of global trade networks, fundamentally reshaping the world economy.

Expansion of Maritime Trade

Facilitation of Long-Distance Trade: Islamic financial instruments, such as the Sakk (cheque) and early forms of credit, were crucial in facilitating long-distance trade. Their adaptation by European merchants enabled more extensive and efficient maritime trade networks.
Role of Joint-Stock Companies: The joint-stock company model, influenced by Islamic partnership concepts, allowed for pooling of resources and risks in maritime ventures, leading to the expansion of European trade networks to the Americas, Asia, and Africa.

Development of Trade Routes and Markets

Establishment of New Trade Routes: European exploration and subsequent colonization, funded and managed by joint-stock companies and utilizing Islamic financial principles, led to the establishment of new global trade routes.
Integration of Markets: These new routes integrated previously disconnected markets, leading to a significant increase in the exchange of goods, capital, and labor across continents, a precursor to today's globalized economy.

Impact on European Economies

Economic Growth: The expansion of global trade networks, facilitated by Islamic financial practices, contributed to significant economic growth in European nations, particularly in maritime powers like Portugal, Spain, England, and the Netherlands.
Shift in Economic Power: The ability to access and control trade routes and resources led to a shift in economic power in Europe, with maritime trading nations gaining prominence over traditional land-based powers.

Cultural and Knowledge Exchange

Spread of Ideas and Technologies: The global trade networks also facilitated the exchange of ideas, technologies, and knowledge between different parts of the world, contributing to scientific advancements and cultural enrichment.
Interaction of Economic Systems: The interaction between Islamic and European economic systems through trade contributed to a mutual influence and adaptation of financial practices.

Influence on Modern Global Economy

Foundations for Modern Trade Practices: The practices established during this period laid the groundwork for modern trade practices, including banking, insurance, and financial markets.
Legacy in Economic Interconnectivity: The development of global trade networks, influenced by Islamic finance, set the stage for the economic interconnectivity that characterizes the modern world economy.

Section 6: Economic Competition and Cooperation

The Interplay of Rivalry and Partnership in Shaping Global Economy

This section examines how Islamic finance principles Influenced the dynamics of economic competition and cooperation between European and Islamic powers, shaping the development of the global trade system and contributing to the evolution of modern economic practices.

Rivalry in Trade and Expansion

Competition for Trade Dominance: The competition for control over lucrative trade routes and markets, particularly between Islamic empires and European maritime powers, was intensified by advancements in financial and commercial practices influenced by Islamic finance.
Military and Naval Rivalries: This economic competition often translated into military and naval confrontations, as European and Islamic powers vied for dominance in key strategic regions.

Cooperative Economic Relations

Trade Alliances and Treaties: Despite periods of conflict, there were also significant instances of cooperation and alliance-building between Islamic and European states, facilitating trade and cultural exchange.

Joint Ventures and Partnerships: Influenced by Islamic financial models of partnership and risk-sharing, joint ventures between merchants and financiers from different cultural backgrounds became more common, enhancing trade and economic collaboration.

Influence on European Economic Practices

Adoption of Islamic Trade Techniques: European traders and financiers adopted and adapted various Islamic trade techniques, such as credit systems and contractual agreements, improving their own commercial efficiency and competitiveness.
Development of International Commerce Law: The interactions between Islamic and European traders contributed to the development of international commerce law, incorporating principles from both legal traditions.

Impact on Global Trade Dynamics

Creation of a Multicultural Trade Network: The competition and cooperation between Islamic and European powers led to the creation of a complex and multicultural trade network, spanning continents and involving a diverse array of actors.
Integration of Global Economy: These interactions were instrumental in integrating various regional economies into a more cohesive global economy, setting the stage for the interconnected world market.

Legacy in Contemporary Economic Systems

Influence on Modern Economic Policies: The historical interplay of competition and cooperation helped shape modern economic policies and practices, including international trade agreements and global economic cooperation frameworks.
Foundations for Economic Globalization: The foundations laid during this period, influenced by Islamic finance, contributed to the emergence of economic globalization, characterized by an integrated and interdependent global economy.

Section 7: Financing the Voyages of Discovery

The Role of Islamic Finance in European Exploration

In this section, we explore how the principles and practices of Islamic finance influenced the financing of European voyages of discovery, examining the mechanisms through which these voyages were funded and the impact this had on the expansion of European influence and the development of the global trade network.

Funding Mechanisms for Exploration

Joint Ventures and Risk-Sharing: Inspired by Islamic models, European explorers and merchants often relied on joint ventures where multiple investors shared the risks and rewards. This approach was crucial in funding expensive and risky voyages.
Adoption of Islamic Financial Instruments: Instruments such as letters of credit and bills of exchange, adapted from Islamic practices, were vital in managing and securing funding for long-distance explorations and trade.

Impact on Maritime Explorations

Enabling Long-Distance Voyages: The financial support facilitated by these Islamic-influenced practices enabled ambitious maritime explorations, including voyages to the Americas, Africa, and Asia.
Promotion of Trade and Colonization: The success of these voyages, underpinned by effective financing, led to the establishment of trade routes and colonies, significantly expanding European influence globally.

Influence on European Economic Development

Stimulation of Economic Growth: The influx of wealth from these voyages contributed to the economic growth of European nations, particularly maritime powers like Spain and Portugal.
Development of Financial Centers: The need to manage exploration and trade financing contributed to the development of financial centers in Europe, such as Amsterdam and London.

Contribution to Global Economic Integration

Integration of Diverse Economies: The voyages financed through these methods connected disparate economies, facilitating the flow of goods, capital, and labor across the world.
Foundation for Modern Globalization: The development of a global trade network, influenced by Islamic financial practices, laid the groundwork for modern economic globalization.

Legacy in Contemporary Finance

Influence on Modern Financial Systems: The financing models developed for these voyages influenced the evolution of modern financial systems, including banking, insurance, and investment sectors.
Reflection in International Trade and Finance: The principles of risk-sharing and joint ventures continue to be reflected in contemporary practices of international trade and finance.

Section 8: Islamic Influence on European Market Practices

Cross-Cultural Exchanges Shaping Commerce

This section delves into how Islamic financial practices and commercial techniques were assimilated into European market practices, influencing the evolution of European trade, banking, and the overall economic landscape.

Adoption of Islamic Commercial Practices

Market Structure and Organization: The structure and organization of markets in Islamic civilization, including the concepts of market regulation and consumer protection, influenced the way European markets were organized and regulated.
Islamic Trade Customs: European merchants adopted various Islamic trade customs, which improved efficiency and reliability in commercial transactions. These included practices for contracting, credit, and business ethics.

Innovation in Banking and Credit

Bills of Exchange and Cheques: The Islamic invention of instruments like the Sakk (cheque) was adapted into the European bill of exchange, facilitating easier and safer transfer of money, a practice critical to expanding trade.
Credit Systems: Islamic finance's approach to credit, emphasizing ethical lending and risk-sharing, influenced the development of European credit systems, contributing to the growth of banking institutions.

Evolution of Market Regulations

Commercial Laws and Regulations: Islamic commercial law, known for its detailed regulations on trade and commerce, provided a model for the development of similar laws in European markets.
Consumer Protection and Ethics: The Islamic emphasis on fairness and consumer protection in trade influenced the ethical foundations of European market practices.

Impact on European Economy

Stimulating Trade and Commerce: The assimilation of these practices stimulated trade and commerce within Europe, contributing to the economic prosperity of the late Middle Ages and the Renaissance.

Foundation for Modern Economic Systems: The integration of Islamic practices laid the groundwork for modern economic systems in Europe, particularly in terms of market operations and financial transactions.

Legacy in Modern Commerce

Influence on Global Trade Practices: The evolution of market practices, influenced by Islamic finance, played a role in shaping the norms and standards of contemporary global trade.
Ethical Finance and Contemporary Relevance: Islamic principles of ethical finance and risk-sharing continue to find resonance in modern economic discussions, particularly in the context of sustainable and ethical financing.

Section 9: Shifts in Global Economic Power

The Redefinition of Economic Leadership

This section discusses how the integration of Islamic financial principles and practices into European economies contributed to significant shifts In global economic power, influencing the rise of Europe as a dominant economic force and the subsequent shaping of the world economy.

Transition of Economic Dominance

Decline of Islamic Economic Preeminence: During the Middle Ages, Islamic civilizations were at the forefront of global trade and finance. However, the incorporation of their financial practices into European systems, combined with geopolitical changes, led to a gradual shift in economic dominance towards Europe.
Rise of European Maritime Powers: The adoption of Islamic financial techniques played a role in the rise of European maritime powers like Portugal, Spain, the Netherlands, and England, facilitating their expansion into global trade networks.

Impact on Trade Routes and Economic Centers

New Global Trade Routes: European exploration and colonization, financed and managed using Islamic-influenced financial practices, established new global trade routes, redirecting the flow of goods and wealth.
Emergence of New Economic Centers: Cities such as Venice, Genoa, Amsterdam, and London emerged as new centers of global trade and finance, taking over roles that were once held by Islamic economic hubs.

Changing Dynamics of Global Trade

Integration of East and West: The new trade routes facilitated by European ventures integrated the economies of the East and West, leading to a more interconnected global economy.
Shift in Commodity Trade: The global trade in commodities such as spices, silk, and precious metals saw a shift in control and distribution, with European powers playing increasingly dominant roles.

Influence on Economic Systems and Policies

Development of Capitalism: The shifts in global economic power, underpinned by Islamic finance principles adapted by Europeans, contributed to the development and spread of capitalism as an economic system.
Evolution of Economic Policies: These shifts influenced the evolution of economic policies in both European and Islamic countries, as they adapted to the changing global economic landscape.

Legacy in Contemporary Global Economy

Foundations for Modern Economic Globalization: The changes in global economic power dynamics laid the foundations for modern economic globalization, characterized by extensive international trade and interconnected markets.
Influence on Economic Development Models: The historical shifts in economic power continue to influence contemporary models of economic development and the policies of nations navigating the global economy.

Section 10: Long-Term Impacts on Western Financial Systems

Integrating Islamic Principles into the Foundation of Modern Finance

This final section of Chapter 5 examines the long-term impacts of Islamic finance on Western financial systems, exploring how principles and practices originating from the Islamic world have been integrated into the fabric of modern Western finance and continue to influence contemporary economic practices and policies.

Foundational Influence on Banking and Finance

Risk Sharing and Ethical Investment: Islamic finance's emphasis on risk-sharing and ethical investment has influenced modern financial practices, including the development of alternative financing models that emphasize equity and fairness.
Asset-Backed Financing: The principle of asset-backed financing, a hallmark of Islamic finance, has parallels in modern financial instruments, promoting responsible lending and borrowing practices.

Influence on Financial Regulations and Markets

Development of Financial Regulations: The ethical and risk-based principles of Islamic finance have contributed to the development of financial regulations in Western economies, particularly in the aftermath of financial crises, emphasizing transparency and consumer protection.
Emergence of Islamic Banking and Finance: The growth of Islamic banking and finance in Western countries reflects the integration and adaptation of these principles within the global financial system, offering alternative financial products and services.

Impact on Global Trade and Investment

Promotion of International Trade: Islamic finance principles, such as partnership and profit-sharing, have influenced international trade agreements and joint ventures, promoting cooperative investment practices.
Influence on Global Investment Strategies: The ethical and risk-sharing aspects of Islamic finance have impacted global investment strategies, with a growing focus on sustainability, social responsibility, and ethical investment.

Modern Economic Theories and Practices

Contribution to Economic Theories: The integration of Islamic financial principles has contributed to the development of modern economic theories, including those related to market structure, financial stability, and ethical economics.
Application in Contemporary Economic Policies: These principles continue to inform contemporary economic policies, especially in the context of addressing economic inequalities, fostering sustainable development, and promoting ethical financial practices.

Legacy in Contemporary Economic Discourse

Reshaping Financial Narratives: Islamic finance principles have played a role in reshaping narratives around finance and economics, challenging conventional models and promoting a more inclusive and ethical financial discourse.
Influence on Future Economic Models: The continued integration of these principles is likely to influence the development of future economic models and policies, particularly in an increasingly interconnected and ethically conscious global economy.

Chapter 6: Philosophical and Cultural Exchange

Section 1: Islamic Philosophy and European Enlightenment

Bridging Civilizations Through Thought and Reason

This section explores the profound influence of Islamic philosophy on the European Enlightenment, focusing on how the intellectual contributions of Muslim scholars helped to shape the philosophical underpinnings of this pivotal era in European history.

Foundations of Islamic Philosophy

Integration of Greek Philosophy: Islamic scholars, during the Islamic Golden Age, engaged deeply with the works of Greek philosophers like Aristotle and Plato. They integrated these teachings with Islamic thought, leading to a flourishing of philosophy in the Muslim world.
Rationalism and Empiricism: Islamic philosophy placed a strong emphasis on rationalism and empiricism, approaches that would later become fundamental to Enlightenment thinking.

Transmission to Europe

Centers of Learning: Centers of learning in the Islamic world, such as Baghdad, Cordoba, and Cairo, became hubs for philosophical and scientific inquiry. These centers played a critical role in preserving and advancing knowledge during periods when Europe was less focused on intellectual pursuits.
Role of Al-Andalus: Al-Andalus (Islamic Spain) was particularly instrumental in transmitting Islamic philosophy to Europe. The region served as a bridge for the transfer of knowledge, especially during the Reconquista.

Impact on European Intellectuals

Influence on Enlightenment Thinkers: Key figures of the European Enlightenment, such as Thomas Aquinas, Roger Bacon, and later Descartes and Kant, were influenced by Islamic philosophical works, either directly or through translations.
Advancement of Rational Thought: The encounter with Islamic philosophy encouraged a shift in Europe from predominantly theological to more rational and empirical modes of thinking, setting the stage for the Enlightenment.

Legacy in Modern Western Thought

Continued Relevance: The impact of Islamic philosophy on European thought continues to be relevant in modern Western philosophy. It contributed to shaping ideas about reason, ethics, and the nature of knowledge that are central to contemporary philosophical discourse.
Recognition and Rediscovery: In recent times, there has been a growing recognition and rediscovery of the contributions of Islamic philosophers to Western intellectual heritage.

Section 2: Transmission of Knowledge: From Al-Andalus to Europe

The Crucible of Cultural and Intellectual Synthesis

This section delves into the role of Al-Andalus (Islamic Spain) as a pivotal center for the transmission of knowledge from the Islamic world to Europe, highlighting how this exchange of ideas and learning played a significant role in the intellectual awakening of Europe.

Al-Andalus as a Center of Learning

Multicultural Hub: Al-Andalus, renowned for its multicultural environment, became a thriving center for scholars, artists, and thinkers. This environment facilitated the synthesis of Islamic, Christian, and Jewish knowledge.
Preservation and Advancement of Knowledge: Islamic Spain was instrumental in preserving the works of ancient Greek philosophers and scientists. Scholars in Al-Andalus not only preserved these works but also expanded upon them with their own significant contributions.

Impact on European Renaissance and Enlightenment

Introduction to Classical Works: Through translations and scholarly works from Al-Andalus, European scholars gained access to classical Greek and Roman texts that had been lost or forgotten in Europe.

Stimulus for Intellectual Curiosity: The knowledge transmitted from Al-Andalus reinvigorated intellectual curiosity in Europe, leading to the Renaissance, a revival of learning and culture based on classical antiquity.

Scholars and Translators

Key Figures: Prominent figures in Al-Andalus, such as Averroes (Ibn Rushd) and Maimonides, played critical roles in this intellectual exchange. Their works, along with others, were translated and studied across Europe.
Translation Movements: The translation of Arabic texts into Latin and other European languages in places like Toledo became a major enterprise, bridging the gap between the Islamic and European worlds.

Legacy in Modern Academia

Foundations for Modern Sciences and Humanities: The transmission of knowledge from Al-Andalus laid the foundations for various fields in modern science and humanities, including mathematics, astronomy, medicine, philosophy, and literature.
Cultural Exchange and Tolerance: The multicultural and interfaith interactions in Al-Andalus serve as a historical example of cultural exchange and tolerance, influencing contemporary ideas about multiculturalism and intellectual collaboration.

Section 3: Influence of Islamic Scholars on European Thinkers

Bridging Civilizations Through Intellectual Exchange

This section examines the profound influence that Islamic scholars had on European thinkers, focusing on specific instances where Islamic philosophy, science, and mathematics shaped the European intellectual landscape, particularly during the Renaissance and Enlightenment.

Islamic Contributions to Philosophy

Philosophers like Averroes (Ibn Rushd) and Avicenna (Ibn Sina): Their commentaries on Aristotle and original philosophical works were instrumental in shaping medieval European philosophy. Averroes, in particular, was known in Europe as "The Commentator" for his comprehensive studies of Aristotle.
Integration of Rationalism and Faith: Islamic philosophers grappled with reconciling faith and reason, an endeavor that significantly influenced Christian thinkers who were facing similar philosophical challenges during the Middle Ages.

Advancements in Science and Mathematics

Algebra and Number Systems: Islamic mathematicians like Al-Khwarizmi made groundbreaking contributions to algebra and introduced the Arabic numeral system to Europe, fundamentally changing European mathematics.

Astronomy and Optics: Islamic contributions to astronomy and optics, including works by scholars like Alhazen (Ibn al-Haytham), were foundational to the development of these sciences in Europe.

Medicine and the Natural Sciences

Medical Knowledge: Islamic medical texts, particularly those by Avicenna, became standard references in European medical schools. The Canon of Medicine by Avicenna was a key medical text in Europe for centuries.

Botany and Chemistry: Islamic scholarship in botany and the early forms of chemistry, including works by Al-Razi (Rhazes), provided a wealth of knowledge that was integrated into European scientific studies.

Impact on Renaissance and Enlightenment Thinkers

Revival of Classical Learning: The Islamic preservation and expansion of classical Greek and Roman knowledge played a critical role in the European Renaissance, which saw a revival of learning based on classical sources.

Influence on Enlightenment Ideals: Islamic emphasis on reason and empirical inquiry influenced Enlightenment thinkers, contributing to the development of ideas such as empiricism, individualism, and secularism.

Enduring Legacy in Western Thought

Recognition of Islamic Influence: There is a growing recognition of the extent to which Islamic scholars influenced Western intellectual history, challenging narratives that have traditionally overlooked this contribution.

Continued Relevance in Modern Academia: The works of Islamic scholars continue to be studied for their contributions to philosophy, science, and humanities, highlighting the interconnectedness of world intellectual traditions.

Section 4: The Renaissance and Arabic Texts

The Revival of Learning Fueled by Islamic Scholarship

This section explores the critical role of Arabic texts in the European Renaissance, highlighting how the translation and study of these works facilitated a revival of learning and intellectual curiosity in Europe.

Transmission of Knowledge through Arabic Texts

Preservation and Expansion of Classical Knowledge: During the Islamic Golden Age, scholars translated, preserved, and expanded upon the works of ancient Greek and Roman thinkers. These texts were later translated into Latin and other European languages, reintroducing lost knowledge to Europe.
Centers of Translation: Cities like Toledo in Spain and centers in Sicily became hubs for the translation of Arabic texts into Latin, serving as gateways for the flow of knowledge from the Islamic world to Europe.

Impact on Renaissance Thinkers

Access to Comprehensive Works: European scholars gained access to comprehensive works in fields like philosophy, medicine, mathematics, and astronomy, which had been preserved and enhanced by Islamic scholars.
Inspiration for Intellectual Exploration: The availability of these texts inspired a new generation of European intellectuals, spurring an era of exploration and discovery in various fields of knowledge.

Contributions to Specific Disciplines

Medicine: Works by Islamic physicians, such as Avicenna's "The Canon of Medicine," became foundational texts in European medical schools.
Mathematics: The introduction of Arabic numerals and algebraic concepts revolutionized mathematics in Europe.
Astronomy and Optics: Islamic advancements in astronomy and optics, seen in works by Alhazen and others, were instrumental in the development of these sciences during the Renaissance.

Cultural and Artistic Influences

Art and Architecture: The influence of Islamic art and architecture, with its distinctive aesthetic and techniques, can be seen in various Renaissance artworks and buildings.
Literature and Linguistics: The translation of Arabic texts also influenced European literature, introducing new themes, styles, and linguistic elements.

Legacy in Modern European Thought

Foundation for Modern Sciences: The knowledge transmitted through Arabic texts laid the groundwork for the scientific revolution in Europe.
Recognition of Cross-Cultural Contributions: Contemporary scholarship increasingly acknowledges the integral role of Arabic texts in shaping the Renaissance, highlighting the interconnected nature of global intellectual history.

Section 5: Medicine, Mathematics, and Astronomy

Islamic Contributions to Key Scientific Fields

In this section, we explore the significant contributions of Islamic scholars to the fields of medicine, mathematics, and astronomy, and how their advancements laid the foundations for European developments in these areas during the Renaissance and beyond.

Advancements in Medicine

Foundational Texts: Islamic medical texts, such as Avicenna's "The Canon of Medicine" and Al-Razi's comprehensive works, became standard references in European medical education.
Innovative Techniques: Islamic medicine introduced innovative techniques and a more systematic approach to diagnosis and treatment, which significantly influenced European medical practices.

Developments in Mathematics

Algebra and Algorithm: The work of Al-Khwarizmi in algebra (a term derived from his book "Al-Kitab al-Mukhtasar fi Hisab al-Jabr wal-Muqabala") and the concept of the algorithm were pivotal in advancing mathematical thought in Europe.
Numerical Systems: The introduction of Arabic numerals, including the concept of zero, revolutionized the European numerical system, making calculations easier and more accurate.

Advancements in Astronomy

Astronomical Observations and Models: Islamic astronomers like Al-Battani and Alhazen made significant contributions to the understanding of celestial movements and optics. Their observations and models were crucial for later European astronomers, including Copernicus and Galileo.
Astronomical Instruments: The development of astronomical instruments such as the astrolabe by Islamic scholars was instrumental in advancing European astronomical studies.

Influence on European Renaissance

Transmission of Knowledge: The translation of these scientific texts into Latin and other European languages during the Renaissance opened up a wealth of knowledge to European scholars.
Inspiration for Further Research: Access to Islamic scientific works inspired European scholars to conduct their own research and experiments, leading to significant scientific discoveries and advancements during the Renaissance and Scientific Revolution.

Legacy in Modern Science

Foundational Role in Modern Disciplines: The contributions of Islamic scholars provided a foundation for the development of modern disciplines in medicine, mathematics, and astronomy.
Recognition of Islamic Influence: There is an increasing acknowledgment in the scientific community of the role Islamic scholarship played in the development of these fields, contributing to a more inclusive understanding of the history of science.

Section 6: Islamic Art and Architecture's Influence

The Aesthetic Legacy Bridging East and West

This section delves into the influence of Islamic art and architecture on European styles, exploring how the aesthetic principles, motifs, and techniques of the Islamic world enriched European artistic and architectural expressions during and after the Renaissance.

Islamic Artistic Principles and Motifs

Geometric Patterns and Calligraphy: Islamic art is renowned for its intricate geometric patterns and the art of calligraphy. These elements found their way into European art, particularly in decorative designs.

Use of Color and Light: The Islamic use of vibrant colors and emphasis on light and its effects influenced European artists, leading to innovations in the use of color and light in paintings and architecture.

Influence on European Architecture

Architectural Features: Features such as pointed arches, domes, and intricate tile work, characteristic of Islamic architecture, were incorporated into European buildings, notably in Moorish and Mudéjar styles in Spain and Portugal.
Garden Design and Ornamentation: The concept of the Persian and Islamic gardens, with their emphasis on symmetry, water features, and lush vegetation, inspired the design of European gardens.

Cultural Exchange through Art and Craft

Trade and Cultural Interactions: Trade routes between the Islamic world and Europe facilitated the exchange of artistic goods and techniques, such as textiles, ceramics, and glassware.
Learning from Master Craftsmen: European craftsmen and artists, through interactions with their Islamic counterparts, learned new techniques and incorporated them into their work, enhancing the quality and diversity of European crafts.

Impact on the Renaissance and Beyond

Renaissance Art and Humanism: Elements of Islamic art contributed to the rich tapestry of Renaissance art, aligning with the humanist focus on beauty, balance, and naturalism.
Baroque and Later Movements: The influence of Islamic aesthetics continued into later artistic movements, including the Baroque, where the grandeur and ornamentation echoed Islamic artistic principles.

Enduring Legacy in Modern Art and Architecture

Continued Inspiration: Islamic art and architecture continue to inspire modern artists and architects, contributing to the global artistic vocabulary.
Recognition of Cross-Cultural Influences: Contemporary scholarship increasingly acknowledges the significance of Islamic influences in the history of European art and architecture, highlighting the interconnected nature of cultural and artistic development.

Section 7: The Role of Translation Movements

Bridging Knowledge through Language

This section highlights the crucial role of translation movements in the transmission of Islamic knowledge to Europe, focusing on how these efforts facilitated a cross-cultural flow of ideas, sciences, and philosophies that significantly contributed to European intellectual advancements.

Translation as a Catalyst for Knowledge Transfer

Translation Hubs: Cities like Toledo in Spain and Palermo in Sicily became centers of translation where Arabic texts on science, philosophy, and medicine were translated into Latin and other European languages.
Multilingual Scholars: These translation efforts were often led by multilingual scholars, who not only translated texts but also provided commentaries and interpretations, making the knowledge more accessible to European audiences.

Impact on European Learning

Access to Lost Knowledge: The translations reopened access to classical Greek and Roman works that had been preserved by Islamic scholars, along with the rich intellectual contributions of the Islamic world itself.
Stimulating Intellectual Curiosity: The influx of new knowledge through translations significantly stimulated intellectual curiosity in Europe, influencing developments in universities and scholarly circles.

Contributions to Specific Fields

Advancements in Science and Philosophy: Translated works in astronomy, mathematics, medicine, and philosophy greatly enriched these fields in Europe, laying the groundwork for the Renaissance and Scientific Revolution.
Influence on Theological and Philosophical Thought: The availability of philosophical and theological works from the Islamic world challenged and enriched European theological and philosophical debates.

The Legacy of the Translation Movement

Foundation for Modern European Thought: The knowledge transmitted through these translations was integral to the formation of modern European scientific and philosophical thought.
Recognition of Interconnected Intellectual Heritage: The translation movement underscores the interconnected nature of the world's intellectual heritage, highlighting the contributions of Islamic civilization to European advancements.

Enduring Significance in Modern Times

Model for Cultural Exchange: The translation movements of the medieval period serve as a historical model for cultural and intellectual exchange, emphasizing the value of translating and sharing knowledge across cultural boundaries.
Inspiration for Contemporary Scholarship: The collaborative and integrative spirit of these translation efforts continues to inspire contemporary academic and cross-cultural endeavors.

Section 8: The Impact on European Education Systems

Integrating Islamic Knowledge into European Academia

This section explores how the influx of Islamic knowledge through translation and cultural exchange influenced the development of European education systems, from universities to scientific methods of inquiry.

Foundation of European Universities

Influence on University Curriculum: The establishment of medieval European universities, such as those in Bologna, Oxford, and Paris, was influenced by the learning models of Islamic madrasas and the wealth of knowledge translated from Arabic texts.
Integration of Islamic Scholarship: Subjects like medicine, mathematics, astronomy, and philosophy, heavily influenced by Islamic scholarship, became integral parts of the curriculum in European universities.

Methodological Influences

Emphasis on Rational Inquiry: Islamic scholars' focus on rationalism and empirical inquiry influenced the teaching methods in European institutions, fostering a shift towards more evidence-based and analytical approaches to learning.

Development of the Scientific Method: The works of Islamic scholars in developing scientific methodologies provided a foundation for the formulation of the scientific method in Europe, later articulated by figures like Francis Bacon.

Cross-Cultural Intellectual Exchange

Scholarly Travel and Exchange: European scholars traveled to Islamic centers of learning, such as Cordoba and Cairo, to study and exchange ideas. Similarly, Islamic scholars and texts found their way to European academic settings, fostering a vibrant intellectual exchange.
Influence on Renaissance Humanism: The broadening of educational subjects and methodologies, influenced by Islamic scholarship, contributed to the humanistic ideals of the Renaissance, emphasizing the value of human potential and creativity.

Legacy in Modern Education Systems

Continued Influence on Academic Disciplines: The impact of Islamic scholarship is evident in the range and depth of disciplines taught in modern universities, particularly in the sciences and humanities.
Recognition of Shared Intellectual Heritage: There is growing acknowledgment in contemporary education systems of the shared intellectual heritage between the Islamic world and Europe, leading to a more inclusive approach to the history of knowledge.

Contemporary Educational Collaboration

Interfaith and Intercultural Academic Programs: Modern education systems increasingly incorporate interfaith and intercultural studies, drawing inspiration from the historical periods of fruitful intellectual exchange, such as that between Islamic and European scholars.
Collaborative Research and Exchange Programs: The spirit of collaboration and knowledge exchange seen in historical interactions is mirrored in modern academic research and student exchange programs that cross cultural and geographical boundaries.

Section 9: Intellectual Debates and Exchanges

The Interplay of Ideas Across Cultures

This section delves into the intellectual debates and exchanges between Islamic and European scholars, highlighting how this cross-cultural dialogue contributed to the evolution of philosophical, scientific, and theological thought in both worlds.

Forums for Debate and Exchange

Centers of Learning: Places like the House of Wisdom in Baghdad, the University of Al-Qarawiyyin in Fez, and the University of Al-Azhar in Cairo, along with European universities and monastic schools, served as forums for intellectual exchange and debate.
Interfaith Dialogues: Interactions in multicultural regions, particularly in places like Al-Andalus and Sicily, provided opportunities for Christians, Muslims, and Jews to engage in philosophical and theological discussions.

Philosophical Interactions

Integration and Reconciliation of Views: Islamic and European philosophers grappled with integrating Greek philosophical thought with their respective religious beliefs, leading to a rich body of work that sought to reconcile faith with reason.
Influence on Major Philosophical Movements: Islamic thought, particularly in areas like metaphysics and ethics, influenced major philosophical movements in Europe, including Scholasticism in the Middle Ages and Rationalism during the Enlightenment.

Scientific Collaborations

Advancements In Astronomy and Mathematics: Collaborative efforts in fields such as astronomy and mathematics led to significant advancements, with European scientists building upon the work of their Islamic counterparts.
Development of Medical Knowledge: Exchange of medical knowledge was particularly notable, with European physicians drawing on the extensive medical texts and practices developed by Islamic scholars.

Theological Discussions

Comparative Theology: The interactions between Islamic and Christian theologians led to comparative studies of religious texts and doctrines, deepening the understanding of each other's faiths.
Impact on Religious Tolerance: These exchanges sometimes fostered a climate of relative religious tolerance and mutual respect, challenging prevailing attitudes of religious exclusivity.

Legacy in Modern Intellectual Thought

Foundation for Contemporary Scholarship: The intellectual debates and exchanges of this era laid the groundwork for modern scholarship, characterized by a multidisciplinary and cross-cultural approach.
Inspiration for Interreligious Dialogue: The historical dialogues between Islamic and European scholars continue to inspire contemporary efforts in interreligious and intercultural dialogue, promoting understanding and cooperation in a diverse world.

Section 10: Enduring Legacies in Western Thought

Continuing Influence of Islamic Scholarship

This section addresses the enduring legacies of Islamic intellectual contributions in Western thought, exploring how the exchange of ideas during the medieval period continues to influence contemporary academic disciplines, cultural perspectives, and philosophical paradigms.

Foundational Role in Modern Sciences

Basis for Scientific Disciplines: The works of Islamic scholars in fields like mathematics, astronomy, and medicine laid foundational stones for the development of these disciplines in the West. Concepts like algebra and algorithms, as well as advancements in optics and medical knowledge, have their roots in Islamic scholarship.
Methodological Contributions: The empirical methods and rational inquiry promoted by Islamic scholars contributed to the formation of the scientific method, which remains central to modern scientific inquiry.

Philosophical Influences

Rationalism and Ethics: Islamic philosophy, with its blend of rationalism and ethical inquiry, continues to influence Western philosophical thought, particularly in areas concerning knowledge, ethics, and the relationship between reason and faith.
Interfaith and Intercultural Philosophy: The dialogues between Islamic and Western philosophers have inspired contemporary interfaith and intercultural philosophical studies, fostering a more inclusive and holistic approach to understanding philosophical questions.

Cultural and Artistic Impact

Influences in Art and Architecture: The aesthetic principles and styles of Islamic art and architecture, characterized by intricate geometric patterns, calligraphy, and emphasis on light and space, continue to inspire modern artists and architects.
Cultural Integration and Diversity: The legacy of Islamic influence in European culture has contributed to a richer, more diverse cultural landscape, promoting appreciation for the interconnectedness of global artistic and cultural traditions.

Educational Impacts

Multidisciplinary Studies: The broad range of disciplines enriched by Islamic scholarship has influenced the multidisciplinary nature of modern education, encouraging a comprehensive approach to learning that crosses traditional academic boundaries.
Global History and Perspectives: The recognition of Islamic contributions has led to more inclusive educational curricula that acknowledge the global nature of intellectual history and the interconnectedness of different cultures' contributions.

Contemporary Relevance

Ongoing Intellectual Exchange: The tradition of intellectual exchange between the Islamic world and the West continues to be relevant, fostering collaboration and dialogue in addressing global challenges and advancing knowledge.
Ethical and Social Considerations: Islamic contributions to fields like economics and finance, particularly ethical investment and social responsibility, are increasingly pertinent in contemporary discussions about sustainable and equitable economic practices.

Chapter 7: Voyages to the Americas: An Islamic Echo

Section 1: Early European Expeditions and Their Motives

Exploring the Drivers Behind the Age of Discovery

This section examines the early European expeditions to the Americas, focusing on the underlying motives, both economic and religious, that drove European powers to embark on these ventures, and how Islamic influences subtly echoed in these explorations.

Economic Ambitions

Search for Wealth: The primary motive for many European expeditions was the search for new trade routes and resources, driven by the desire for wealth, particularly in spices and precious metals.
Competition for Trade Dominance: European nations, eager to break the Muslim monopoly over the lucrative trade routes to Asia, were motivated to find alternative routes, leading to westward voyages.

Religious and Ideological Motives

Spread of Christianity: In addition to economic motives, there was a strong desire to spread Christianity. This was partly influenced by the ongoing conflict with Islamic powers in the Mediterranean and the desire to find Christian allies against the Muslims.
Reconquista Legacy: The completion of the Reconquista in Spain, ending centuries of Muslim rule, fueled a zeal for further religious conquests and missionary activities in the New World.

Influence of Islamic Naval Technology

Adoption of Islamic Navigational Techniques: European explorers utilized navigational techniques and maritime technology that had been developed by Islamic scholars and seafarers, including advancements in cartography and ship design.
Knowledge of the Monsoon Winds: Knowledge of the monsoon wind patterns, crucial for navigating to and from Asia, was initially gathered by Arab traders and later utilized by European explorers.

Role of Individual Explorers

Figures like Columbus and Vasco da Gama: Prominent explorers like Christopher Columbus and Vasco da Gama were motivated by a combination of personal ambition, economic gain, and religious fervor, embodying the complex motivations of the Age of Discovery.

Legacy of the Early Expeditions

Opening of the New World: These early expeditions led to the opening of the Americas to European exploration, colonization, and exploitation, setting the stage for profound global transformations.

Echoes of Islamic Influence: The influence of Islamic scholarship, navigation, and trade practices subtly echoed in these voyages, demonstrating the interconnected nature of medieval global knowledge and exploration.

Section 2: Navigation Technology: An Islamic Inheritance

Tracing the Roots of Maritime Advancements

This section explores how Islamic contributions to navigation technology played a crucial role in enabling European explorers to embark on their voyages to the Americas, highlighting the specific Islamic innovations that were integral to these maritime endeavors.

Islamic Contributions to Navigational Sciences

Astrolabe and Compass: Islamic advancements in the astrolabe, an instrument used for celestial navigation, and the early use of the magnetic compass were critical tools adopted by European sailors.
Cartography: Islamic cartographers created detailed maps and charts of known world routes, including the Indian Ocean and the Atlantic, which influenced European mapmaking and the planning of voyages.

Transmission of Knowledge to Europe

Centers of Learning: Places like Al-Andalus in Spain and the major trade cities of the Islamic world were key in transmitting navigational knowledge to European explorers and cartographers.
Maritime Manuals and Texts: Islamic maritime manuals and texts, which included sophisticated knowledge of tides, stars, and sea currents, were translated into European languages and studied by sailors and explorers.

Impact on European Voyages

Preparation for Long-Distance Travel: Islamic navigational tools and knowledge equipped European sailors for long-distance oceanic travel, allowing for more precise and safer voyages.
Exploration Routes: The understanding of monsoon winds and ocean currents, gleaned from Islamic sources, was crucial in planning routes to the Americas and later to Asia.

Influences on Ship Design

Adaptation of Shipbuilding Techniques: European shipbuilders adopted techniques from Islamic shipbuilding, including the design of hulls and the use of lateen sails, which were more suitable for long voyages.
Enhancement of Maritime Capabilities: These advancements in ship design enhanced the maritime capabilities of European vessels, making them more maneuverable and seaworthy for transoceanic expeditions.

Legacy in Modern Navigation

Foundations for Modern Maritime Exploration: The Islamic contributions to navigation technology laid the foundations for modern maritime exploration and navigation.
Acknowledgment of Cross-Cultural Exchange: The role of Islamic science and technology in the Age of Discovery highlights the importance of cross-cultural exchanges in shaping global history and technological progress.

Section 3: The Quest for Alternative Trade Routes

Navigating New Paths in Response to Economic and Political Pressures

This section discusses the European quest for alternative trade routes to Asia and the Americas, delving into how this pursuit was driven by economic ambitions to bypass Islamic-controlled territories and the desire to find new sources of wealth.

Motivation Behind Seeking New Routes

Bypassing Islamic Trade Monopolies: Islamic empires controlled key trade routes to Asia, especially the Silk Road and routes through the Indian Ocean. European powers sought new routes to avoid paying high tariffs and to gain direct access to Asian markets.
Economic Rivalry and Independence: The desire to establish independent trade routes was fueled by economic rivalry with Islamic powers and the aspiration to establish direct trade relationships with Asian kingdoms.

Exploratory Ventures and Discoveries

Voyages of Columbus: Christopher Columbus's voyages, initially aimed at finding a westward route to Asia, led to the unexpected discovery of the Americas, opening up new opportunities for trade and colonization.

Vasco da Gama's Route to India: Vasco da Gama's successful sea voyage around Africa to India marked the beginning of European maritime dominance and the establishment of sea routes that bypassed Islamic territories.

Technological Advancements and Navigation

Maritime Technology: The development of caravels and advancements in navigation technology, influenced by Islamic maritime knowledge, enabled longer and more daring sea voyages.
Mapping and Cartography: Improved maps and navigational charts, incorporating Islamic and Asian knowledge, played a crucial role in these explorations.

Impact on Global Trade Dynamics

Shift in Trade Power: The establishment of new trade routes diminished the control of Islamic empires over global trade, gradually shifting economic power to Europe.
Globalization of Trade: These new routes contributed to the early phases of globalization, connecting distant parts of the world through commerce and exchange.

Legacy and Historical Significance

Opening of the New World: The search for alternative trade routes led to the European encounter with the Americas, profoundly impacting indigenous civilizations and leading to significant cultural and demographic changes.
Reconfiguration of World Economy: The opening of new maritime routes reconfigured the world economy, setting the stage for European colonialism and the rise of the West in the global economic order.

Section 4: Columbus and the Drive Westward

Unraveling the Motives and Influences Behind Columbus's Voyages

This section focuses on Christopher Columbus's voyages to the Americas, examining the complex web of motivations behind his expeditions, including the desire to find a westward route to Asia, and the influence of Islamic geographical knowledge on his journey.

Columbus's Ambition and Vision

Seeking a Westward Route to Asia: Columbus was driven by the goal of finding a westward sea route to Asia, intending to access its riches directly and bypass the Islamic-controlled trade routes.
Influence of Marco Polo's Travels: Columbus was inspired by the accounts of Marco Polo and other travelers who described the wealth of Asia, fueling his ambition to establish a direct trade route.

Islamic Influence on Columbus's Navigation

Geographical Knowledge: Columbus utilized maps and navigational knowledge that were significantly influenced by Islamic scholars. This included understanding of the trade winds and ocean currents, which were crucial for his transatlantic voyage.
Miscalculations and Misconceptions: Columbus's underestimation of the Earth's circumference, a miscalculation partly influenced by his interpretation of Islamic geographical texts, led to his unexpected landing in the Americas.

Financial and Political Backing

Support from Spanish Monarchs: Columbus's voyages were financially backed by Queen Isabella and King Ferdinand of Spain, particularly after the completion of the Reconquista. This support was partly motivated by the desire to expand Spanish power and spread Christianity.
Navigating Court Politics: Columbus had to navigate the complex politics of European courts, leveraging the growing rivalry with Islamic powers and the eagerness of European monarchies to find new trade routes.

Impact and Consequences of Columbus's Discoveries

Encounter with the New World: Columbus's discovery of the Americas, while initially seen as a new route to Asia, opened up a new continent to European exploration, exploitation, and colonization.
Cultural and Demographic Shifts: The arrival of Europeans in the Americas led to significant cultural, demographic, and ecological changes, marking the beginning of a new era in global history.

Legacy of Columbus's Voyages

Historical Controversy: Columbus's legacy is complex and controversial, encompassing both the opening of the Americas to European influence and the subsequent negative impacts on indigenous populations.
Echoes of Islamic Influence: The indirect influence of Islamic scholarship on Columbus's voyage highlights the interconnected nature of knowledge and exploration in the medieval world.

Section 5: Interactions with Indigenous Peoples

Encounters and Consequences of European and Indigenous Contact

This section discusses the interactions between European explorers and indigenous peoples of the Americas, focusing on the nature of these encounters, the impact on indigenous societies, and the legacy of these interactions in shaping the New World.

First Encounters

Initial Contact: The first encounters between European explorers, beginning with Columbus, and indigenous peoples were marked by curiosity and mutual misunderstanding. Europeans were often mistaken for divine figures or seen with suspicion.
Exchange of Goods and Ideas: These early interactions involved the exchange of goods, knowledge, and cultural practices. Europeans introduced items like metal tools and firearms, while indigenous peoples shared knowledge of local agriculture and geography.

Cultural and Ethical Misunderstandings

Misinterpretation of Cultures: European explorers often misinterpreted indigenous customs and social structures, viewing them through a Eurocentric and often condescending lens.
Religious Perspectives: The European perception of indigenous religions and practices was heavily influenced by their Christian background, leading to efforts to convert indigenous peoples and sometimes to outright destruction of native religious symbols.

Impact on Indigenous Societies

Diseases and Population Decline: The introduction of European diseases, such as smallpox, to which indigenous peoples had no immunity, resulted in catastrophic population declines.

Social and Political Disruption: European colonization and settlement disrupted indigenous social structures, economies, and political systems, leading to the displacement and subjugation of many native communities.

Resistance and Adaptation

Indigenous Resistance: Indigenous peoples employed various strategies of resistance, from armed conflict to diplomatic negotiations, in response to European encroachment.
Cultural Adaptation and Syncretism: In some cases, indigenous societies adapted to the new realities, blending European and native practices in areas such as religion, language, and governance.

Legacy of European-Indigenous Interactions

Enduring Impact on Indigenous Cultures: The legacy of these early interactions continues to affect indigenous communities, with ongoing challenges related to cultural preservation, land rights, and political autonomy.
Historical Reevaluation: Contemporary scholarship and societal perspectives are increasingly reevaluating these interactions, recognizing the complexities of cultural exchange and the often-devastating impact of European colonization on indigenous peoples.

Section 6: The Role of Religion in Colonization

Faith as a Driving Force in the New World

This section explores the significant role of religion in the European colonization of the Americas, examining how Christian missionary efforts, religious justifications for conquest, and the interaction with indigenous belief systems shaped the colonial experience.

Christian Missionary Endeavors

Evangelization Efforts: One of the primary motives for many European explorers and colonizers was the spread of Christianity. Missionary orders, such as the Jesuits, Franciscans, and Dominicans, played a pivotal role in this endeavor.
Impact on Indigenous Populations: The missionary efforts led to the conversion of many indigenous people to Christianity, often accompanied by the suppression of native religions and practices.

Religious Justifications for Conquest

Doctrine of Discovery: European powers often used religious doctrines, such as the Papal Bull "Inter Caetera," to justify the conquest and colonization of the Americas, claiming a divine mandate to spread Christianity and civilize indigenous peoples.
Moral and Ethical Dilemmas: The process of colonization raised complex moral and ethical questions for both colonizers and indigenous peoples, particularly regarding issues of sovereignty, human rights, and religious freedom.

Syncretism and Cultural Resistance

Blending of Religious Traditions: In many parts of the Americas, a syncretism of Christian and indigenous religious traditions emerged, leading to unique forms of worship and belief that combined elements of both.
Resistance Through Religion: Indigenous peoples often used religion as a form of cultural resistance, preserving aspects of their traditional beliefs and practices within the framework of imposed Christian traditions.

Legacy of Religious Colonization

Enduring Religious Influence: The religious landscape of the Americas today is heavily influenced by these early missionary efforts, with Christianity being the dominant religion in many regions.
Reevaluation of Missionary Legacy: Modern perspectives are increasingly critical of the missionary legacy, acknowledging the cultural and spiritual loss experienced by indigenous peoples and the complex legacy of religious colonization.

Section 7: European Settlement Strategies

Strategies and Motivations Behind European Colonization

This section examines the various strategies employed by European powers in establishing settlements in the Americas, exploring how these strategies were influenced by economic, religious, and political factors, and their impact on the indigenous populations and the environment.

Diverse Colonial Approaches

Spanish and Portuguese Models: The Spanish and Portuguese primarily pursued a model of direct control and exploitation, establishing encomiendas and missions, focusing on resource extraction and conversion of indigenous peoples to Christianity.
French and English Methods: The French and English approaches were initially more oriented towards trade, particularly in fur, and establishing alliances with indigenous groups. Over time, however, they also moved towards more direct forms of colonization and settlement.

Economic Drivers

Resource Exploitation: The primary motive for many European settlements was the exploitation of natural resources, such as gold, silver, and agricultural products. This often led to the enslavement and exploitation of indigenous populations.
Trade and Mercantilism: European powers sought to establish colonies that could provide raw materials for the home country and serve as markets for European goods, in line with mercantilist economic policies.

Religious and Ideological Factors

Spread of Christianity: The religious mission to convert indigenous peoples to Christianity was a significant factor in European colonization, influencing settlement patterns and interactions with native populations.
Utopian Visions: Some European settlements, particularly English ones in North America, were also motivated by religious and ideological visions of creating "utopian" societies based on particular religious or social ideals.

Impact on Indigenous Societies

Displacement and Cultural Disruption: The establishment of European settlements often led to the displacement of indigenous communities, disruption of their traditional ways of life, and significant cultural and demographic changes.
Resistance and Accommodation: Indigenous responses varied from resistance and conflict to accommodation and alliance, depending on local circumstances and the nature of European settlement.

Environmental Changes

Introduction of New Species: European colonization led to the introduction of new plants and animals to the Americas, significantly altering local ecosystems – a process known as the Columbian Exchange.

Land Use and Ecological Impact: European agricultural practices and land use strategies, such as deforestation and mining, had profound impacts on the American landscape and environment.

Section 8: The Impact of Islamic Naval Power

Navigating the Influence of Islamic Maritime Strength

This section explores the impact of Islamic naval power on European voyages and colonization efforts in the Americas, focusing on how the maritime strength of Islamic states influenced European naval strategies and the course of exploration.

Islamic Dominance in the Mediterranean

Control of Mediterranean Trade: For much of the medieval period, Islamic states, particularly the Ottoman Empire, exerted significant control over Mediterranean trade routes. This dominance forced European powers to seek alternative routes to Asia and the New World.

Naval Technology and Tactics: Islamic advancements in naval technology and tactics, including shipbuilding and navigation, indirectly influenced European maritime developments.

Response to Islamic Naval Power

Driving Exploration Westward: The need to circumvent Islamic-controlled routes was a key factor motivating European explorations westward, leading to the discovery of the Americas.

Adaptation of Maritime Techniques: European powers adapted and improved upon naval technologies and tactics encountered through interactions with Islamic states, enhancing their own maritime capabilities.

European Naval Expansion

Development of Ocean-Going Fleets: In response to Islamic naval strength, European nations developed ocean-going fleets capable of longer voyages, which were instrumental in the exploration and colonization of the Americas.

Competition and Conflict: The competition with Islamic powers also led to increased naval conflict in the Mediterranean and the Indian Ocean, influencing European naval strategies and shipbuilding.

Influence on Colonial Strategies

Protecting Trade Routes: The presence of Islamic naval power influenced European strategies to protect their newly established trade routes to the Americas and Asia.
Establishing Naval Bases: The need to support long-distance trade and naval operations led to the establishment of European naval bases and colonies along key maritime routes.

Legacy of Islamic Naval Influence

Shaping Global Maritime History: The interplay between Islamic and European naval powers significantly shaped the course of global maritime history and the patterns of world trade.
Continued Study and Appreciation: Modern historical and naval studies continue to recognize and explore the influence of Islamic naval power on the Age of Exploration and the development of naval warfare and trade.

Section 9: Resource Exploitation and Trade Dynamics

The Economic Implications of European Expansion

This section examines the patterns of resource exploitation and the resulting trade dynamics established by European powers in the Americas, highlighting how these practices were influenced by and diverged from Islamic economic models.

Patterns of Resource Exploitation

Extraction of Precious Metals: The exploitation of gold and silver, particularly by the Spanish in South and Central America, became a primary objective, fueling European economies and global trade.
Agricultural Commodities: European colonizers established plantations in the Americas, cultivating crops like sugar, tobacco, and cotton, often using forced labor from indigenous populations and African slaves.

Influence of Islamic Trade Practices

Mercantilism vs. Islamic Trade Ethics: European mercantilism, focused on state control and the accumulation of wealth, contrasted with Islamic principles of trade, which emphasized fair dealings and ethical practices.
Adaptation of Navigational Knowledge: European exploitation of American resources was facilitated by navigational and maritime knowledge, some of which was inherited from Islamic traditions.

Development of Transatlantic Trade Networks

Creation of New Trade Routes: The colonization of the Americas led to the establishment of new transatlantic trade routes, connecting Europe, Africa, and the Americas.
Columbian Exchange: The exchange of goods, plants, animals, and diseases between the Old and New Worlds, known as the Columbian Exchange, had profound economic and ecological impacts.

Economic Impact on Indigenous Societies

Disruption of Local Economies: European economic activities disrupted indigenous economies and ways of life, leading to social and economic upheavals.
Forced Labor and Enslavement: The demand for labor in mining and plantation agriculture led to the widespread use of forced labor, including the enslavement of indigenous peoples and the importation of African slaves.

Legacy of Colonial Economic Practices

Foundations for Global Capitalism: The economic models and trade networks established during this period laid the groundwork for the development of global capitalism.
Reevaluation of Economic Impact: Contemporary perspectives increasingly scrutinize the economic legacy of European colonization in the Americas, recognizing the detrimental effects on indigenous populations and the long-term ecological consequences.

Section 10: The Transformation of the New World

Enduring Changes in the Americas Post-European Contact

This final section of Chapter 7 discusses the profound transformations in the Americas resulting from European exploration and colonization, examining the lasting impacts on the continents' demographics, cultures, economies, and environments.

Demographic Changes

Population Decline: The introduction of European diseases, coupled with the effects of conquest and colonization, led to a dramatic decline in the indigenous population of the Americas. Immigration and Settlement: European colonization brought significant European and African population movements to the Americas, leading to demographic shifts and the creation of diverse societies.

Cultural Transformations

Syncretism and Cultural Blending: The encounter between European and indigenous cultures led to syncretic blends in religion, language, and customs, giving rise to unique cultural identities in the Americas.
Loss of Indigenous Cultures: Despite instances of cultural blending, many indigenous cultures, languages, and traditions were lost or heavily suppressed under European influence.

Economic Impact

Shift in Global Trade: The Americas became integral to the global trade network, with the flow of silver, gold, and agricultural commodities reshaping global economic dynamics.
Development of Colonial Economies: The establishment of plantation economies and resource extraction industries in the Americas set the stage for the region's economic development, often based on exploitative labor practices.

Environmental Changes

Columbian Exchange: The transatlantic exchange of plants, animals, and diseases led to significant ecological changes in both the Old and New Worlds.
Altered Landscapes: European agricultural practices, mining, and urban development dramatically altered the landscapes of the Americas, impacting local ecosystems and biodiversity.

Legacy of European Colonization

Foundations of Modern Nations: The political and social structures established during colonization played a significant role in the development of modern nation-states in the Americas.
Ongoing Repercussions: The legacy of European colonization continues to be felt in various aspects, including social and economic disparities, debates over land rights and indigenous sovereignty, and the ongoing efforts to preserve and revive indigenous cultures.

Chapter 8: The Jewish Community: Between Worlds

Section 1: Jewish Life in Islamic and Christian Lands

Examining the Varied Experiences of Jewish Communities

This section explores the experiences of Jewish communities living under Islamic and Christian rule, highlighting the differences in cultural, social, and legal aspects of Jewish life in these contrasting environments.

Jewish Life in Islamic Lands

Generally Tolerant Environment: In many Islamic lands, Jews lived as "dhimmis" – non-Muslim citizens with certain protections under Islamic law. They were allowed to practice their religion and participate in economic and cultural life, albeit with restrictions and special taxes.
Cultural and Intellectual Flourishing: Jewish communities in Islamic territories, notably in places like Al-Andalus and the Ottoman Empire, experienced periods of cultural and intellectual flourishing, contributing significantly to the fields of philosophy, medicine, and poetry.

Jewish Communities under Christian Rule

Varied Experiences: The experience of Jews in Christian Europe varied greatly over time and between regions, ranging from relative tolerance to severe persecution and expulsion.

Pogroms and Expulsions: In many parts of medieval and early modern Europe, Jews faced periods of intense persecution, including pogroms (violent riots aimed at Jewish communities) and mass expulsions, most notably from Spain in 1492.

Economic Roles and Restrictions

Occupational Specialization: Due to religious and legal restrictions, Jews in both Islamic and Christian lands often specialized in certain professions, such as finance, trade, and medicine.
Ghettoization and Segregation: In Europe, Jews were frequently confined to ghettos and faced various social and economic restrictions. In contrast, Jewish quarters in Islamic cities were often less restrictive.

Religious and Cultural Developments

Development of Jewish Thought: Living in diverse cultural environments led to 'significant developments in Jewish religious thought, including the creation of major works like the Talmud and various Kabbalistic texts.
Interfaith Interactions: Jewish communities often served as intermediaries in cultural and intellectual exchanges between the Islamic and Christian worlds.

Legacy and Historical Significance

Resilience and Adaptability: The history of Jewish communities in Islamic and Christian lands is marked by resilience and adaptability in the face of changing political and social circumstances.
Influence on Jewish Identity: These experiences have had a lasting impact on Jewish religious, cultural, and social identity, shaping the diverse nature of contemporary Jewish communities.

Section 2: Expulsion from Spain and Its Consequences

The Far-Reaching Impact of the Alhambra Decree

This section delves into the expulsion of the Jews from Spain in 1492, also known as the Alhambra Decree, examining its causes, the immediate consequences for the Jewish community, and the wider implications for European and Mediterranean societies.

Background and Causes

Religious Intolerance: The expulsion was part of a broader policy of religious unification in Spain under Catholic monarchs Ferdinand and Isabella, following the completion of the Reconquista.

Political and Economic Motives: Beyond religious factors, the expulsion was also motivated by economic and political reasons, including the consolidation of power and the desire to confiscate Jewish wealth.

Immediate Effects on the Jewish Community

Forced Migration: The decree forced hundreds of thousands of Jews to flee Spain, leading to a massive diaspora. Many sought refuge in nearby Portugal, North Africa, the Ottoman Empire, and other parts of Europe.

Loss of Community and Heritage: The expulsion led to the disintegration of one of the most vibrant Jewish communities in Europe, resulting in a significant loss of cultural, intellectual, and economic contributions.

Impact on Spain and Europe

Economic and Cultural Decline: The expulsion of the Jews, along with the subsequent expulsion of Muslims (Moriscos), is believed to have contributed to the economic and cultural decline of Spain.

Precedent for Religious Intolerance: The Alhambra Decree set a precedent for religious intolerance and ethnic cleansing in Europe, echoed in later events like the Inquisition and pogroms.

Influence on the Jewish Diaspora

Cultural and Intellectual Contributions: The Jewish diaspora resulting from the expulsion contributed significantly to the cultures and economies of their new host countries, particularly in the Ottoman Empire.

Development of Sephardic Culture: The expelled Jews, known as Sephardim, maintained their unique cultural and religious identity, influencing Jewish life and customs in their new communities.

Legacy and Historical Reflection

Recognition of Historical Injustice: In recent years, there has been a growing recognition of the injustice of the expulsion, with Spain offering citizenship to descendants of expelled Jews.

Enduring Impact on Jewish History: The expulsion from Spain remains a defining moment in Jewish history, symbolizing both the resilience of the Jewish community and the destructive impact of religious and ethnic intolerance.

Section 3: Jewish Diaspora and Their Role in Exploration

The Contribution of the Jewish Diaspora to Age of Discovery

This section examines the role of the Jewish diaspora in the Age of Discovery, highlighting how Jewish navigators, financiers, and intellectuals contributed to European exploration efforts and the eventual discovery of the New World.

Jewish Navigators and Explorers

Participation in Voyages: Jews participated in various capacities in European voyages of exploration, often as navigators, cartographers, and interpreters. Their expertise in these fields was invaluable in the success of many expeditions.
Notable Figures: Some notable Jewish figures involved in exploration include Abraham Zacuto, a Jewish astronomer and mathematician whose works were used by Portuguese navigators like Vasco da Gama.

Financial Contributions

Funding Expeditions: Jewish financiers played a significant role in funding exploration voyages. Their involvement was partly due to their extensive networks and expertise in international trade and finance.
Economic Impact: The investments made by Jewish financiers in these expeditions helped spur the economic growth and expansion of European maritime powers.

Intellectual Contributions

Cartography and Geography: Jewish cartographers and geographers contributed to the mapping of uncharted territories and the development of new navigation techniques, essential for long-distance sea voyages.
Scientific and Astronomical Knowledge: Jewish scholars contributed to the scientific knowledge crucial for exploration, particularly in astronomy and navigation.

Impact of the Expulsion from Spain

Dispersal of Knowledge: The expulsion of Jews from Spain led to the dispersal of their accumulated knowledge and expertise across Europe and into the Ottoman Empire, where many found refuge and continued their work.

Influence on Trade Networks: The Jewish diaspora, through their extensive trade networks, also played a role in establishing contacts and trade routes that were later utilized in European exploration.

Legacy and Recognition

Acknowledgment of Contributions: The role of the Jewish diaspora in the Age of Discovery has gained more recognition in recent historical studies, highlighting their integral contributions to maritime exploration and the interconnected nature of cultural and scientific exchange.
Influence on Global Trade and Exploration: The contributions of the Jewish community during this era had lasting effects on the development of global trade networks and the course of maritime exploration.

Section 4: Contributions to Nautical Science and Cartography

Jewish Innovations in Maritime Exploration

This section discusses the significant contributions made by the Jewish community to nautical science and cartography during the Age of Discovery, highlighting their pivotal role in advancing maritime navigation and mapmaking.

Advancements in Nautical Science

Astronomical and Navigational Knowledge: Jewish scholars, well-versed in astronomy, played a crucial role in improving navigational techniques. Their understanding of celestial navigation was critical for the development of more accurate methods for sea voyages.
Development of Navigational Instruments: Jewish inventors and scientists contributed to the design and refinement of navigational instruments like astrolabes and sextants, enhancing the precision of maritime navigation.

Impact on Cartography

Mapping Uncharted Territories: Jewish cartographers were instrumental in mapping newly discovered lands, using their expertise to create more accurate and detailed maps. These maps were vital for future explorations and territorial claims.
Exchange of Geographic Knowledge: The Jewish diaspora, with its extensive trade networks and multilingual abilities, facilitated the exchange of geographic knowledge across Europe and the Mediterranean.

Influential Figures

Notable Jewish Cartographers: Prominent Jewish figures in cartography, such as Abraham Cresques of Majorca, produced works that were highly valued in maritime circles and used by explorers for navigation.
Collaboration with Explorers: Jewish cartographers often worked in collaboration with explorers, providing them with valuable maps and charts for their voyages.

Role in the Age of Discovery

Supporting Exploration Efforts: The contributions of Jewish scientists and cartographers supported the efforts of European explorers, indirectly aiding in the discovery of new trade routes and lands.
Advancing Maritime Knowledge: The advancements in nautical science and cartography by Jewish scholars played a significant role in the progress of maritime exploration during the Age of Discovery.

Legacy and Recognition

Acknowledgment of Contributions: Recent historical research has begun to acknowledge the significant contributions of the Jewish community to nautical science and cartography, highlighting their role in shaping maritime exploration history.
Influence on Modern Cartography: The methods and techniques developed by Jewish cartographers laid the foundations for modern cartography, demonstrating the long-lasting impact of their work.

Section 5: Financing Voyages: The Jewish Contribution

The Role of Jewish Financiers in Maritime Expeditions

This section examines the critical role played by Jewish financiers in funding the voyages of discovery during the Age of Discovery, highlighting their contributions to the exploration and colonization efforts of European powers.

Jewish Involvement in Maritime Financing

Capital for Expeditions: Jewish financiers, often among the few groups in Europe who could amass and manage large sums of capital, played a key role in funding maritime expeditions. Their involvement was crucial in an era where such ventures required substantial investment.

Networks and Expertise: Leveraging their extensive trade networks and expertise in international finance, Jewish financiers were able to mobilize resources across different regions, providing essential support for long-distance voyages.

Notable Examples

Financing Columbus's Voyages: There is historical evidence suggesting that Jewish financiers were among those who provided funds for Christopher Columbus's voyage to the New World. Their contribution was significant, given the speculative nature of such an endeavor.
Support for Other Explorers: Jewish financiers also supported other explorers and maritime ventures, contributing to various European nations' efforts to explore and colonize distant lands.

Impact on European Expansion

Enabling Exploration and Trade: The financial backing of Jewish financiers was instrumental in enabling the Age of Discovery, facilitating European expansion into the Americas and other parts of the world.
Economic Benefits: The successful voyages funded by Jewish capital brought substantial economic benefits to the European powers involved, often enhancing their global standing.

Challenges and Risks

Navigating Political and Religious Restrictions: Jewish financiers had to navigate the complex political and religious landscape of Europe, where anti-Semitic sentiments and restrictions on Jewish economic activities were prevalent.
Risk of Financial Ventures: The financing of maritime expeditions was fraught with risk, including the potential loss of ships and cargo, making the involvement of Jewish financiers a high-stakes endeavor.

Legacy and Historical Recognition

Acknowledgment of Jewish Contributions: Recent scholarship has begun to recognize and appreciate the role of Jewish financiers in the Age of Discovery, highlighting their crucial contributions to key historical events.
Influence on Global Trade and Economics: The involvement of Jewish financiers in maritime expeditions had a lasting impact on global trade patterns and the development of international finance.

Section 6: The Jewish Experience in the New World

Adapting and Thriving in a New Environment

This section explores the experiences of Jewish communities in the New World, focusing on their adaptation, contributions, and challenges in the Americas during the period of European colonization and expansion.

Early Jewish Settlers in the Americas

Arrival in the New World: Some of the first Jews arrived in the Americas with early European expeditions, often fleeing persecution in Europe. They established communities in places like New Amsterdam (later New York), Brazil, and the Caribbean.
Crypto-Jews and Conversos: Many Jews in the New World were forced converts (Conversos) or Crypto-Jews, publicly practicing Christianity while privately maintaining Jewish traditions due to the pervasive threat of the Inquisition.

Economic and Social Contributions

Trade and Commerce: Jewish settlers played significant roles in the trade and economic development of the colonies, using their extensive networks and mercantile expertise.
Cultural Impact: Despite often facing restrictions and discrimination, Jewish communities contributed to the cultural and social fabric of colonial societies, bringing diverse traditions and practices.

Religious and Community Life

Establishing Synagogues and Institutions: In regions where religious freedom was more tolerated, such as in some of the Dutch and English colonies, Jews established synagogues and community institutions, laying the foundations for vibrant Jewish life.
Navigating Religious Tolerance: The degree of religious tolerance varied significantly across the Americas, with Jewish communities continually navigating challenges to maintain their religious identity.

Challenges and Persecution

Anti-Semitism in the Colonies: Jews in the New World faced anti-Semitism and legal restrictions, mirroring the discrimination they had faced in Europe.

Impact of the Inquisition: In territories under Spanish and Portuguese control, the Inquisition was a constant threat, leading to trials and persecution of Jews and Conversos.

Legacy of Jewish Communities in the Americas

Enduring Presence: The descendants of these early Jewish settlers have continued to play influential roles in the Americas, contributing to the religious, cultural, and economic landscapes. Recognition of Historical Struggles: Contemporary understanding of the Jewish experience in the New World acknowledges the resilience and adaptability of Jewish communities in the face of adversity and their lasting impact on American societies.

Section 7: Religious Tolerance and Persecution

Navigating the Complex Landscape of Faith in New Societies

This section examines the varying degrees of religious tolerance and persecution experienced by Jewish communities in Islamic and Christian lands, highlighting how these dynamics shaped their social, cultural, and religious identities.

Religious Tolerance in Islamic Lands

Dhimmi Status: In many Islamic societies, Jews were granted "dhimmi" status, allowing them certain rights and protections while subjecting them to specific taxes and social restrictions. Periods of Coexistence: There were periods and regions within the Islamic world where Jews experienced significant tolerance, contributing to flourishing cultural and intellectual life, notably in Al-Andalus and the Ottoman Empire.

Experiences of Persecution

Pogroms and Expulsions in Christian Europe: In contrast, in Christian Europe, Jews frequently faced persecution, including pogroms, expulsions, and forced conversions, with the Spanish Inquisition and the expulsion of 1492 being among the most notable instances. Varied Experiences Across the Islamic World: While there was a general trend of tolerance in Islamic lands, this was not uniform, and instances of persecution and discrimination did occur, influenced by political, social, and economic factors.

Impact of Religious Tolerance and Persecution

Cultural and Religious Resilience: The Jewish response to these varying experiences has been marked by a resilience in preserving religious and cultural identity, often adapting practices to fit the constraints of their environments.
Community Cohesion and Survival: The challenges faced, particularly in Christian Europe, led to a strengthening of community bonds and a focus on survival and mutual support.

Legacy in Modern Contexts

Influence on Jewish Diaspora: The historical experiences of tolerance and persecution have had a lasting impact on the Jewish diaspora, influencing communal structures, cultural practices, and religious traditions.
Contemporary Relevance: The historical narrative of Jewish tolerance and persecution remains relevant in contemporary discussions on religious freedom, minority rights, and interfaith relations.

Reevaluation and Acknowledgment

Recognition of Jewish Contributions: There is increasing acknowledgment of the contributions made by Jewish communities to the societies in which they lived, despite the challenges they faced.
Understanding Historical Complexities: Modern scholarship and societal perspectives are reevaluating these historical experiences, seeking a deeper understanding of the complexities and nuances of Jewish life in diverse cultural contexts.

Section 8: Intellectual Exchange Among Jews, Christians, and Muslims

The Interplay of Ideas Across Religious Boundaries

This section examines the rich intellectual exchange that occurred among Jewish, Christian, and Muslim communities, especially during the medieval period, highlighting how these interactions contributed to advancements in various fields of knowledge.

Centers of Learning and Dialogue

Cultural Hubs: Cities like Cordoba, Toledo, and Baghdad served as vibrant centers of learning where scholars from Jewish, Christian, and Muslim backgrounds engaged in intellectual discourse.

Translation Movements: The translation of texts from Arabic to Hebrew and Latin in places like the Toledo School of Translators facilitated the spread of knowledge across religious and cultural boundaries.

Contributions to Philosophy and Theology

Philosophical Interactions: Jewish philosophers like Maimonides were influenced by Muslim thinkers such as Ibn Rushd (Averroes) and Al-Farabi, contributing to a rich dialogue on matters of philosophy, ethics, and theology.
Theological Debates: Interfaith debates and discussions among scholars provided opportunities to explore and challenge theological concepts, fostering a deeper understanding of each faith's doctrines.

Advancements in Science and Medicine

Collaborative Contributions: Scholars from different religious backgrounds collaborated in fields like astronomy, mathematics, and medicine, leading to significant advancements.
Preservation and Enhancement of Knowledge: Jewish scholars played a key role in preserving and enhancing the knowledge acquired from Islamic sources, which was later transmitted to Christian Europe.

Cultural and Artistic Exchanges

Influence on Literature and Art: The interaction among Jewish, Christian, and Muslim artists and writers led to cross-cultural influences in literature, poetry, and art, enriching the cultural heritage of each community.
Musical and Architectural Synthesis: These exchanges also manifested in music and architecture, with elements from each culture blending into unique artistic expressions.

Impact on Modern Thought

Foundation for Modern Learning: The intellectual exchange among these communities laid the groundwork for the Renaissance and the scientific revolution in Europe.
Legacy of Interfaith Dialogue: The history of collaboration and dialogue serves as a model for contemporary interfaith and intercultural interactions, promoting mutual respect and understanding.

Section 9: Influence on Early American Settlements

Jewish Contributions to the Formation of the Americas

This section explores the role and influence of Jewish communities in the early settlements of the Americas, highlighting their contributions to the economic, cultural, and political development of the New World.

Economic Contributions

Trade and Commerce: Jewish settlers often played significant roles in the trade networks of early American colonies, contributing to their economic vitality. Their expertise in finance and international trade helped establish important commercial connections.
Agricultural Development: In some colonies, Jewish settlers were involved in agricultural development, introducing new crops and farming techniques.

Cultural and Social Impact

Cultural Diversity: Jewish settlers added to the cultural diversity of early American colonies, bringing unique traditions, languages, and customs. This contributed to the multicultural tapestry of the New World.
Community Building: Despite facing religious restrictions in some colonies, Jewish settlers established tight-knit communities, contributing to the social fabric of early American society.

Political Involvement

Advocacy for Religious Freedom: Jewish settlers were among those who advocated for religious freedom in the colonies. Their experiences of persecution in Europe made them vocal proponents of religious tolerance and rights.
Participation in Colonial Governance: In colonies where they were allowed to participate in governance, Jewish settlers contributed to the political discourse and development of early American political structures.

Religious Contributions

Establishment of Synagogues: The establishment of synagogues in early American settlements, such as in New York and Rhode Island, played a crucial role in preserving Jewish religious and cultural identity.

Interfaith Relations: Jewish settlers often engaged in interfaith dialogues and collaborations, contributing to a climate of religious tolerance in some colonies.

Legacy in American Society

Foundations for Future Communities: The early Jewish settlers laid the foundations for future Jewish communities in the United States and other parts of the Americas, influencing their subsequent growth and development.
Influence on American Values: The efforts of Jewish settlers in promoting religious freedom and tolerance had a lasting impact on the development of American values and the country's approach to religious diversity.

Section 10: Legacy of Jewish Communities in Western Development

Enduring Impact of Jewish Presence in the West

This final section of Chapter 8 discusses the lasting legacy of Jewish communities in the development of Western societies, focusing on their contributions to culture, science, economics, and the ongoing challenges and achievements of the Jewish diaspora.

Cultural and Intellectual Contributions

Advancements in Arts and Sciences: Jewish individuals and communities have significantly contributed to the arts, sciences, and philosophy throughout Western history, often leading innovation and intellectual discourse.
Preservation and Development of Heritage: Jewish communities have preserved a rich cultural and religious heritage, including literature, music, and religious practices, which have enriched the cultural diversity of Western societies.

Economic and Commercial Impact

Role in Commerce and Finance: Historically, Jews have played a pivotal role in the development of commerce and finance in Western countries, often pioneering banking and trade practices.
Entrepreneurship and Innovation: The entrepreneurial spirit and innovation within Jewish communities have driven economic growth and technological advancement in various sectors.

Social and Political Influence

Advocacy for Civil Rights and Equality: Jewish communities have been at the forefront of civil rights movements and advocacy for equality and justice, contributing to social and political reforms in Western countries.
Political Participation: Jews have actively participated in the political life of Western nations, contributing to policy-making and governance.

Challenges and Resilience

Facing Anti-Semitism: Despite their contributions, Jewish communities have continually faced anti-Semitism in various forms, from discrimination to violent persecution.
Resilience and Adaptability: The history of Jewish communities is marked by resilience and adaptability in the face of these challenges, maintaining their identity and traditions while integrating into broader societies.

Legacy in Modern Society

Recognition of Jewish Contributions: There is a growing recognition of the multifaceted contributions of Jewish communities to Western development, across cultural, scientific, economic, and social spheres.
Contemporary Jewish Identity: The legacy of Jewish communities continues to evolve, shaping contemporary Jewish identity and its interaction with broader global and Western contexts.

Chapter 9: The Ottomans: Europe's Eastern Neighbor

Section 1: Rise and Expansion of the Ottoman Empire

Tracing the Ottoman Empire's Ascent to Power

This section examines the rise and expansion of the Ottoman Empire, focusing on its origins, military conquests, and the establishment of a vast empire that would become a significant player in European and Middle Eastern politics.

Foundations of the Ottoman Empire

Origins: The Ottoman Empire emerged in the late 13th and early 14th centuries in Anatolia, founded by Osman I, from whom the empire gets its name.

Early Conquests: The Ottomans initially expanded by conquering territories in Anatolia and the Balkans, gradually asserting their dominance over rival Turkish principalities and Byzantine territories.

Military Successes and Expansion

Use of Gunpowder Technology: The Ottomans were among the early adopters of gunpowder technology in military tactics, giving them a significant advantage in battles and sieges.
Conquest of Constantinople: The fall of Constantinople in 1453 to Sultan Mehmed II marked a turning point, establishing the Ottomans as a major power in the region and ending the Byzantine Empire.

Consolidation of the Empire

Administration and Governance: The Ottomans established an efficient administrative system to govern their vast territories, blending Turkish, Islamic, and Byzantine traditions.
Cultural and Religious Policies: The empire was known for its relatively tolerant religious and cultural policies, allowing various ethnic and religious groups to coexist under Ottoman rule.

Economic Growth and Trade

Control of Key Trade Routes: The Ottoman Empire controlled critical trade routes between Europe and Asia, playing a pivotal role in East-West trade during the Renaissance period.
Urban and Economic Development: Major Ottoman cities like Istanbul, Cairo, and Baghdad became centers of commerce, culture, and learning, contributing to the empire's economic strength.

Impact on Europe and the Middle East

Shifting Power Dynamics: The rise of the Ottoman Empire significantly altered the political and military dynamics of Europe and the Middle East.
Cultural Exchanges: The expansion of the Ottomans facilitated cultural exchanges between East and West, influencing art, architecture, science, and cuisine in both regions.

Legacy of the Ottoman Expansion

Foundation for Modern Nations: The territories and cultures encompassed by the Ottoman Empire laid the foundations for several modern nations in the Middle East and Southeast Europe.

Historical and Cultural Significance: The legacy of the Ottoman Empire's rise and expansion continues to be felt in the cultural, political, and religious landscapes of the region.

Section 2: Ottoman Influence on European Politics and Warfare

Exploring the Ottoman Impact on European Affairs

This section delves into how the Ottoman Empire influenced European politics and warfare, examining the empire's role as a major power in shaping the political landscape of Europe and its contributions to military strategy and technology.

Diplomatic Relations and Rivalries

Balancing European Powers: The Ottoman Empire's presence as a formidable power in Eastern Europe forced European states to consider Ottoman interests in their diplomatic calculations, often leading to complex alliances and rivalries.
Diplomatic Engagements: The Ottomans engaged in diplomatic relations with various European states, using these connections to influence European politics and maintain a balance of power in the region.

Military Conflicts and Strategies

Frequent Warfare with European Powers: The Ottomans were frequently involved in military conflicts with European powers, notably the Habsburgs, Venetians, and Russians, influencing the course of European history.
Adoption and Innovation in Military Technology: The Ottomans were known for their effective use and innovation in military technology, particularly in artillery and siege warfare, which European powers often sought to emulate.

Contributions to Military Tactics

Siege Warfare: The Ottoman mastery of siege warfare, exemplified in the conquest of Constantinople, spurred advancements in fortification and siege tactics across Europe.
Use of Janissaries: The Ottoman Janissaries, an elite military corps, were among the first standing armies in Europe and influenced European military organization and tactics.

Economic and Trade Implications

Control of Trade Routes: Ottoman control over key trade routes, including access to the Black Sea and the Eastern Mediterranean, impacted European trade and economic policies.
Competition for Maritime Dominance: Ottoman naval power in the Mediterranean led to competition with European maritime states, driving advancements in naval technology and tactics.

Cultural and Religious Impact

Perception of the Ottoman Threat: The perceived threat of the Ottoman Empire had significant cultural and religious implications in Europe, often being portrayed as the principal antagonist in a Christian-Muslim dichotomy.
Influence on European Renaissance: The Ottoman expansion contributed indirectly to the European Renaissance by prompting the movement of scholars and texts from Byzantium to Italy following the fall of Constantinople.

Legacy in European History

Shaping European Identity: The Ottoman Empire's interactions with Europe played a key role in shaping European political and cultural identity during the early modern period.
Recognition of Ottoman Influence: Contemporary scholarship increasingly acknowledges the significant impact of the Ottoman Empire on European politics, warfare, and cultural development.

Section 3: Trade and Diplomacy Between Ottomans and Europeans

Interactions Shaping Commerce and International Relations

This section explores the complex trade relationships and diplomatic interactions between the Ottoman Empire and European powers, highlighting how these engagements influenced economic and political dynamics in both regions.

Trade Agreements and Commerce

Key Trade Routes: The Ottoman Empire controlled vital trade routes connecting Europe to Asia and Africa, playing a central role in the lucrative spice and silk trades.

Commercial Treaties: European states, seeking access to Eastern goods, negotiated commercial treaties with the Ottomans. These agreements often included provisions for trade privileges and the establishment of consulates.

Diplomatic Engagements

Ambassadorial Exchanges: Diplomatic relations were established through the exchange of ambassadors, with European states and the Ottoman Empire maintaining permanent diplomatic missions.
Negotiating Alliances and Conflicts: Diplomatic negotiations were key in managing conflicts, alliances, and territorial disputes between the Ottomans and European states.

Cultural Exchanges and Influence

Cultural and Knowledge Transfer: Trade and diplomacy facilitated the exchange of ideas, technologies, and cultural practices, enriching both Ottoman and European societies.
European Fascination with the Orient: The interactions with the Ottoman Empire contributed to a European fascination with "Oriental" culture, influencing European art, literature, and fashion.

Impact on European Politics

Balancing Ottoman Power: European powers often had to balance their relations with the Ottomans against internal European rivalries and conflicts, affecting the broader political landscape of Europe.
Shaping Foreign Policy: The need to maintain favorable trade relations with the Ottomans influenced the foreign policies of many European states.

Economic Impact

Boosting European Economies: Access to Ottoman-controlled trade routes significantly boosted the economies of European states, contributing to the wealth and power of nations like Venice and France.
Influence on Global Trade Patterns: The Ottoman-European trade interactions played a role in shaping global trade patterns, paving the way for the emergence of a more interconnected world economy.

Legacy of Ottoman-European Trade Relations

Foundations for Modern Diplomacy: The diplomatic practices established between the Ottomans and Europeans laid some of the foundations for modern international diplomacy.
Enduring Cultural Influences: The cultural exchanges that occurred through trade and diplomacy have left lasting influences, evident in the architecture, cuisine, and art of both regions.

Section 4: Ottoman Naval Power and Mediterranean Dynamics

The Influence of Ottoman Maritime Strength in the Mediterranean

This section delves into the role of Ottoman naval power in shaping the dynamics of the Mediterranean region, examining how the Ottoman fleet influenced trade, politics, and conflicts in this crucial maritime space.

Development of Ottoman Naval Power

Establishment of a Strong Navy: Under leaders like Sultan Suleiman the Magnificent, the Ottoman Empire built a formidable navy, challenging European powers for control of the Mediterranean.
Technological and Tactical Advancements: The Ottomans adopted and innovated maritime technologies and tactics, contributing to their naval dominance.

Impact on Mediterranean Trade

Control of Key Maritime Routes: Ottoman control over strategic points like the Dardanelles and the Suez region allowed them to influence trade flows between the Mediterranean and the Red Sea/Indian Ocean.
Competition with European Powers: The Ottoman navy's presence in the Mediterranean led to intense competition with maritime powers such as Venice, Spain, and Portugal for control of trade routes and territories.

Major Naval Engagements

Battles for Dominance: The Ottoman fleet engaged in several key battles with European navies, including the Battle of Preveza (1538) and the Battle of Lepanto (1571). These battles significantly influenced the balance of power in the Mediterranean.
Piracy and Privateering: Ottoman-sponsored corsairs, like Barbarossa, played a role in Mediterranean conflicts, attacking European shipping and coastal settlements.

Diplomatic and Political Ramifications

Influence on European Alliances: The threat of Ottoman naval power influenced the formation of military alliances among European states, such as the Holy League.
Negotiations and Treaties: The Ottomans engaged in diplomatic negotiations and treaties with European powers to manage conflicts and establish maritime boundaries.

Cultural Exchanges and Perceptions

Cross-Cultural Interactions: The Ottoman navy facilitated cultural and technological exchanges between the East and West, with sailors and merchants from diverse backgrounds interacting in port cities.
European Views of the Ottomans: The strength and activities of the Ottoman navy shaped European perceptions of the Ottoman Empire, often viewed as both a formidable adversary and a key player in regional politics.

Legacy of Ottoman Maritime Dominance

Enduring Influence in Naval History: The Ottoman Empire's naval history remains an important part of the broader narrative of maritime power and conflict in the Mediterranean.
Shaping Modern Maritime Strategies: The strategies and tactics employed by the Ottoman navy influenced the development of modern naval warfare and maritime diplomacy.

Section 5: Cultural and Artistic Exchange

The Interplay of Ottoman and European Cultures

This section explores the cultural and artistic exchanges between the Ottoman Empire and Europe, highlighting how these interactions enriched the arts, architecture, and cultural practices in both regions.

Ottoman Influences on European Art and Culture

Artistic Inspiration: European artists were often inspired by Ottoman art, adopting elements like intricate patterns, vibrant textiles, and unique motifs in their works.
Orientalism in European Art: The fascination with the Ottoman and wider Islamic world led to the emergence of Orientalism in European art, characterized by depictions of exotic Eastern scenes and lifestyles.

European Influences in the Ottoman Empire

Adoption of European Styles: The Ottomans incorporated various European artistic and architectural styles, particularly in the later periods of the empire, blending them with traditional Ottoman and Islamic designs.
Diplomatic Gifts and Exchanges: Diplomatic interactions often involved the exchange of luxurious gifts, including artworks and artifacts, which influenced artistic tastes and practices in both Europe and the Ottoman Empire.

Architectural Synthesis

Ottoman Architecture: Ottoman architecture, renowned for its grand mosques and palaces, incorporated diverse elements, including Byzantine, Persian, and later European influences.
European Adoption of Ottoman Motifs: Some European architecture, especially in regions close to the Ottoman borders, incorporated Ottoman motifs and styles, reflecting the cultural interplay.

Cultural Exchanges through Trade

Spread of Goods and Ideas: Trade between the Ottoman Empire and Europe facilitated the spread of cultural goods like textiles, ceramics, and spices, which influenced lifestyles and artistic practices.
Culinary Influences: The exchange of culinary practices and ingredients enriched the cuisines of both regions, introducing new flavors and cooking techniques.

Music and Performing Arts

Musical Influences: Ottoman music influenced European composers, with some incorporating Turkish themes and rhythms into their compositions.
Cross-Cultural Performances: The Ottoman Empire was a site of diverse cultural performances, including traditional dances, music, and theater, some of which were influenced by European styles.

Legacy of Cultural Exchange

Enduring Artistic Influence: The artistic and cultural exchanges between the Ottoman Empire and Europe have left a lasting legacy, evident in the rich cultural heritage of both regions.
Recognition of Shared Heritage: Modern appreciation of this shared heritage highlights the importance of cultural exchange in enriching and diversifying artistic and cultural landscapes.

Section 6: The Siege of Vienna and Its Aftermath

A Turning Point in Ottoman-European Relations

This section examines the significance of the Siege of Vienna in 1683, a critical event in Ottoman-European history, and its aftermath, which had profound implications for both the Ottoman Empire and European powers.

The Siege of Vienna

Ottoman Objectives: The Ottoman Empire, under the leadership of Grand Vizier Kara Mustafa Pasha, aimed to capture Vienna, a strategic gateway to further expansion into Europe.
European Resistance: The siege, a culmination of centuries-long conflicts between the Ottomans and European powers, was marked by intense fighting and significant mobilization of forces on both sides.

Impact on the Ottoman Empire

Military and Political Setback: The failure to capture Vienna and subsequent losses in battles marked a turning point, signaling the beginning of the Ottoman Empire's gradual decline in military and political power in Europe.
Internal Repercussions: The siege's outcome led to political changes within the Ottoman administration, including the execution of Kara Mustafa and shifts in the empire's strategic focus.

Consequences for Europe

Boost in European Confidence: The successful defense of Vienna bolstered European confidence and was celebrated as a key victory against Ottoman expansion.
Formation of the Holy League: The siege led to the formation of the Holy League, an alliance of European powers, including the Habsburg Monarchy, the Polish-Lithuanian Commonwealth, and the Papal States, aimed at pushing back Ottoman forces.

Cultural and Symbolic Significance

Symbol of European Resilience: The siege became a symbol of European resilience and unity in the face of external threats, often portrayed in art and literature.
Influence on European Identity: The event played a role in shaping European identity, reinforcing the perception of a Christian Europe united against a Muslim Ottoman Empire.

Long-term Implications

Shift in Power Dynamics: The aftermath of the siege marked a shift in the balance of power, with European states gaining more influence at the expense of the Ottoman Empire.
Legacy in Historical Memory: The Siege of Vienna remains a significant event in the historical memory of both Europe and Turkey, symbolizing different aspects of their shared history.

Section 7: European Perceptions of the Ottomans

The Evolving Views of the Ottoman Empire in European Thought

This section explores how European perceptions of the Ottoman Empire evolved over time, examining the complex interplay of fear, admiration, and misunderstanding that characterized European views of their Eastern neighbor.

Early Perceptions and Exoticism

Initial Views: In the early stages of Ottoman expansion, Europeans often viewed the empire with a mixture of fear and fascination, seeing it as a formidable military adversary and a culturally exotic realm.
Orientalism: The Ottoman Empire played a significant role in the development of Orientalism in European art and literature, which romanticized and exoticized Eastern cultures, including the Ottomans.

The Ottoman Threat

Military and Religious Fears: The military successes of the Ottomans and their control over key trade routes led to perceptions of the empire as a significant threat to Christian Europe.
Propaganda and Misinformation: European narratives about the Ottomans were often influenced by religious and political propaganda, leading to widespread misconceptions and generalizations.

Diplomatic and Intellectual Interactions

Ambassadorial Writings: European ambassadors and travelers who visited the Ottoman Empire provided more nuanced and informed perspectives, contributing to a better understanding of Ottoman society and governance.

Intellectual Curiosity: The Ottoman Empire's culture, administration, and military organization became subjects of study and interest among European intellectuals, influencing their views on governance and society.

Changing Perceptions Over Time

From Admiration to Critique: As the Ottoman Empire's power waned, European perceptions shifted from viewing it as a formidable adversary to a "sick man of Europe," a term used to describe its perceived decline.
Appreciation of Cultural Contributions: Despite changing political dynamics, there was a growing appreciation in Europe for the Ottoman Empire's cultural and artistic contributions.

Legacy of European Perceptions

Influence on European Identity: The perception of the Ottoman Empire played a role in shaping European identity, often serving as a contrasting 'Other' against which Europe defined itself.
Continued Relevance: Contemporary discussions about East-West relations continue to be influenced by historical perceptions of the Ottoman Empire, highlighting the importance of understanding these complex views.

Section 8: Ottoman Legacy in European Architecture and Art

The Enduring Influence of Ottoman Aesthetics

This section delves into the influence of the Ottoman Empire on European architecture and art, examining how Ottoman aesthetic and architectural principles contributed to the European artistic landscape.

Ottoman Influence on European Architecture

Adoption of Architectural Elements: European architects borrowed elements from Ottoman architecture, such as domes, minarets, and decorative tile work, integrating them into their designs.
Mudéjar Style in Spain: In Spain, the Mudéjar style, which reflects a blend of Islamic and Christian architectural elements, was particularly influenced by Ottoman motifs.

Artistic Exchanges and Inspirations

Orientalist Art Movement: The Ottoman Empire was a significant inspiration for the Orientalist art movement in Europe, where artists depicted exoticized scenes of Eastern life, influenced by their perceptions of the Ottoman world.
Textiles and Decorative Arts: Ottoman textiles, ceramics, and metalwork were highly prized in Europe, influencing European decorative arts with their intricate designs and techniques.

Cultural Interactions through Trade

Import of Ottoman Goods: The import of goods from the Ottoman Empire, such as carpets, silks, and spices, influenced European tastes and artistic practices.
European Merchants in Ottoman Lands: European merchants and diplomats living in Ottoman lands contributed to the exchange of artistic ideas and goods.

Influence in Gardens and Landscape Design

Ottoman-style Gardens: The layout and design of Ottoman gardens, characterized by water features, geometric patterns, and lush plantings, influenced garden design in Europe, particularly in areas like Andalusia.

Music and Performing Arts

Musical Influence: Ottoman military music, particularly the Janissary bands, influenced European military music and classical composers like Mozart and Beethoven.
Cultural Festivals and Performances: European cultural festivals and performances occasionally featured Ottoman-themed spectacles and music, reflecting the fascination with Ottoman culture.

Legacy in Modern European Art and Architecture

Continued Appreciation: Ottoman-influenced art and architecture continue to be appreciated for their aesthetic value and historical significance in Europe.
Recognition of Cross-Cultural Influences: Modern scholarship recognizes the Ottoman influence on European art and architecture as an example of rich cross-cultural exchange and interaction.

Section 9: Ottoman Decline and European Ascendancy

Shifts in Power Dynamics Between the Ottoman Empire and Europe

This section examines the period of the Ottoman Empire's decline and the simultaneous rise of European powers, exploring the factors that contributed to these shifts in power dynamics and their implications for both regions.

Factors Leading to Ottoman Decline

Military Setbacks: Significant military defeats, such as the loss at the Battle of Vienna in 1683, marked the beginning of the Ottoman Empire's gradual decline in military prowess.

Administrative and Economic Challenges: Internal administrative inefficiencies, corruption, and economic difficulties weakened the empire's ability to manage its vast territories effectively.

Technological Lag: As European nations advanced in technology and industrialization, the Ottoman Empire struggled to keep pace, leading to a growing technological gap.

Rise of European Powers

Advancements in Technology and Industry: European nations experienced significant advancements in technology, industry, and military capabilities, which bolstered their global influence and power.

Colonial Expansion: The age of European colonialism saw the expansion of European influence across the globe, often at the expense of Ottoman interests and territories.

Impact on Trade and Economics

Shift in Trade Routes: The discovery of new sea routes to Asia by European explorers reduced the importance of Ottoman-controlled land routes, impacting the empire's trade revenues.

Economic Competition: European economic growth and the rise of mercantilism presented significant competition to Ottoman trade and commerce.

Cultural and Social Changes

European Cultural Influence: As European powers ascended, European culture, ideas, and styles began to have a more significant influence in Ottoman territories.

Reforms in the Ottoman Empire: In response to these challenges, the Ottoman Empire initiated a series of reforms, known as the Tanzimat, aimed at modernizing the empire and preventing further decline.

Legacy of the Shift in Power

End of the Ottoman Era: The decline of the Ottoman Empire eventually led to its dissolution after World War I, marking the end of a significant era in Middle Eastern and European history. Formation of Modern Europe and the Middle East: The shifting power dynamics significantly shaped the political and cultural landscapes of modern Europe and the Middle East, with the legacy of the Ottoman Empire still evident in these regions today.

Section 10: Lasting Impacts on European Identity

The Ottoman Empire's Enduring Influence in Europe

This final section of Chapter 9 discusses the lasting impacts of the Ottoman Empire on European identity, exploring how centuries of interaction, conflict, and exchange with the Ottomans have shaped aspects of European culture, politics, and societal norms.

Cultural and Social Influence

Influence on European Arts and Architecture: Ottoman artistic and architectural styles left an indelible mark on European culture, particularly in regions that were once under Ottoman influence or in close proximity, such as the Balkans and parts of Eastern Europe. Ottoman Legacy in Cuisine and Customs: The culinary and lifestyle influences of the Ottoman Empire are still evident in various European countries, contributing to the diversity of European cuisine and customs.

Political and Historical Legacy

Shaping National Boundaries: The Ottoman Empire's history of territorial control and eventual disintegration played a significant role in shaping the national boundaries and political structures of many Southeast European countries. Influence on European Political Thought: The presence of a powerful Islamic empire at Europe's borders influenced political thought and discourse, contributing to the development of European concepts of statehood and sovereignty.

Religious and Intellectual Impact

Interreligious Dialogue and Tolerance: Centuries of coexistence and conflict with the Ottoman Empire contributed to the evolution of religious tolerance and interfaith dialogue in Europe.

Contribution to European Learning and Scholarship: Intellectual exchanges between the Ottoman and European worlds enriched European scholarship, particularly in fields like history, linguistics, and Oriental studies.

Perceptions and Representations

Continued Representation in Media and Literature: The depiction of the Ottoman Empire in European literature, media, and art continues to evolve, reflecting changing perceptions and understandings of this historical period.
Reassessment of Historical Narratives: There is an ongoing reassessment of the historical narratives surrounding the Ottoman Empire in Europe, with a growing appreciation for its complex role in European history.

Legacy in Modern Europe

Cultural Diversity and Heritage: The legacy of the Ottoman Empire contributes to the rich tapestry of cultural diversity in modern Europe, evident in various cultural practices, traditions, and architectural landmarks.
Understanding Contemporary Issues: The historical Ottoman-European interactions provide context for understanding contemporary issues in Europe, including migration, cultural integration, and regional conflicts.

Chapter 10: Comparative Religious Studies: Islam, Christianity, Judaism

Section 1: Fundamental Beliefs of Islam, Christianity, and Judaism

Exploring Core Tenets of the Three Abrahamic Faiths

This section provides an overview of the fundamental beliefs of Islam, Christianity, and Judaism, highlighting their origins, key teachings, and the elements that both distinguish and connect these three major Abrahamic religions.

Islam

Origins and Prophet Muhammad: Islam, founded in the 7th century in Arabia by Prophet Muhammad, is based on the belief in one God (Allah) and the teachings of Muhammad as the final prophet.

The Quran and Five Pillars: Central to Islamic belief is the Quran, considered the word of God, and the practice of the Five Pillars: declaration of faith, prayer, almsgiving, fasting during Ramadan, and pilgrimage to Mecca.

Christianity

Jesus Christ and the Holy Trinity: Christianity, emerging from Jewish traditions in the 1st century CE, centers on the life and teachings of Jesus Christ, viewed as the Son of God and the savior of humanity. Central to many Christian denominations is the concept of the Holy Trinity.
The Bible and Salvation: The Bible, comprising the Old and New Testaments, is the sacred scripture. Central themes include the redemption of sin through Jesus Christ and the promise of eternal life.

Judaism

Ancient Hebrew Roots and Monotheism: Judaism, one of the oldest monotheistic religions, originates from the ancient Hebrews. It is centered on the belief in a single, omniscient, omnipotent, and benevolent God.
Torah and Jewish Law: The Torah, the first five books of the Hebrew Bible, is the primary scripture, accompanied by rabbinical interpretations. Jewish law (Halakha) and traditions play a crucial role in guiding daily life and practices.

Commonalities and Differences

Shared Heritage: All three religions share a common heritage, with roots in the ancient Near East and stories of figures like Abraham, Moses, and David.
Divergent Theologies and Practices: Despite commonalities, each religion has distinct theological beliefs, rituals, and religious practices, shaping their unique identities.

Influence on Society and Culture

Ethical and Moral Frameworks: The teachings of Islam, Christianity, and Judaism have significantly influenced the ethical and moral frameworks of societies where they are practiced.
Cultural and Historical Impact: The art, literature, laws, and cultures of numerous societies have been shaped by the principles and narratives of these religions.

Section 2: Theological Similarities and Differences

Examining the Common Grounds and Divergences in Abrahamic Theologies

This section delves into the theological similarities and differences between Islam, Christianity, and Judaism, exploring how these faiths interpret key religious concepts and principles differently, yet also share common theological foundations.

Similarities in Belief and Practice

Monotheism: All three religions are monotheistic, believing in one God, who is the creator and sustainer of the universe.
Abrahamic Tradition: They share a common heritage in the Abrahamic tradition, with figures like Abraham, Moses, and David being central in their religious narratives.
Ethical Teachings: The emphasis on ethical living, compassion, justice, and care for the needy is a common thread across these religions.

Differences in Theological Perspectives

Concept of God: While all three faiths believe in one God, Christianity's concept of the Trinity distinguishes it from the strictly monotheistic views of Judaism and Islam.
Role of Jesus: Christianity views Jesus as the Son of God and the savior, while Islam regards him as a prophet and Judaism does not ascribe any divine status to him.
Scriptural Interpretations: Each religion has its unique scriptures and interpretations, leading to different religious laws, practices, and spiritual understandings.

Salvation and Afterlife

Christianity: Emphasizes salvation through faith in Jesus Christ and his resurrection, with eternal life in heaven as the ultimate goal.
Islam: Stresses submission to God's will (Islam) and good deeds as the path to salvation, with paradise as the reward for the faithful.
Judaism: Focuses more on righteous living in this world and the collective fate of the Jewish people, with varied beliefs about the afterlife.

Rituals and Worship

Prayer Practices: Prayer is central in all three, but the methods, frequency, and nature of prayer vary, from the ritualistic Salat in Islam to Sabbath services in Judaism and Sunday worship in Christianity.
Observance of Holy Days: Each religion has its specific holy days and festivals, such as Ramadan in Islam, Passover in Judaism, and Easter in Christianity.

Interpretations of Religious Law

Sharia, Halakha, and Canon Law: Islamic Sharia, Jewish Halakha, and Christian Canon Law represent the diverse legal interpretations and applications of religious principles in each faith.

Influence on Individual and Community Life

Guidance in Personal Conduct: The religions provide guidelines for personal conduct, family life, and community relations, though the specifics of these guidelines differ.
Role of Religious Leadership: The roles of religious leaders, such as imams, rabbis, and priests, vary in authority and function across these faiths.

Section 3: Historical Intersections and Conflicts

Tracing the Interwoven Histories of the Three Faiths

This section explores the historical intersections and conflicts between Islam, Christianity, and Judaism, examining how these interactions have shaped the course of history and the relationships between these religious communities.

Early Intersections

Shared Origins: All three religions have their roots in the Middle East, with intertwined histories dating back to ancient times.
Influence of Judaism on Early Christianity and Islam: As the oldest of the three, Judaism significantly influenced the early development of Christianity and Islam, both of which emerged in a world where Jewish communities were already established.

Conflicts and Conquests

Islamic Expansion and Christian Response: The rapid expansion of Islam in the 7th and 8th centuries brought it into direct contact and often conflict with Christian territories, leading to centuries of military engagements, including the Crusades.
Jewish Communities in Islamic and Christian Lands: Jewish communities often found themselves caught in the middle of these conflicts, facing varying degrees of tolerance or persecution depending on the ruling powers.

Periods of Coexistence

Convivencia in Al-Andalus: In medieval Spain, Muslims, Christians, and Jews coexisted in a period known as "Convivencia," marked by cultural and intellectual exchanges despite occasional tensions.
Ottoman Millet System: The Ottoman Empire's millet system allowed for a degree of religious autonomy for Christians and Jews, leading to periods of peaceful coexistence.

Impact of Religious Conflicts

Shaping Political Borders: Religious conflicts, such as the Crusades and the Reconquista, played significant roles in shaping the political borders and power dynamics of Europe and the Middle East.
Cultural and Religious Impact: These conflicts also influenced cultural perceptions and religious narratives within each community, often reinforcing identities and differences.

Modern Repercussions

Legacy in Contemporary Relations: The historical intersections and conflicts continue to influence contemporary relations and perceptions among Muslims, Christians, and Jews.
Efforts at Reconciliation and Dialogue: In recent times, there have been increased efforts to acknowledge this shared history and promote interfaith dialogue and reconciliation.

Section 4: Influence of Religious Thought on Governance

Examining the Role of Religion in Shaping Political Systems

This section explores how the religious doctrines and principles of Islam, Christianity, and Judaism have influenced governance and political systems throughout history, reflecting on the varying degrees to which religion has intersected with state affairs.

Islam and Governance

The Caliphate System: In Islamic history, the concept of the Caliphate, representing the political and religious leadership of the Muslim community, exemplifies the integration of religious principles in governance.
Sharia Law: Islamic law (Sharia) has played a central role in the legal and administrative systems of various Islamic states, influencing aspects of civil and criminal law.

Christianity's Influence on Western Politics

The Church and State: Throughout history, especially in medieval Europe, the Christian Church held significant political power, influencing monarchies and shaping state policies.
Secularization Movements: Over time, the rise of secularism in Europe led to the separation of church and state, though Christian values and ethics continue to influence Western political thought and policies.

Judaism and Political Organization

Ancient Israel and Theocracy: In ancient times, Judaism functioned within a theocratic system in Israel, where religious leaders also held political authority.
Diaspora Influence: In the diaspora, Jewish communities often developed autonomous systems of governance, relying on religious laws and principles to manage internal affairs.

Common Themes and Divergences

Religion as a Source of Law and Order: In all three religions, religious texts and teachings have been used as sources of law and ethical guidelines for governance.
Differing Approaches to Theocracy and Secularism: Each religion has navigated the spectrum between theocracy and secularism differently, reflecting diverse historical and cultural contexts.

Modern Implications

Contemporary Debates: The role of religion in governance remains a topic of debate in many societies, with discussions around secularism, religious freedom, and the place of religious laws in secular states.
Influence on International Relations: Religious principles and affiliations continue to influence international relations and policies, particularly in regions with strong religious identities.

Legacy of Religious Governance

Enduring Influence: The historical influence of these religions on governance has left an enduring legacy, shaping modern legal systems, political structures, and social norms.
Dynamic Interplay: The dynamic interplay between religion and politics continues to evolve, reflecting ongoing changes in societal values and global interactions.

Section 5: The Role of Religion in Exploration and Colonization

Intersecting Faith and Expansionism in History

This section examines the role that Islam, Christianity, and Judaism played in the historical contexts of exploration and colonization, exploring how religious motivations and justifications were intertwined with these expansive endeavors.

Christianity and the Age of Discovery

Missionary Zeal: Christian missionary work was a key driver in European exploration and colonization, with the goal of spreading Christianity to new lands and peoples.
Doctrine of Discovery: European powers used Christian doctrines, such as the Papal Bulls that sanctioned the exploration, to justify the claim and colonization of non-Christian lands.
Impact on Indigenous Peoples: The spread of Christianity often resulted in the displacement and conversion of indigenous cultures, leading to significant cultural and religious changes in colonized regions.

Islamic Expansion and Influence

Spread of Islam through Trade and Conquest: The expansion of Islam in the early centuries was facilitated through both trade and military conquest, spreading Islamic culture and religious practices across vast regions, including parts of Europe, Africa, and Asia.
Cultural and Religious Integration: In many cases, Islamic rulers allowed for a degree of religious tolerance, leading to the coexistence and integration of different cultural and religious groups under Islamic governance.

Judaism and Diaspora Movements

Jewish Migration and Settlement: While not a colonizing force, Jewish diaspora movements throughout history were often in response to persecution or in search of trade opportunities, leading to the establishment of Jewish communities in diverse geographical regions.

Influence on Local Economies and Cultures: Jewish settlers contributed to the economic and cultural life of the regions they settled in, often acting as intermediaries in trade and cultural exchange.

Common Themes and Differences

Religion as a Motivation and Justification: In both Christianity and Islam, religion served as both a motivation for exploration and a justification for political and territorial expansion.
Diverse Outcomes and Impacts: The impacts of religiously motivated exploration and colonization varied, from the spread of religious beliefs and practices to the alteration or suppression of local cultures and religions.

Contemporary Reflections

Reevaluation of Historical Narratives: Modern perspectives are reevaluating the role of religion in exploration and colonization, recognizing the complex interplay of faith, power, and cultural exchange.
Legacy in Global Religions and Cultures: The historical role of these religions in exploration and colonization has left a lasting impact on global religious landscapes and cultural identities.

Section 6: Religious Tolerance and Persecution Across Cultures

The Dynamics of Acceptance and Conflict Among Faiths

This section investigates the historical and contemporary aspects of religious tolerance and persecution in Islam, Christianity, and Judaism, examining how these religions have interacted with each other and with different cultures over time.

Historical Contexts of Tolerance and Persecution

Periods of Coexistence: There have been notable periods of religious tolerance, such as during the Islamic Golden Age and in parts of medieval Spain, where scholars and believers of different faiths coexisted and collaborated.
Instances of Persecution: Conversely, history is replete with instances of religious persecution, including the Crusades, the Spanish Inquisition, and various pogroms against Jews in Christian Europe.

Islamic Tolerance and Challenges

Dhimmi Status in Islamic Rule: Non-Muslims living under Islamic rule were often accorded a protected status (dhimmi), though they were subject to certain taxes and social restrictions.
Contemporary Issues: In modern times, the concept of tolerance in Islamic societies varies, with some nations embracing pluralism while others face criticism for religious discrimination.

Christian Approaches to Other Faiths

Conversion Efforts and Colonialism: Christianity's history includes efforts to convert non-believers, sometimes interwoven with colonialism and cultural suppression.
Ecumenism and Interfaith Dialogue: Modern Christian movements have increasingly focused on ecumenism and dialogue with other faiths, promoting religious tolerance and understanding.

Judaism's Experiences and Responses

Diaspora and Coexistence: Throughout history, Jewish communities have often lived as minorities, leading to diverse experiences of tolerance and persecution.
Adaptation and Resilience: Jewish responses to these dynamics have shaped a tradition marked by adaptation, resilience, and a strong emphasis on community solidarity.

Influences on Societal Norms and Laws

Shaping Legal Systems: The treatment of religious minorities and the concept of religious tolerance have significantly influenced the development of legal systems and human rights norms worldwide.
Cultural and Ethical Impact: The interplay of tolerance and persecution in religious contexts has also affected cultural and ethical perspectives in various societies.

Modern Perspectives and Challenges

Ongoing Debates: Issues of religious tolerance and persecution remain relevant, with ongoing debates about the role of religion in public life, freedom of belief, and the rights of religious minorities.
Efforts Towards Greater Tolerance: Across the globe, there are efforts to promote greater religious tolerance, understanding, and peaceful coexistence among different faiths.

Section 7: Mysticism and Philosophical Thought

Exploring the Mystical and Philosophical Dimensions of the Abrahamic Faiths

This section delves into the mystical traditions and philosophical schools of thought within Islam, Christianity, and Judaism, examining how they have shaped spiritual practices, theological interpretations, and intellectual discourse within and beyond these religions.

Mysticism in Islam: Sufism

Sufism: Sufism is the mystical Islamic belief and practice in which Muslims seek to find divine love and knowledge through direct personal experience with God.
Prominent Sufi Figures: Figures like Rumi and Al-Ghazali have been influential, with their poetry and writings emphasizing the inner, spiritual journey of the believer.

Christian Mysticism

Variety of Traditions: Christian mysticism spans a diverse range of traditions, with figures like St. Teresa of Ávila and St. John of the Cross in Catholicism, emphasizing the personal experience of union with the divine.
Impact on Christian Thought: These mystical traditions have significantly influenced Christian theology and spiritual practices, often focusing on contemplation, prayer, and the transformative power of divine love.

Jewish Mysticism: Kabbalah

Kabbalah: Jewish mysticism, known as Kabbalah, explores the mystical aspects of the Torah and Jewish belief, seeking a deeper understanding of the divine, the universe, and the soul's journey.
Influence on Jewish Practice: Kabbalistic teachings have deeply influenced certain Jewish rituals and interpretations of religious texts, contributing to a rich spiritual tradition within Judaism.

Philosophical Contributions

Islamic Philosophy: Islamic philosophers like Avicenna (Ibn Sina) and Averroes (Ibn Rushd) contributed significantly to metaphysics, ethics, and the reconciliation of reason with religious faith.

Christian Philosophy: Christian thinkers such as St. Augustine and Thomas Aquinas explored the intersections of faith and reason, influencing Western philosophical thought.

Jewish Philosophical Thought: Jewish philosophers, including Maimonides and Spinoza, have made substantial contributions to ethical, metaphysical, and religious philosophy, often in dialogue with Islamic and Christian thought.

Interfaith Influence and Exchange

Cross-Pollination of Ideas: Throughout history, there has been significant interplay and exchange of mystical and philosophical ideas among these faiths, enriching each tradition.

Modern Relevance: The mystical and philosophical traditions of these religions continue to influence contemporary spiritual practices and philosophical inquiries.

Section 8: Religious Reforms and Their Impacts

Transformations within the Abrahamic Faiths

This section discusses significant religious reforms in Islam, Christianity, and Judaism, exploring how these movements have reshaped practices, beliefs, and institutional structures within these faiths, and their broader societal impacts.

Reforms in Christianity

The Protestant Reformation: Initiated by figures like Martin Luther and John Calvin, the Protestant Reformation in the 16th century fundamentally altered the landscape of Christianity, leading to the formation of various Protestant denominations.

Catholic Counter-Reformation: In response, the Catholic Church underwent its own reform, known as the Counter-Reformation, aimed at revitalizing the church and responding to Protestant critiques.

Impact on European Society: These reforms had profound effects on European society, politics, and culture, contributing to the rise of religious pluralism and influencing the development of modern nation-states.

Islamic Reform Movements

19th and 20th Century Reforms: Various reform movements within Islam, such as Wahhabism and the modernist reforms of leaders like Atatürk in Turkey, sought to address issues of modernity, tradition, and the role of religion in state affairs.

Contemporary Debates: Modern Islamic reform efforts continue to generate debate within Muslim communities, focusing on issues like gender equality, religious pluralism, and the interpretation of Sharia law.

Judaism and Reform

Rise of Reform Judaism: In the 19th century, Reform Judaism emerged, advocating a more liberal interpretation of Jewish laws and practices, adapting to contemporary life while maintaining Jewish identity.
Orthodox and Conservative Responses: In response to Reform Judaism, Orthodox and Conservative movements reinforced traditional practices and interpretations, leading to a diversification of Jewish religious expression.

Common Themes in Religious Reforms

Adaptation to Modernity: A common theme in these reforms is the challenge of adapting religious traditions and practices to the changing conditions of modern life.
Tension Between Tradition and Change: Reforms often generate internal tensions within religious communities, balancing the desire to maintain traditional beliefs with the need to address contemporary issues.

Societal and Global Implications

Influence on Social Norms and Laws: These religious reforms have influenced social norms, legal systems, and ethical frameworks in societies where these religions are practiced.
Global Religious Dynamics: The reform movements have contributed to the global dynamics of religious exchange and interaction, affecting interfaith relations and religious diversity.

Section 9: Scriptural Interpretations and Their Influence

Diverse Readings of Sacred Texts Across Religions

This section explores how the interpretations of sacred scriptures in Islam, Christianity, and Judaism have evolved over time, influencing theological thought, religious practices, and even societal norms within these faiths.

Scriptural Interpretation in Islam

The Quran and Hadith: Interpretations of the Quran, Islam's central religious text, along with the Hadith (sayings and actions of Prophet Muhammad), have shaped Islamic law (Sharia) and practice.
Exegetical Traditions: Exegetical traditions, including Tafsir (Quranic commentary), have provided diverse perspectives on Quranic verses, influencing theological and legal interpretations within Islam.

Christian Biblical Exegesis

Interpreting the Bible: The interpretation of the Bible, comprising the Old and New Testaments, has varied greatly among different Christian denominations, influencing theology, liturgy, and ethical teachings.
Historical-Critical Method: The development of the historical-critical method in biblical scholarship has led to new understandings of biblical texts, examining their historical context and literary composition.

Jewish Approaches to Torah Interpretation

Rabbinic Commentary and Talmud: In Judaism, the interpretation of the Torah is supplemented by rabbinic commentary and the Talmud, a central text in Jewish tradition that explores legal and ethical issues.
Kabbalistic Interpretations: Kabbalah, Jewish mysticism, offers esoteric interpretations of the Torah, providing a mystical dimension to Jewish understanding of scripture.

Impact of Scriptural Interpretation

Influence on Religious Practice: Interpretations of sacred texts directly impact religious practices and rituals in each of these faiths, shaping worship and community life.
Theological Debates and Schisms: Differing interpretations have often led to theological debates and, in some cases, schisms within these religious traditions.

Societal and Cultural Influence

Ethical and Moral Guidelines: The scriptural interpretations provide ethical and moral guidelines for adherents, influencing personal behavior and societal norms.
Influence on Art and Literature: Sacred texts and their interpretations have profoundly influenced art, literature, and culture, inspiring countless works and cultural expressions.

Contemporary Challenges and Dialogues

Relevance in the Modern World: Contemporary religious scholars and leaders grapple with interpreting sacred texts in ways that are relevant to modern societal issues and ethical dilemmas.
Interfaith Interpretative Dialogues: There is an increasing trend in interfaith dialogues focusing on scriptural interpretations, fostering mutual understanding and respect among these faiths.

Section 10: Modern Reflections on Interreligious Dynamics

Contemporary Interplay and Challenges Among the Three Faiths

This final section of Chapter 10 explores the current state of interactions and dynamics among Islam, Christianity, and Judaism, focusing on contemporary challenges, dialogues, and the role of these religions in a globalized world.

Interfaith Dialogue and Cooperation

Promoting Understanding: Initiatives aimed at interfaith dialogue have increased, with leaders and organizations from each faith engaging in discussions to promote mutual understanding and respect.
Joint Humanitarian Efforts: Collaborative efforts in addressing global issues like poverty, injustice, and climate change showcase the potential for interreligious cooperation.

Challenges in Modern Contexts

Religious Extremism: All three faiths face challenges from extremist groups who claim religious justification for their actions, leading to tensions both within and between the faiths.
Secularism and Religious Identity: The rise of secularism poses questions about the role and influence of religion in public life, affecting the practice and expression of these faiths.

Impact of Globalization

Increased Interaction: Globalization has led to more frequent and diverse interactions among followers of these religions, resulting in both opportunities for dialogue and instances of conflict.
Cultural Exchange and Influence: The global spread of religious ideas and practices has influenced cultural trends, artistic expressions, and societal norms across different regions.

Role in Peacebuilding and Conflict

Religion in Conflict Resolution: Religious leaders and institutions from these faiths have played roles in peacebuilding initiatives and conflict resolution in various parts of the world.
Religious Conflicts: At the same time, religious differences have been a factor in conflicts, necessitating efforts towards religious tolerance and coexistence.

Educational and Academic Contributions

Religious Studies and Scholarship: Academic study of these religions has contributed to a deeper understanding of their histories, doctrines, and interrelations.
Educational Programs for Mutual Understanding: Educational initiatives aimed at teaching about the beliefs and practices of different faiths have been instrumental in reducing stereotypes and misconceptions.

Contemporary Religious Identity and Practice

Adaptation to Modern Life: Followers of Islam, Christianity, and Judaism continue to explore ways to adapt their religious practices and beliefs to contemporary life and societal changes.
Youth Engagement: Engaging the younger generation in religious traditions and interfaith activities is a focus area, ensuring the continuity and evolution of these faiths.

Chapter 11: Military Strategies: From Crusades to Colonial Wars

Section 1: Crusades as a Prelude to Modern Warfare

Examining the Impact of the Crusades on Military Evolution

This section discusses the Crusades, focusing on their role as a significant prelude to modern warfare, examining how these medieval military campaigns influenced subsequent military strategies, tactics, and the evolution of warfare.

Overview of the Crusades

Historical Context: The Crusades were a series of religiously motivated military expeditions by European Christians, primarily aimed at recapturing the Holy Land from Muslim control during the 11th to 13th centuries.

Diverse Participants: Crusaders included a range of participants from different regions of Europe, each bringing their own military techniques and equipment.

Military Innovations and Tactics

Siege Warfare: The Crusades saw significant developments in siege warfare, including the use of siege engines and new tactics for assaulting fortified cities.
Cavalry and Infantry Tactics: The Crusades led to changes in the use of cavalry and infantry, with adaptations to counter the military techniques of Middle Eastern armies.

Impact on European Military Thought

Cross-Cultural Exchanges: The Crusades facilitated the transfer of military knowledge between Europe and the Middle East, leading to the adoption of new weapons, armor, and tactics in European warfare.
Influence on Military Organization: Experiences from the Crusades influenced the organization and structure of European armies, contributing to the evolution towards more professional and standing armies.

Technological Advancements

Introduction of Gunpowder: Although gunpowder was not widely used during the Crusades, the campaigns contributed to its eventual introduction and adoption in European warfare.
Naval Engagements: The Crusades also spurred advancements in naval warfare, including ship design and naval tactics, crucial for later maritime explorations and conflicts.

Sociopolitical Implications

Feudalism and Centralized Power: The Crusades played a role in the decline of feudalism and the rise of centralized monarchies, which began to assume more direct control over military affairs.
Legacy in Warfare: The tactics, strategies, and organizational changes from the Crusades had lasting impacts, setting the stage for subsequent developments in military history.

Section 2: Islamic Military Tactics and European Adaptations

The Interplay of Islamic and European Military Approaches

This section explores the influence of Islamic military tactics on European warfare, detailing how European powers adapted and integrated these tactics into their own military strategies over the centuries.

Origins of Islamic Military Tactics

Early Islamic Conquests: The rapid expansion of the Islamic caliphates in the 7th and 8th centuries was facilitated by innovative military tactics, including mobile cavalry and effective use of archery.
Siege Warfare: Islamic armies excelled in siege warfare, employing advanced techniques for besieging and defending fortifications.

European Observation and Adaptation

Learning from the East: Through encounters during the Crusades and subsequent conflicts, Europeans observed and learned from Islamic military tactics.
Adoption of Cavalry Techniques: European knights and armies adopted and adapted cavalry tactics, such as the use of light cavalry for reconnaissance and raiding, influenced by Islamic practices.

Technological Exchanges

Weaponry and Armor: Europeans incorporated elements of Islamic weaponry and armor into their arsenals, including improvements in swordsmanship and the use of chainmail.
Gunpowder Technology: While initially introduced to Europe from China, Islamic innovations in gunpowder technology also influenced European warfare.

Impact on Naval Warfare

Shipbuilding and Naval Engagements: Islamic maritime prowess, especially in the Mediterranean, spurred European advancements in shipbuilding and naval tactics.
Mediterranean Conflicts: Conflicts with Islamic powers in the Mediterranean, such as the Ottoman Empire, pushed European states to develop stronger navies and new naval strategies.

Cultural and Tactical Exchanges

Cultural Perceptions and Misconceptions: The exchange of military tactics was often accompanied by cultural perceptions and misconceptions, influencing the way these tactics were viewed and adopted.

Integration into Military Doctrine: Over time, Islamic influences were integrated into European military doctrine, contributing to the evolution of European warfare.

Legacy and Continued Relevance

Enduring Influence on Military Strategies: The influence of Islamic military tactics on European warfare has had a lasting impact, shaping military strategies and practices beyond the medieval period.
Study in Military History: The study of these exchanges remains a significant topic in military history, illustrating the importance of cross-cultural influences in the development of warfare.

Section 3: Naval Battles and Technological Advances

Evolving Maritime Warfare from the Middle Ages to the Colonial Era

This section highlights the developments in naval battles and maritime technology from the Crusades through the colonial wars, focusing on how advancements in shipbuilding, navigation, and weaponry transformed naval warfare.

Naval Engagements During the Crusades

Mediterranean Battles: Naval battles in the Mediterranean during the Crusades were crucial in controlling key sea routes and ports. These conflicts showcased early strategies in maritime warfare and the importance of naval power.
Techniques and Tactics: Crusader and Islamic fleets employed various tactics, including boarding actions, use of Greek fire, and ramming, laying the groundwork for future naval warfare.

Shipbuilding Innovations

Advancements in Design: The need for more durable and maneuverable ships led to innovations in shipbuilding, including the development of the caravel and galleon during the Age of Exploration.
Improved Navigation: Advances in navigation, such as the astrolabe and more accurate maps, allowed for longer and more precise voyages, essential for both exploration and warfare.

The Age of Exploration and Naval Dominance

European Exploration: European exploratory voyages, driven by the search for new trade routes and territories, were made possible by advancements in naval technology.
Control of Sea Lanes: Control of key sea lanes became increasingly vital, leading to naval conflicts between emerging colonial powers like Spain, Portugal, England, and the Netherlands.

Naval Armaments and Tactics

Gunpowder and Cannonry: The introduction and refinement of gunpowder weapons, particularly cannons, revolutionized naval combat, leading to changes in ship design and battle tactics.
Boarding to Broadside: The shift from boarding-focused tactics to broadside engagements marked a significant evolution in naval warfare.

Impact of Naval Power on Colonialism

Projection of Military Power: The ability to project military power across oceans enabled European powers to establish and maintain colonies, reshape global trade networks, and dominate large parts of the world.
Naval Battles for Imperial Control: Major naval battles often determined the fate of colonies and trade routes, influencing the rise and fall of colonial empires.

Legacy and Modern Implications

Foundation for Modern Navies: The developments in naval technology and tactics during this period laid the foundations for modern naval warfare.
Study in Technological Advancement: The evolution of naval battles and technology remains a key area of study, highlighting the interplay between technology, strategy, and historical outcomes.

Section 4: The Role of Fortifications: From Castles to Colonial Forts

Evolution of Defensive Structures in Military History

This section explores the development and significance of fortifications in military strategy, tracing their evolution from medieval castles to colonial forts, and examining how changes in warfare technology and tactics influenced their design and use.

Medieval Castles and Fortifications

Castles as Power Symbols and Defensive Structures: In medieval Europe, castles served as both symbols of feudal power and key defensive structures against invasions and local conflicts. Design and Evolution: Castle designs evolved from motte-and-bailey structures to massive stone fortresses, reflecting advancements in siege technology and defensive needs.

Islamic Fortifications

Influence of Islamic Architecture: Islamic architecture contributed significantly to fortification design, particularly in the Middle East and North Africa. Techniques included complex layouts and the use of towers and battlements.
Adaptation to Local Environments: Islamic fortifications were often adapted to local environments, using materials and designs suitable for desert or urban settings.

Transition to Gunpowder Era

Impact of Gunpowder: The advent of gunpowder weaponry, especially cannons, necessitated major changes in fortification design, leading to the development of star forts and bastion fortresses.
European and Islamic Adaptations: Both European and Islamic military engineers adapted their fortifications to withstand or utilize gunpowder-based weaponry, resulting in significant architectural innovations.

Colonial Forts

Establishment of Colonial Forts: In the age of exploration and colonial expansion, European powers built forts in the Americas, Africa, and Asia to protect trading posts and territorial claims.
Design and Function: Colonial forts combined traditional European designs with adaptations to local conditions and materials, serving both as military strongholds and centers of colonial administration.

Legacy and Modern Significance

Historical and Cultural Landmarks: Many of these fortifications remain today as historical and cultural landmarks, reflecting the military, architectural, and political histories of their regions.
Influence on Urban Development: The placement and design of these forts influenced the development of surrounding towns and cities, some of which grew into major urban centers.

Study in Military Architecture

Reflection of Military and Social Changes: The evolution of fortifications offers insights into changes in military technology, tactics, and the broader social and political dynamics of the periods in which they were built.
Archaeological and Academic Interest: Fortifications continue to be a subject of archaeological and academic study, shedding light on the past and informing preservation efforts.

Section 5: European Conquests in the New World

The Dynamics of European Military Expansion Overseas

This section examines the European conquests in the Americas, focusing on the military strategies, tactics, and technologies employed by European powers and how these shaped the colonization and transformation of the New World.

Overview of European Expansion

Age of Exploration: The European conquests in the Americas began with the voyages of explorers like Christopher Columbus, leading to the establishment of European colonies.
Diverse European Powers: Different European nations, including Spain, Portugal, England, France, and the Netherlands, engaged in the conquest and colonization of the Americas.

Military Strategies and Tactics

Combination of Naval and Land Warfare: European conquests involved both naval power to reach and supply distant territories and land warfare to subjugate and control them.
Role of Alliances with Indigenous Peoples: Europeans often formed strategic alliances with certain indigenous groups to gain advantage over others, altering local power dynamics.

Technological Superiority

Firearms and Artillery: The technological superiority of European firearms and artillery played a significant role in their military successes against indigenous armies.
Impact of Horses and War Dogs: The introduction of horses and the use of war dogs significantly changed the nature of warfare in the Americas.

Disease as an Unintended Ally

Devastating Impact of Diseases: European contact led to the spread of diseases like smallpox among indigenous populations, which had catastrophic effects and often weakened resistance to European conquests.

Psychological Warfare

Use of Fear and Intimidation: European conquerors sometimes used tactics of fear and intimidation, including displays of military power and harsh punishments, to subdue indigenous populations.
Religious Justifications: The spread of Christianity was used both as a justification for conquest and as a tool for cultural control and conversion.

Consequences of Conquests

Transformation of the Americas: The European conquests led to significant demographic, cultural, and environmental changes in the New World.
Legacy of Colonialism: The legacy of these conquests, including issues of colonialism, cultural suppression, and economic exploitation, continues to influence the Americas today.

Modern Reflections

Reevaluation of Historical Narratives: Contemporary perspectives are reevaluating the narratives of European conquests, considering the impacts on indigenous populations and the ethical implications of colonialism.

Section 6: Guerrilla Warfare and Indigenous Resistance

The Dynamics of Asymmetric Warfare in Colonial Contexts

This section examines the role of guerrilla warfare as a method of resistance used by indigenous peoples against European colonial forces, analyzing its effectiveness, strategies, and impact on colonial military tactics.

Origins and Nature of Guerrilla Warfare

Definition and Tactics: Guerrilla warfare refers to a form of irregular warfare in which small groups of combatants use military tactics, including ambushes, sabotage, and hit-and-run strategies, to fight larger and less-mobile traditional armies.
Adaptation to Local Environments: Indigenous groups often used their knowledge of local terrain and environment to their advantage in guerrilla warfare against European colonizers.

Notable Examples of Indigenous Resistance

Native American Warfare: In North America, various Native American tribes engaged in guerrilla tactics against European settlers and armies, notably during the American Indian Wars.
Resistance in South America: In South America, indigenous groups like the Mapuche used guerrilla tactics to resist the Spanish conquest, achieving notable successes.

Impact on European Colonial Tactics

Adaptation and Counter-Strategies: European colonial forces had to adapt their military strategies to counter guerrilla tactics, often leading to the development of more mobile and flexible military units.
Psychological and Moral Challenges: Guerrilla warfare posed not only tactical challenges but also psychological and moral dilemmas for colonial forces, as it blurred the lines between combatants and civilians.

Influence on Modern Warfare

Lessons in Military Strategy: The experiences of guerrilla warfare during colonial times influenced modern military strategies and doctrines, particularly in dealing with asymmetric warfare.
Legacy in National Liberation Movements: The use of guerrilla tactics by indigenous peoples served as a model for later national liberation and resistance movements in various parts of the world.

Contemporary Perspectives

Recognition of Indigenous Resistance: Modern historical narratives increasingly recognize and acknowledge the role and significance of indigenous resistance through guerrilla warfare.
Reassessment of Colonial Military History: The study of guerrilla warfare in colonial contexts contributes to a more nuanced understanding of the complexities and impacts of colonialism.

Section 7: Arms Trade and Military Alliances

The Global Impact of Arms Trade and Alliances in Military History

This section explores the historical significance of the arms trade and the formation of military alliances, focusing on how they influenced warfare strategies from the medieval period through the colonial era.

Development of the Arms Trade

Early Arms Trade: The trade in weapons and military technology dates back to ancient times but expanded significantly during the medieval and Renaissance periods.
Globalization of the Arms Trade: With the age of exploration and colonial expansion, the arms trade became a global enterprise, influencing conflicts worldwide.

European Powers and Arms Trading

European Dominance: European powers, with their advancements in weaponry and shipbuilding, dominated the global arms trade, supplying weapons to various parts of the world.
Impact on Non-European Societies: The introduction of European weapons and military technology had profound impacts on the balance of power in non-European societies, often altering local warfare dynamics.

Military Alliances and Their Impact

Formation of Alliances: The formation of military alliances, both within Europe and between European and non-European powers, played a significant role in the strategies and outcomes of numerous conflicts.
Alliances in the Colonial Context: In the colonial era, alliances between European powers and local groups were crucial in establishing and maintaining colonial rule, as well as in resisting it.

Economic and Political Implications

Arms Trade as a Political Tool: The arms trade often served as a tool of political influence, with European powers using it to gain leverage in diplomatic and colonial affairs.
Economic Benefits and Costs: The arms trade was a lucrative business for weapon-producing countries but also had significant economic costs for purchasing nations.

Ethical and Moral Considerations

Debate on the Arms Trade: The ethics of the arms trade have been debated throughout history, particularly concerning its role in fueling conflicts and contributing to human suffering.
Regulation and Control: Efforts to regulate and control the arms trade have been a part of international relations, though with varying degrees of success.

Modern Perspectives

Continued Relevance: The history of the arms trade and military alliances continues to be relevant in modern times, influencing contemporary discussions on arms control, international security, and geopolitics.
Legacy in International Relations: The dynamics of the arms trade and the formation of military alliances have left a lasting legacy in the field of international relations, shaping current policies and strategies.

Section 8: The Impact of Gunpowder

Tracing the Revolutionary Role of Gunpowder in Warfare

This section analyzes the transformative impact of gunpowder on military strategies and tactics from its introduction in warfare to its role in the colonial wars, underscoring how this technological innovation reshaped the nature of combat and military organization.

Introduction of Gunpowder in Warfare

Origins in China: Originally invented in China, gunpowder made its way to the Islamic world and Europe, where it began to be used in warfare by the 13th century.
Early Uses: Initially used for incendiary and explosive devices, gunpowder's potential in projectile weaponry was soon realized, leading to the development of cannons and firearms.

Transformation of Siege Warfare

Effect on Fortifications: The advent of gunpowder-based artillery rendered traditional high-walled fortresses vulnerable, leading to the development of new styles of fortifications, such as bastion forts.
Changing Tactics: The use of cannons significantly changed siege tactics, making sieges more destructive and altering the balance of power between besiegers and besieged.

Gunpowder in Field Battles

Introduction of Firearms: The incorporation of handheld firearms (muskets and arquebuses) transformed infantry tactics, diminishing the dominance of heavy cavalry on the battlefield.
New Formations and Strategies: The use of gunpowder weapons led to the development of new military formations, such as the Spanish Tercio, and necessitated changes in battlefield strategies.

Impact on Naval Warfare

Gunpowder in Naval Battles: The application of gunpowder in naval warfare led to the development of heavily armed warships, changing naval tactics and leading to the era of ship-of-the-line battles.
Global Maritime Dominance: Gunpowder-enabled naval power played a crucial role in the European exploration and colonization of the Americas, Africa, and Asia.

Socio-Political Implications

Military and Political Power: The ability to produce and utilize gunpowder weapons became a key factor in determining military and political power, influencing the rise and fall of empires.
Economic Impact: The production of gunpowder and firearms became an important industry, impacting economies and trade.

Ethical and Humanitarian Considerations

Increased Lethality and Destruction: The use of gunpowder increased the lethality and destructiveness of warfare, raising ethical and humanitarian concerns.
Legacy in Warfare: The introduction and evolution of gunpowder weaponry have had a lasting impact on military history, with its influence still evident in modern warfare.

Section 9: Siege Warfare: A Comparative Study

Analyzing the Evolution and Techniques of Siege Warfare

This section delves into the history and evolution of siege warfare, comparing different techniques and strategies used across various cultures and time periods, from the medieval era through the colonial wars.

Fundamentals of Siege Warfare

Purpose and Tactics: Siege warfare involves surrounding and attacking fortified places to compel the surrender of the defenders. Techniques include blockades, bombardments, and breaching fortifications.
Historical Significance: Throughout history, sieges have played a crucial role in warfare, often determining the outcome of broader conflicts.

Medieval and Islamic Siege Techniques

Castle Sieges in Europe: Medieval European sieges revolved around castles and walled cities, with attackers using trebuchets, battering rams, and siege towers.
Islamic Siege Craft: Islamic military engineers developed sophisticated siege techniques, including the use of counterweight trebuchets and mining.

Gunpowder and the Transformation of Sieges

Introduction of Artillery: The advent of gunpowder artillery transformed siege warfare, making it possible to breach thick stone walls and leading to changes in fortification design.
Development of Star Forts: The star fort, or trace italienne, with its angled bastions and low walls, emerged in response to the effectiveness of artillery.

Sieges in the Age of Exploration and Colonialism

European Colonial Sieges: In the colonial era, sieges were instrumental in the European conquests of the Americas, Africa, and Asia, with European powers often facing indigenous fortifications.
Adaptation to Local Conditions: In various colonial contexts, European siege techniques were adapted to local environments and conditions.

Technological Innovations and Strategies

Evolution of Siege Weapons: Throughout history, siege weapons evolved from simple mechanical devices to complex artillery pieces.
Tactical Innovations: Innovations in tactics, such as sapping and bombardment strategies, were developed to make sieges more effective.

Impact on Civilian Populations

Sieges and Civilians: Sieges often had devastating effects on civilian populations within fortified places, leading to famine, disease, and hardship.
Psychological Warfare: The psychological impact of sieges, both on defenders and civilians, was an important aspect of this form of warfare.

Legacy and Historical Study

Sieges in Military History: The study of siege warfare offers insights into historical military strategies, technological advancements, and the human cost of war.
Enduring Influence: The principles and tactics of siege warfare continue to influence modern military thinking, particularly in urban warfare contexts.

Section 10: Military Legacy in Modern Warfare

Tracing the Historical Influence on Contemporary Military Practices

This final section of Chapter 11 examines how the military strategies, tactics, and innovations from the Crusades to the colonial wars have influenced modern warfare, shedding light on the lasting legacies of these historical periods in contemporary military thought and practice.

Legacy of the Crusades

Tactical and Strategic Lessons: The Crusades influenced modern military strategies, particularly in the areas of logistics, siege warfare, and the use of cavalry.
Psychological and Cultural Impact: The Crusades also left a lasting psychological and cultural legacy, shaping Western perceptions of the Middle East and influencing military and political policies.

Gunpowder Revolution

Artillery and Firearms: The development and refinement of gunpowder weapons during the colonial era revolutionized warfare, leading to the dominance of firearms in modern combat.
Impact on Naval Warfare: The introduction of gunpowder significantly changed naval warfare, a legacy seen in modern naval tactics and ship design.

Fortification and Siege Warfare

Evolution of Fortifications: The adaptation of fortifications in response to artillery in the colonial era influences the design and concept of defensive structures in modern military architecture.
Urban Warfare: The principles of siege warfare continue to be relevant in urban warfare scenarios, where control of cities and strongholds remains a key objective.

Military Alliances and Arms Trade

Global Alliances: The formation of military alliances during the colonial period set precedents for modern international military coalitions and alliances.
Continued Arms Trade Dynamics: The global arms trade, which expanded significantly during the colonial era, remains a significant factor in international relations and conflict.

Guerrilla Warfare and Asymmetric Tactics

Legacy of Irregular Warfare: The use of guerrilla tactics by indigenous peoples against colonial powers influenced modern asymmetric and unconventional warfare methods.
Counterinsurgency Strategies: Modern militaries continue to develop strategies to counter guerrilla warfare, drawing on historical experiences.

Ethical and Legal Developments

Warfare and International Law: The conduct of warfare during these historical periods contributed to the development of international laws and conventions regulating armed conflict.
Humanitarian Considerations: The impact of warfare on civilian populations in the Crusades and colonial wars underscores ongoing concerns about the humanitarian aspects of modern conflict.

Technological Innovation and Adaptation

Continuous Evolution: The continuous innovation in military technology and tactics, a theme from the Crusades to the colonial era, persists in the modern era, with militaries constantly adapting to new challenges and technologies.

Chapter 12: Cultural Assimilation and Resistance in the New World

Section 1: Indigenous Cultures and European Settlers

Encounters and Impacts Between Native and European Cultures

This section explores the initial encounters between indigenous cultures and European settlers in the New World, focusing on the diverse ways these interactions unfolded and their profound impacts on native societies.

First Contacts

Early Encounters: The initial contacts between European explorers and indigenous peoples varied greatly, from peaceful trade and interaction to hostility and conflict.
Perceptions and Misunderstandings: These early encounters were often marked by mutual curiosity, but also significant misunderstandings and misinterpretations of each other's cultures and intentions.

Cultural Impact on Indigenous Peoples

Introduction of European Goods and Technologies: The arrival of Europeans introduced new goods, technologies, and practices to indigenous societies, altering their way of life and economic systems.
Disease and Population Decline: European contact brought devastating diseases to which indigenous populations had no immunity, leading to massive population declines and societal disruption.

European Adaptation and Influence

Adopting Indigenous Knowledge: European settlers often adapted indigenous knowledge and practices for survival, including agriculture, navigation, and medicinal uses of native plants.
Cultural Exchange: Despite conflicts, there was a degree of cultural exchange, with Europeans integrating certain aspects of indigenous culture into their own lives.

Resistance and Accommodation

Variations in Indigenous Responses: Indigenous responses to European settlement ranged from resistance and warfare to accommodation and alliances, depending on local circumstances and European approaches.
Shifting Power Dynamics: The interactions between indigenous cultures and European settlers reshaped the power dynamics within native societies, often leading to internal changes and realignments.

Long-Term Cultural Effects

Preservation and Loss of Indigenous Cultures: While some indigenous cultures were able to preserve key aspects of their identity, others faced significant cultural loss and erosion due to European colonization.
Foundations of New Societies: The intermingling of indigenous and European cultures laid the foundations for the diverse cultural landscapes of modern nations in the Americas.

Section 2: Models of Cultural Assimilation

Understanding the Processes and Patterns of Cultural Integration

This section delves into the various models of cultural assimilation that emerged in the New World as a result of European colonization, analyzing how indigenous peoples and European settlers navigated the complex process of cultural integration.

Forced Assimilation

Imposition of European Culture: In many cases, European colonizers attempted to impose their culture, language, religion, and social norms on indigenous populations, often through coercive means.
Residential Schools and Cultural Eradication: The establishment of residential schools aimed to eradicate indigenous cultures and languages, promoting a European way of life.

Voluntary Assimilation

Adoption of European Practices: Some indigenous individuals and groups voluntarily adopted certain European practices, whether for survival, economic benefit, or social mobility.
Intermarriage and Cultural Blending: Intermarriage between Europeans and indigenous peoples led to cultural blending and the emergence of mixed-heritage communities.

Syncretism

Combining Cultural Elements: Syncretism involved the blending of indigenous and European cultural elements, particularly in religion and art, creating unique hybrid cultures.
Religious Syncretism: In religion, syncretic practices combined indigenous beliefs with Christianity, resulting in distinctive religious practices.

Resistance to Assimilation

Maintaining Indigenous Identity: Despite pressures to assimilate, many indigenous communities strived to maintain their cultural identity, language, and traditions.
Cultural Revival Movements: In some cases, indigenous peoples actively resisted assimilation through cultural revival movements and the reassertion of traditional practices.

Government Policies and Their Impact

Colonial Policies on Assimilation: The policies of colonial governments significantly influenced the process of assimilation, often favoring and enforcing European cultural norms.
Contemporary Reevaluation: Modern societies are reevaluating past assimilation policies, recognizing their detrimental impacts on indigenous cultures and seeking reconciliation and redress.

Legacy of Assimilation in the New World

Cultural Diversity and Tensions: The legacy of cultural assimilation is complex, contributing to the rich cultural diversity of the Americas but also to ongoing tensions and challenges in addressing historical injustices.
Influence on Modern Cultural Identities: The processes of cultural assimilation have shaped the identities and social fabric of nations in the New World, influencing contemporary discussions on multiculturalism and heritage preservation.

Section 3: Resistance and Revolt Against Colonizers

Exploring Indigenous Opposition to European Domination

This section examines the various forms of resistance and revolt by indigenous peoples against European colonizers in the New World, highlighting the strategies, motivations, and impacts of these acts of defiance.

Forms of Resistance

Armed Revolts: Indigenous groups often resorted to armed revolts against European settlers and colonial authorities, seeking to defend their territories and way of life.
Guerrilla Warfare: Utilizing their knowledge of the local terrain, many indigenous groups engaged in guerrilla tactics, conducting hit-and-run attacks and ambushes against colonial forces.

Notable Uprisings

The Pueblo Revolt: In 1680, the Pueblo peoples in present-day New Mexico successfully revolted against Spanish rule, expelling the colonizers from their lands for several years.
Pontiac's Rebellion: In the 1760s, a confederation of Native American tribes led by Pontiac, an Ottawa leader, rose against British post-colonial rule in the Great Lakes region.

Cultural and Spiritual Resistance

Preservation of Traditions: Beyond physical resistance, indigenous peoples sought to preserve their cultural and spiritual practices in the face of European suppression.
Secret Societies and Rituals: Secret societies and the clandestine practice of traditional rituals became means of maintaining cultural identity and resistance.

Impact of Resistance Movements

Temporary Victories and Reprisals: While some revolts achieved temporary success, they often led to harsh reprisals and increased suppression by colonial powers.
Enduring Symbolism: These acts of resistance became enduring symbols of indigenous resilience and defiance, inspiring future generations.

Influence on Colonial Policies

Changes in Colonial Approach: In some cases, indigenous resistance led to changes in colonial policies, with authorities adopting more conciliatory approaches or granting certain concessions.
Legacies of Resistance: The legacies of these resistance movements are visible in contemporary indigenous rights movements and efforts to reclaim historical narratives.

Modern Reflections and Recognition

Reevaluation of Historical Narratives: Modern scholarship and societal perspectives are increasingly acknowledging and reevaluating the role and significance of indigenous resistance to colonization.
Commemoration and Education: Efforts to commemorate and educate about these resistance movements contribute to a broader understanding of colonial history and its impacts.

Section 4: The Role of Religion in Cultural Exchange

Intersections of Faith and Culture in the Colonization Era

This section examines the significant role of religion in the cultural exchange between European settlers and indigenous peoples in the New World, highlighting how religious interactions shaped both groups and influenced cultural assimilation and resistance.

Religious Imposition and Conversion Efforts

Missionary Activities: European colonization was often accompanied by missionary efforts aimed at converting indigenous peoples to Christianity, particularly by Catholic and later Protestant missionaries.
Forced Conversions: In some regions, conversion to Christianity was enforced through coercion, with indigenous spiritual practices being suppressed or outlawed.

Syncretism and Hybrid Religions

Blending of Beliefs: Despite efforts to eradicate indigenous religions, syncretism occurred, with elements of indigenous beliefs and practices blending with Christianity to form unique hybrid religions.
Examples of Syncretism: The Virgin of Guadalupe in Mexico and Vodou in Haiti are examples of syncretic religious traditions that combine Christian and indigenous elements.

Indigenous Spiritual Practices and Resistance

Preservation of Traditions: Indigenous communities often sought to preserve their spiritual traditions secretly or by integrating them into Christian practices.
Religion as a Form of Resistance: In some cases, indigenous religious leaders led resistance against colonial forces, using spiritual authority to unite communities against European domination.

Impact on European Settlers

Influence of Indigenous Spirituality: European settlers were sometimes influenced by indigenous spiritual views, leading to a broader understanding and, in some cases, adoption of certain practices or concepts.
Reevaluation of Religious Practices: Encounters with indigenous spirituality led some European settlers to reevaluate their own religious beliefs and practices.

Religious Institutions and Colonial Administration

Church and State: The church often played a significant role in colonial administration, influencing policies and decisions regarding indigenous peoples.
Education and Indoctrination: Religious institutions frequently established educational systems as a means of cultural assimilation and religious indoctrination.

Contemporary Perspectives

Recognition of Religious Impact: Modern scholarship recognizes the complex role of religion in cultural exchanges during the colonial period, acknowledging both its oppressive aspects and its contributions to cultural diversity.
Reclamation and Revival: Contemporary indigenous movements often involve the reclamation and revival of traditional spiritual practices, reflecting a continuing effort to preserve cultural identity.

Section 5: Syncretism: Blending of Cultures and Beliefs

The Fusion of European and Indigenous Cultural Elements

This section explores the phenomenon of syncretism in the New World, highlighting how European and indigenous cultures and beliefs merged to create unique hybrid traditions, practices, and forms of expression.

Definition and Dynamics of Syncretism

Cultural and Religious Fusion: Syncretism refers to the blending of different cultural and religious elements, forming new, hybrid traditions. This often occurs in contexts where diverse cultures interact, such as in colonization.

Mechanism of Adaptation: Syncretism can be seen as a mechanism of adaptation and survival, allowing indigenous cultures to retain elements of their identity while adapting to the dominant culture.

Examples of Religious Syncretism

Afro-American Religions: In the Caribbean and Latin America, religions like Santería, Candomblé, and Vodou emerged, blending African religious traditions with Catholicism.
Native American Christian Traditions: Indigenous peoples in North America often incorporated Christian symbols and practices into their spiritual traditions, creating unique forms of worship.

Cultural Syncretism

Art and Architecture: Syncretism is evident in art and architecture, with indigenous and European styles merging to create distinct artistic expressions.
Language and Literature: The fusion of languages and literary traditions resulted in new dialects and literary forms, reflecting the combined heritage of the colonizers and the colonized.

Impact on Identity and Society

Creation of New Identities: Syncretic cultures contributed to the formation of new social and cultural identities, particularly in regions with significant mestizo (mixed heritage) populations.
Cultural Resilience and Resistance: Syncretism served as a form of cultural resilience and resistance, enabling indigenous peoples to maintain aspects of their heritage under colonial rule.

Challenges and Controversies

Tensions in Cultural Preservation: Syncretism sometimes led to tensions over the preservation of "pure" cultural forms, with debates on authenticity and cultural erosion.
Religious Conflicts: Syncretic practices were often at odds with orthodox religious teachings, leading to conflicts with religious authorities.

Contemporary Relevance

Recognition and Revival: Today, there is growing recognition and revival of syncretic traditions, seen as important cultural legacies and expressions of historical resilience.
Role in Intercultural Understanding: Understanding syncretism can foster greater intercultural understanding and appreciation of the complex histories that shape modern societies.

Section 6: Language and Literature as Tools of Assimilation

The Role of Language in Shaping Cultural Identities

This section examines how language and literature were used as tools of cultural assimilation in the New World, impacting indigenous populations and contributing to the formation of new cultural identities.

Language Policies and Assimilation

Imposition of European Languages: European colonial powers often imposed their languages on indigenous populations, viewing this as a key aspect of assimilation into European culture. Suppression of Indigenous Languages: In many regions, indigenous languages were actively suppressed, with policies prohibiting their use in public life, education, and religious practice.

Literature as a Means of Cultural Transmission

European Literary Traditions: European settlers brought their literary traditions to the New World, which often included religious texts, histories, and classical literature that reflected European values and worldviews.
Creation of Colonial Literature: In the colonies, a new body of literature emerged that blended European styles with local experiences and perspectives, contributing to the development of distinct literary traditions.

Resistance through Language and Literature

Preservation of Indigenous Languages: Despite efforts at suppression, many indigenous communities managed to preserve their languages, passing them down through generations.
Indigenous Literary Forms: Indigenous peoples also used oral traditions, storytelling, and, in some cases, written forms to keep their narratives and cultural heritage alive.

Impact on Identity and Communication

Formation of Creole Languages: The interaction between European and indigenous (as well as African) languages led to the development of creole languages, reflecting the blended cultural environments of the colonies.
Language as a Cultural Marker: Language served as an important marker of cultural identity, with the choice of language often reflecting social status, cultural alignment, and resistance or adaptation to colonial rule.

Educational Role of Language

Language in Colonial Education Systems: European languages were often the medium of instruction in colonial education systems, shaping the way knowledge was transmitted and received.
Literacy and Access to Knowledge: Literacy in the colonial language became a key factor in accessing education, economic opportunities, and political power.

Modern Perspectives on Language and Literature

Reevaluation and Revival: Contemporary efforts focus on the reevaluation and revival of indigenous languages and literature, recognizing their value and the need to preserve linguistic diversity.
Cultural Resurgence: Language and literature continue to play a central role in cultural resurgence movements, with indigenous and mestizo communities reclaiming their linguistic heritage as a form of empowerment and identity.

Section 7: Education and Indoctrination Strategies

The Role of Education in Shaping Societal Dynamics in the Colonies

This section addresses how education was used as a strategic tool for cultural assimilation and indoctrination in the New World, analyzing its impacts on indigenous populations and the shaping of colonial societies.

Educational Policies of Colonial Powers

Establishment of Schools: European colonizers established schools in the colonies, often run by religious missions, with the aim of educating indigenous populations in European ways of life and Christian doctrine.
Curriculum and Content: The curriculum in these schools emphasized European history, literature, and values, often neglecting or misrepresenting indigenous cultures and histories.

Indoctrination and Cultural Erasure

Assimilationist Objectives: The primary objective of colonial education was often to assimilate indigenous children, encouraging them to abandon their traditional cultures and languages.
Suppression of Indigenous Knowledge: Traditional indigenous knowledge systems and educational practices were suppressed or undervalued, leading to a loss of cultural heritage.

Resistance and Adaptation

Indigenous Responses: Indigenous communities responded in various ways, from outright resistance and the establishment of alternative education systems to adaptation and the use of colonial education for their own purposes.
Preservation of Culture: In some cases, indigenous peoples covertly maintained their cultural practices and languages, even while participating in the colonial education system.

Long-Term Impacts

Cultural and Linguistic Impact: Colonial education had lasting impacts on the cultural and linguistic landscape of the colonies, with many indigenous languages and traditions becoming endangered or extinct.
Formation of Elites: The colonial education system often created a new elite class within indigenous societies, which sometimes led to social stratification and conflicts.

Reevaluation and Reform

Contemporary Critiques: Modern perspectives critically assess the role of colonial education systems, acknowledging their role in cultural suppression and advocating for the incorporation of indigenous knowledge and languages in education.
Revival and Inclusion: Efforts to revive indigenous languages and cultures include reforming educational policies to be more inclusive and representative of indigenous histories and perspectives.

Education as a Tool for Empowerment

Empowering Indigenous Voices: Education is increasingly seen as a tool for empowering indigenous voices and perspectives, fostering a more diverse and inclusive understanding of history and culture.

Section 8: Economic Exploitation and Its Cultural Effects

Assessing the Interplay Between Economic Practices and Cultural Changes

This section explores the economic exploitation of indigenous peoples and resources by European colonizers in the New World and its profound effects on the cultural landscapes of both indigenous and colonial societies.

Economic Practices and Exploitation

Resource Extraction: European colonization often involved the extraction of natural resources, such as gold, silver, and agricultural products, heavily relying on indigenous labor and knowledge.
Encomienda and Hacienda Systems: Systems like the encomienda and hacienda in Latin America exemplified the economic exploitation of indigenous peoples, often under harsh and oppressive conditions.

Cultural Impacts on Indigenous Peoples

Disruption of Traditional Economies: The introduction of European economic systems and the demand for labor and resources disrupted traditional indigenous economies and ways of life.
Loss of Land and Autonomy: The loss of land and autonomy under colonial rule had significant cultural implications, leading to the erosion of indigenous social structures and traditions.

Resistance and Adaptation

Economic Resistance: Indigenous peoples employed various forms of resistance, from revolts against oppressive labor systems to subtle forms of work slowdowns and sabotage.
Adaptation to New Economic Realities: Some indigenous communities adapted to the new economic realities by engaging in trade with Europeans, modifying agricultural practices, or participating in the colonial economy.

Formation of New Social Classes

Creation of Mestizo and Casta Systems: The colonial economy contributed to the formation of new social classes, including mestizos (mixed European and indigenous heritage) and complex casta systems, which had significant cultural implications.
Stratification and Social Mobility: These new social structures led to stratification within indigenous societies and opportunities for social mobility, albeit often limited.

Long-Term Cultural Consequences

Persistence of Economic Disparities: The economic models established during colonization have had lasting effects, contributing to ongoing economic disparities in many regions of the New World.

Cultural Resilience and Revival: Despite economic exploitation, indigenous cultures have shown resilience, with contemporary efforts focusing on the revival of traditional practices and economic systems.

Contemporary Perspectives and Reforms

Reevaluation of Colonial Economic Impact: Modern scholarship and policy reforms are increasingly reevaluating the impact of colonial economic practices on indigenous cultures, advocating for more equitable and sustainable approaches.
Indigenous Economic Empowerment: Current initiatives aim to empower indigenous communities economically, recognizing the value of traditional knowledge and practices in sustainable development.

Section 9: The Persistence of Indigenous Cultures

Enduring Heritage and Resilience Amidst Colonization

This section focuses on the remarkable persistence and resilience of indigenous cultures in the New World, despite the profound impacts of European colonization, exploring how these cultures have maintained their identity and traditions.

Survival of Cultural Practices

Retention of Traditional Practices: Indigenous communities have managed to retain many of their traditional cultural practices, including language, art, music, and spiritual rituals, often adapting them to changing circumstances.
Secret Preservation: In some cases, cultural practices were preserved secretly, especially when they were prohibited or discouraged by colonial authorities.

Cultural Revival Movements

Revival of Indigenous Languages and Traditions: Recent decades have seen a resurgence in the revival of indigenous languages and traditions, with communities reclaiming their cultural heritage.
Cultural Festivals and Celebrations: Cultural festivals, ceremonies, and celebrations have played a significant role in maintaining and revitalizing indigenous cultural practices.

Role of Oral History and Storytelling

Preservation through Oral Traditions: Oral history and storytelling have been crucial in preserving indigenous knowledge, history, and cultural values across generations.
Adaptation of Narratives: These narratives have adapted over time, incorporating elements of the colonial experience while maintaining core indigenous perspectives.

Intermingling with Colonial Cultures

Syncretism and Hybrid Cultures: The intermingling of indigenous and colonial cultures has led to the development of syncretic and hybrid cultural forms, reflecting a blend of influences.
Influence on Broader Society: Indigenous cultures have influenced the broader societies of the New World, contributing to the rich cultural diversity of the Americas.

Contemporary Recognition and Challenges

Increased Recognition and Rights: There is increasing recognition of indigenous cultures and rights, including efforts to protect and promote indigenous heritage and languages.
Challenges of Modernization and Globalization: Indigenous cultures face challenges in maintaining their traditions in the face of modernization, globalization, and changing demographics.

Resilience and Adaptation

Resilience in the Face of Adversity: The persistence of indigenous cultures is a testament to their resilience and ability to adapt in the face of adversity and change.
Continued Evolution of Indigenous Cultures: Indigenous cultures continue to evolve, reflecting both their traditional heritage and their interactions with modern society.

Section 10: Long-Term Cultural Impacts of Colonization

Examining the Enduring Effects of European Colonization on New World Societies

This final section of Chapter 12 discusses the long-term cultural impacts of European colonization in the New World, exploring how these historical events have shaped the contemporary cultural landscapes of both indigenous and settler societies.

Cultural Hybridization

Formation of New Cultural Identities: Colonization led to the creation of new cultural identities, particularly in regions with significant mestizo and mulatto populations, blending indigenous, European, and African elements.
Syncretic Traditions: The fusion of different cultural traditions has resulted in unique syncretic forms in art, music, religion, and other cultural expressions.

Language and Linguistic Diversity

Dominance of European Languages: European languages like Spanish, Portuguese, English, and French became dominant in many regions, often at the expense of indigenous languages.
Linguistic Revival and Preservation: Efforts to preserve and revive indigenous languages are underway, recognizing their importance in cultural heritage and identity.

Impact on Social Structures and Norms

Class and Racial Hierarchies: Colonialism established class and racial hierarchies that have had lasting impacts on societal structures and relationships in the Americas.
Continued Social and Racial Tensions: The legacy of these hierarchies continues to influence social and racial dynamics, contributing to ongoing tensions and disparities.

Influence on Art and Architecture

Colonial and Indigenous Art Forms: The blending of European and indigenous styles created distinctive art and architectural forms, visible in historical and contemporary works.
Cultural Heritage and Tourism: Many colonial and indigenous art forms and architectural sites have become important cultural heritage landmarks and tourist attractions.

Religious and Spiritual Legacies

Spread and Adaptation of Christianity: The widespread adoption and adaptation of Christianity have had profound effects on religious practices and beliefs in the New World.
Persistence and Revival of Indigenous Spirituality: Indigenous spiritual practices have persisted and are experiencing revival, often coexisting with or incorporated into Christian practices.

Modern Cultural Identity and Expression

Complex Identities: The cultural legacies of colonization have contributed to complex, multi-layered identities in the New World, reflecting diverse historical influences.
Contemporary Cultural Expression: Artists, writers, and cultural practitioners in the New World continue to explore and express these complex identities, often addressing themes of colonization, resistance, and cultural fusion.

Reflections on Historical Narratives

Reexamining History: There is an ongoing reexamination of historical narratives about colonization, with increased emphasis on indigenous perspectives and experiences.
Educational and Policy Implications: This reexamination is influencing educational curricula and cultural policies, promoting a more inclusive and accurate understanding of the New World's history.

Chapter 13: European Enlightenment and Islamic Legacy

Section 1: Defining the European Enlightenment

Exploring the Intellectual Movement that Transformed Europe

This section offers an overview of the European Enlightenment, a pivotal intellectual movement that profoundly influenced European thought, culture, and society, and sets the stage for examining its interactions with Islamic thought.

Origins and Context

Time Period: The Enlightenment, often referred to as the "Age of Reason," primarily spanned the 17th and 18th centuries.
Roots in the Scientific Revolution: Building on the scientific advances of the 16th and 17th centuries, the Enlightenment represented a shift towards rational thought, empirical science, and skepticism of traditional authority.

Key Philosophies and Ideas

Rationalism and Empiricism: Enlightenment thinkers emphasized rationalism—the reliance on reason as the primary source of knowledge—and empiricism, which stressed observation and experience.
Secularism and Humanism: The movement fostered secularism, separating religious influence from public life and governance, and humanism, focusing on human potential and achievements.

Notable Enlightenment Thinkers

Diverse Intellectual Contributions: Philosophers like John Locke, Voltaire, and Immanuel Kant, among others, contributed diverse ideas ranging from political theory to ethics and epistemology.
Advocacy for Political and Social Reforms: Enlightenment thinkers often advocated for political and social reforms, including democratic governance, individual rights, and freedom of expression.

Impact on Society and Culture

Influence on Political Revolutions: The Enlightenment played a key role in shaping the intellectual backdrop of the American and French Revolutions.
Cultural and Educational Shifts: It also influenced cultural and educational norms, encouraging scientific inquiry, critical thinking, and a questioning of traditional dogmas.

Contemporary Relevance

Legacy in Modern Thought: The Enlightenment's emphasis on reason, science, and individual rights continues to influence modern Western thought and democratic ideals.
Ongoing Debates and Critiques: The movement's legacy is subject to ongoing debate, with critiques focusing on aspects such as its Eurocentric perspective and its role in colonialism.

Section 2: Islamic Contributions to European Thought

The Influence of Islamic Scholarship on the European Enlightenment

This section examines the significant contributions of Islamic scholars to European intellectual thought, particularly how their works and ideas influenced the development of various disciplines during the Enlightenment period.

Transmission of Knowledge

Transmission through Al-Andalus and the Crusades: The interaction between Islamic and Christian worlds in places like Al-Andalus (Muslim Spain) and during the Crusades facilitated the transfer of Islamic knowledge to Europe.
Role of Translation Movements: Translation movements, especially in places like Toledo, played a crucial role in bringing Islamic works on science, philosophy, and medicine to a European audience.

Advancements in Science and Mathematics

Astronomy and Mathematics: Islamic scholars like Al-Khwarizmi and Al-Battani made significant contributions to mathematics and astronomy, which were later integrated into European scientific thought.
Medicine: Works by Islamic physicians, such as Ibn Sina (Avicenna) and Al-Razi, were foundational in the development of European medicine.

Philosophy and Rational Thought

Aristotelian Philosophy: Islamic philosophers like Al-Farabi and Averroes (Ibn Rushd) played a key role in preserving and commenting on the works of Aristotle, which significantly influenced European philosophers.
Integration into Scholasticism: The integration of Aristotelian philosophy from Islamic sources into Christian Scholasticism laid the groundwork for rational inquiry during the Enlightenment.

Technological Innovations

Adoption of Inventions: European advancements were often built upon Islamic innovations in areas like optics, engineering, and navigation.
Paper and the Printing Revolution: The Islamic introduction of paper production to Europe facilitated the spread of printed books, aiding the dissemination of knowledge during the Enlightenment.

Cultural and Artistic Influence

Islamic Art and Architecture: The influence of Islamic art and architecture was evident in various parts of Europe, inspiring new artistic movements and styles.

Literary Works: Literary works from the Islamic world, including poetry and tales like those from "One Thousand and One Nights," also left an imprint on European literature.

Impact on European Intellectual Renaissance

Foundation for Renaissance Thought: The contributions of Islamic scholars provided a foundation for the intellectual renaissance in Europe, paving the way for the Enlightenment.
Recognition of Interconnected Histories: Modern scholarship increasingly acknowledges the interconnected histories of Islamic and European thought, highlighting the role of Islamic contributions in shaping the European intellectual landscape.

Section 3: Philosophers Influenced by Islamic Works

Tracing the Impact of Islamic Scholarship on European Enlightenment Thinkers

This section delves into the influence of Islamic scholars and their works on key European philosophers during the Enlightenment, revealing the depth of intellectual exchange between the Islamic and European worlds.

Influence on Medieval European Scholars

Transmission of Aristotelian Thought: Islamic philosophers like Averroes (Ibn Rushd) and Avicenna (Ibn Sina) played a crucial role in transmitting and interpreting Aristotelian philosophy, which significantly influenced medieval European scholars such as Thomas Aquinas.
Integration into Scholasticism: The works of Islamic philosophers were integrated into the Scholastic tradition, forming a bridge between classical philosophy and the European Renaissance.

Renaissance and Enlightenment Figures

Roger Bacon: Known for his empirical approach to science, Bacon was influenced by Islamic works on optics and scientific methodology.
René Descartes: Descartes, a key figure in the development of modern philosophy, was influenced by the Islamic emphasis on reason and rational inquiry.

Scientific Advances

Advancements in Mathematics and Astronomy: European mathematicians and astronomers, including Copernicus and Kepler, were influenced by the mathematical and astronomical works of Islamic scholars.
Medicine and Natural Sciences: Islamic medical texts and studies in natural sciences had a lasting impact on European medical and scientific thought.

Philosophical and Ethical Ideas

Moral and Ethical Philosophy: The ethical and moral philosophies developed by Islamic thinkers contributed to European discourses on ethics, governance, and the nature of society.
Political Philosophy: Islamic political philosophy, especially the works discussing governance and the role of rulers, influenced European political thought.

Cultural and Artistic Inspiration

Literary Influence: The translation of literary works from the Islamic world inspired European writers and poets, contributing to the rich tapestry of European literature.
Art and Architecture: The aesthetic principles and architectural styles of Islamic art influenced European art and architecture, seen in various motifs and designs.

Recognition and Scholarship

Acknowledgment of Contributions: Contemporary scholarship increasingly acknowledges the contributions of Islamic scholars to European thought, recognizing the interconnectedness of intellectual histories.
Revisiting Historical Narratives: This recognition has led to a reevaluation of historical narratives about the origins and development of European philosophical and scientific ideas.

Section 4: Enlightenment Ideals and Islamic Philosophy

Exploring the Convergence and Divergence of Thought

This section analyzes the intersections and divergences between the ideals of the European Enlightenment and Islamic philosophy, offering insights into how these two intellectual traditions influenced and contrasted with each other.

Foundations of Enlightenment Thought

Reason and Rational Inquiry: The Enlightenment was marked by an emphasis on reason, rational inquiry, and a questioning of traditional authority and dogma.
Individual Rights and Liberties: Enlightenment thinkers advocated for individual rights, liberties, and the separation of church and state, principles that would shape modern democratic societies.

Islamic Philosophical Traditions

Emphasis on Reason and Logic: Islamic philosophy, especially during its Golden Age, placed a strong emphasis on reason and logic, with thinkers like Al-Farabi and Averroes making significant contributions.
Integration of Faith and Reason: Unlike the secular orientation of much of Enlightenment thought, Islamic philosophy often sought to integrate faith and reason, viewing them as complementary paths to truth.

Points of Convergence

Rationalism and the Pursuit of Knowledge: Both traditions valued rationalism and the pursuit of knowledge, albeit with different orientations and ultimate goals.
Ethical and Moral Reasoning: Islamic and Enlightenment thinkers both engaged in ethical and moral reasoning, exploring questions about the nature of good governance, justice, and the role of the individual in society.

Divergences in Thought

Secularism vs. Faith-Centered Worldview: A key divergence lies in the Enlightenment's move towards secularism, contrasting with the more faith-centered worldview of Islamic philosophy.
Different Historical and Cultural Contexts: The different historical and cultural contexts of these intellectual traditions led to distinct philosophical developments and societal impacts.

Influence on European Enlightenment

Islamic Influence on Key Concepts: The influence of Islamic thought can be seen in several key Enlightenment concepts, particularly in the fields of science, mathematics, and philosophical reasoning.

Adaptation and Transformation of Ideas: European thinkers adapted and transformed these influences, integrating them into the distinct cultural and intellectual context of the Enlightenment.

Contemporary Relevance

Ongoing Dialogue Between Traditions: The dialogue between Islamic philosophy and Enlightenment ideals continues to be relevant, informing contemporary discussions on multiculturalism, global ethics, and the integration of diverse intellectual traditions.
Reassessing Contributions and Interactions: Modern scholarship increasingly seeks to reassess the contributions and interactions between these two rich intellectual traditions, providing a more nuanced understanding of their historical interplay.

Section 5: Scientific Revolution: An Intersection of Cultures

Tracing the Contributions of Islamic Scholarship to the European Scientific Awakening

This section explores the critical role Islamic scholarship played in the European Scientific Revolution, highlighting how the transfer of knowledge from the Islamic world contributed to pivotal advancements in science during the Enlightenment.

Islamic Foundations of the Scientific Revolution

Preservation and Advancement of Knowledge: Islamic scholars preserved and expanded upon the scientific knowledge of ancient civilizations, including Greek, Persian, and Indian.
Innovations in Various Fields: Contributions in fields such as mathematics, astronomy, medicine, and optics by scholars like Al-Khwarizmi, Ibn Al-Haytham (Alhazen), and Avicenna (Ibn Sina) were foundational for later developments in Europe.

Transmission to Europe

Translation Movements: The translation of Islamic scientific works into Latin during the medieval period, especially in centers like Toledo, Spain, played a crucial role in introducing Islamic knowledge to Europe.
Universities and Learning Centers: The establishment of universities and learning centers in Europe facilitated the study and expansion of this knowledge, setting the stage for the Scientific Revolution.

Key Areas of Influence

Mathematics and Algebra: Islamic advancements in algebra and the introduction of Arabic numerals had a profound impact on European mathematics.
Astronomy and Observational Techniques: Islamic astronomers' work on celestial observations and refinements to Ptolemaic models influenced European astronomers, including Copernicus.
Medicine and Anatomy: Islamic medical texts and their holistic approach to health and medicine were influential in European medical schools.

Renaissance and Enlightenment Thinkers

Adoption and Adaptation of Ideas: European thinkers during the Renaissance and Enlightenment, such as Kepler, Galileo, and Newton, adopted and adapted these ideas, further advancing scientific thought.
Building on a Multicultural Foundation: The Scientific Revolution in Europe was built on a multicultural foundation, incorporating and expanding upon the knowledge from the Islamic world.

Impact on European Thought

Shift to Empirical Research: The influence of Islamic scholarship contributed to the shift towards empirical research and observation in Europe, a hallmark of the Scientific Revolution.
Questioning of Traditional Beliefs: The infusion of new ideas and knowledge challenged traditional beliefs and paved the way for more critical and independent scientific inquiry during the Enlightenment.

Modern Recognition

Acknowledging Cross-Cultural Contributions: Modern scholarship increasingly acknowledges the cross-cultural contributions to the Scientific Revolution, recognizing the interconnected nature of scientific progress.
Revisiting Historical Narratives: This recognition has led to a revisiting of historical narratives about the origins and development of modern science, highlighting the diverse contributions of Islamic scholars.

Section 6: The Role of Rationalism and Empiricism

Interweaving Islamic and European Philosophical Traditions

This section examines how Islamic philosophy influenced the development of rationalism and empiricism in Europe, particularly during the Enlightenment, highlighting the interplay between these intellectual traditions.

Rationalism in Islamic Philosophy

Emphasis on Reason: Islamic philosophers like Al-Farabi, Avicenna (Ibn Sina), and Averroes (Ibn Rushd) placed a strong emphasis on reason and rational analysis, significantly contributing to the field of logic and metaphysics.
Reconciliation of Philosophy and Religion: These thinkers often sought to reconcile philosophical reasoning with Islamic theology, arguing for the compatibility of faith and reason.

Impact on European Rationalism

Transmission of Ideas: The transmission of Islamic philosophical works to Europe, particularly those of Averroes and Avicenna, played a crucial role in shaping European rationalist thought.
Influence on European Thinkers: European philosophers, including Thomas Aquinas and later Descartes, were influenced by the rationalist approach of Islamic philosophy.

Development of Empiricism

Islamic Foundations: Islamic scholars' emphasis on empirical observation, especially in fields like medicine and astronomy, laid the groundwork for the empirical approach in science.
Contribution to the Scientific Method: The methodological approaches developed by Islamic scholars contributed to the formulation of the scientific method, which became a cornerstone of empirical science during the Enlightenment.

Enlightenment and the Synthesis of Rationalism and Empiricism

Integration in European Thought: Enlightenment thinkers synthesized rationalist and empiricist approaches, using reason as a tool to interpret empirical observations.
Advancement of Scientific Inquiry: This synthesis advanced scientific inquiry, encouraging a critical examination of the natural world and leading to numerous scientific discoveries.

Contemporary Perspectives

Reassessment of Intellectual History: Modern scholarship increasingly acknowledges the role of Islamic philosophy in the development of rationalism and empiricism in European thought.
Recognition of Cross-Cultural Influences: There is growing recognition of the cross-cultural influences that shaped the intellectual landscape of the Enlightenment, moving beyond a Eurocentric view of the period.

Section 7: Political Theories and Islamic Governance

Exploring the Interplay Between Islamic Political Thought and Enlightenment Ideals

This section examines the influence of Islamic political philosophy on European political theories during the Enlightenment, highlighting how ideas from the Islamic world contributed to shaping concepts of governance, statehood, and civil society in Europe.

Islamic Contributions to Political Thought

Foundational Works: Islamic political thinkers, such as Al-Farabi, Avicenna (Ibn Sina), and Al-Mawardi, developed sophisticated theories on governance, statecraft, and the responsibilities of rulers.
Concepts of Justice and Ethics in Governance: Islamic political philosophy emphasized the importance of justice, ethical governance, and the welfare of the community, ideas that resonated with European Enlightenment thinkers.

Transmission and Influence

Introduction to Europe: Through the translation of Islamic texts and interaction with the Muslim world, European scholars were exposed to Islamic political ideas.
Influence on European Philosophers: Thinkers like Thomas Aquinas, John Locke, and Montesquieu were influenced, directly or indirectly, by the political concepts developed in the Islamic world.

Enlightenment and the Reimagining of Governance

Reformulation of Sovereignty and Statehood: Enlightenment thinkers reformulated concepts of sovereignty and statehood, incorporating ideas of social contract and popular sovereignty, which had parallels in Islamic political thought.

Advocacy for Rational and Ethical Governance: The Enlightenment's emphasis on rational and ethical governance echoed similar principles found in Islamic philosophy.

Comparative Analysis

Differences in Context and Application: While there were similarities in political thought, the context and application of these ideas differed significantly between the Islamic world and Europe, shaped by different historical, cultural, and religious landscapes.
Synthesis of Ideas: The Enlightenment period saw a synthesis of various ideas, including those from Islamic political thought, leading to new conceptions of governance and civil liberties.

Legacy and Modern Implications

Influence on Modern Political Systems: The political theories developed during the Enlightenment, influenced in part by Islamic thought, laid the foundations for modern democratic systems and political philosophies.
Reassessing the Origins of Political Concepts: Modern scholarship is increasingly recognizing the diverse origins of key political concepts, including the contributions of Islamic political thought to European Enlightenment ideas.

Section 8: Social Contract Theory and Islamic Law

Examining the Parallels and Influences in Political and Legal Philosophies

This section delves into the similarities and potential influences between the concept of the social contract in European Enlightenment thought and principles found in Islamic law and governance.

Social Contract Theory in the Enlightenment

Development of the Theory: The social contract theory, as developed by thinkers like Thomas Hobbes, John Locke, and Jean-Jacques Rousseau, posits that political and moral society is founded on an implicit agreement between individuals and the state.
Rights and Sovereignty: This theory emphasizes the rights of individuals and the idea that sovereignty ultimately resides with the people, a cornerstone of modern democratic thought.

Principles of Islamic Law and Governance

Sharia and Social Order: Islamic law, or Sharia, encompasses a comprehensive system of governance and social order, based on the Quran and Hadith (sayings and actions of Prophet Muhammad).
Community and Justice: Central to Islamic governance is the concept of justice and the welfare of the community (Ummah), with a focus on ethical conduct and mutual obligations between rulers and the ruled.

Comparative Analysis

Concept of Mutual Obligations: Both social contract theory and Islamic law emphasize the idea of mutual obligations and rights between the governed and the governing, albeit in different cultural and theological contexts.
Governance and Ethical Principles: The emphasis on ethical principles in governance and the accountability of rulers is a common thread in both traditions.

Potential Influences and Interactions

Cross-Cultural Exchanges: The potential influence of Islamic thought on European social contract theory could have come through the translation of Islamic works and interactions between the Islamic world and Europe.
Independent Development: While there are similarities, it is also possible that these concepts developed independently in response to different societal needs and philosophical traditions.

Modern Interpretations and Implications

Reassessing Intellectual Histories: Modern scholarship often involves reassessing the intellectual histories of political concepts, acknowledging the potential contributions of non-European traditions.
Islamic Law in Contemporary Contexts: The principles of Islamic law continue to be relevant in contemporary discussions about governance, human rights, and the intersection of religious and secular law.

Section 9: Enlightenment in Art and Architecture

The Confluence of Islamic Influence and European Enlightenment Aesthetics

This section explores the influence of Islamic art and architecture on European aesthetic developments during the Enlightenment, highlighting how cross-cultural exchanges enriched artistic expression in this era.

Islamic Artistic Traditions

Richness and Diversity: Islamic art is characterized by its richness and diversity, incorporating intricate geometric patterns, calligraphy, and a strong emphasis on decorative arts.
Architectural Marvels: Islamic architecture, renowned for its ornate mosques and palaces, introduced innovative structural solutions and aesthetic forms.

Influence on European Art and Architecture

Adoption of Aesthetic Elements: European art and architecture during the Enlightenment were influenced by Islamic elements, particularly in countries like Spain and Portugal, where Islamic presence had been significant.
Orientalism in Art: The Enlightenment also saw the rise of Orientalism in art, where European artists depicted stylized and often romanticized scenes of the Islamic world.

Synthesis in Architectural Styles

Mudéjar and Moorish Revival: Architectural styles such as Mudéjar in Spain and the later Moorish Revival in Europe demonstrate a direct influence of Islamic art and architecture, blending these elements with European designs.
Gardens and Landscape Design: Islamic influences were also evident in European garden and landscape design, incorporating elements like water features and geometric layouts.

Impact on Decorative Arts

Ceramics and Textiles: The techniques and designs of Islamic ceramics and textiles were adopted and adapted in European decorative arts, influencing patterns and motifs used in various crafts.
Influence on Book Design: Islamic contributions to bookmaking and calligraphy influenced European book design, particularly in the use of decorative elements and manuscript illumination.

Cross-Cultural Artistic Dialogue

Artistic Exchange: The artistic exchange between Islamic and European cultures during this period was a two-way dialogue, with Islamic artisans also adopting European techniques and styles.
Representation of Cultural Diversity: Art and architecture from this period represent a cultural diversity that was a hallmark of the Enlightenment, reflecting openness to ideas and styles from different parts of the world.

Reevaluating Artistic Heritage

Modern Appreciation: In contemporary times, there is an increasing appreciation of the Islamic influence on European art and architecture, recognizing it as an integral part of Europe's cultural heritage.
Influence on Modern Art and Design: The aesthetic principles derived from Islamic art continue to influence modern art and design, celebrated for their creativity and intricacy.

Section 10: The Enlightenment's Legacy in Modern Western Thought

Tracing the Enduring Influences of the Enlightenment and Islamic Contributions

This final section of Chapter 13 explores the lasting legacy of the European Enlightenment in modern Western thought, including how the integration of Islamic intellectual contributions shaped contemporary ideologies, philosophies, and practices.

Foundations of Modern Western Ideals

Rationalism and Secularism: The Enlightenment's emphasis on rationalism and secularism remains foundational in Western intellectual traditions, influencing modern scientific inquiry, ethical reasoning, and political theory.
Democratic Principles and Human Rights: Ideas about democracy, human rights, and individual liberties that were central to Enlightenment thought continue to underpin Western political and legal systems.

Islamic Influences on Contemporary Thought

Legacy of Islamic Scholarship: The contributions of Islamic scholars to science, mathematics, philosophy, and arts during the medieval period set the stage for the Enlightenment and continue to be recognized for their role in shaping modern Western thought.

Interplay of Ideas: The interplay between Islamic and European ideas during the Enlightenment contributed to a rich intellectual heritage that has influenced contemporary discussions on multiculturalism, global ethics, and interfaith dialogue.

Cultural and Artistic Impact

Art and Architecture: The aesthetic principles and artistic styles influenced by Islamic art during the Enlightenment have left a lasting imprint on Western art and architecture.
Literature and Education: The literary and educational contributions from the Islamic world during the medieval period laid the groundwork for the Enlightenment's cultural and literary advancements.

Challenges and Reinterpretations

Revisiting Enlightenment Ideals: In contemporary times, there is an ongoing process of revisiting and reinterpreting Enlightenment ideals, considering their implications in a globalized and multicultural world.
Critiques and Expansions: Critiques of the Enlightenment, such as its Eurocentric perspective and role in colonialism, have led to an expansion of its intellectual legacy, incorporating diverse global perspectives.

Continued Dialogue and Exchange

Ongoing Intellectual Exchange: The dialogue between Western and Islamic intellectual traditions continues, with scholars from both traditions engaging in mutual learning and exchange.
Influence on Global Discourse: This ongoing exchange influences global discourse on issues such as governance, human rights, science, and intercultural understanding.

Educational and Policy Implications

Incorporation in Curricula: The legacy of the Enlightenment and its interactions with Islamic thought are increasingly incorporated into educational curricula, fostering a more inclusive understanding of intellectual history.
Policy and Global Relations: Understanding this legacy also has implications for policy-making and international relations, highlighting the importance of diverse intellectual traditions in shaping a shared global future.

Chapter 14: Diplomacy and Alliances: East Meets West

Section 1: Early Diplomatic Contacts Between Muslims and Christians

The Foundations of Cross-Cultural Interactions

This section examines the initial diplomatic contacts between the Muslim and Christian worlds, highlighting how these early interactions set the stage for subsequent relations and exchanges.

Initial Encounters and Exchanges

Early Islamic Expansion: Following the rapid expansion of Islam in the 7th and 8th centuries, Muslim empires came into contact with Christian kingdoms in Europe, initiating the first diplomatic interactions.
Byzantine and Islamic Relations: Initial diplomatic contacts were often marked by the Byzantine Empire's engagements with various Islamic caliphates, involving both conflict and negotiation.

Trade and Diplomatic Missions

Trade as a Catalyst: Trade was a significant catalyst for early diplomatic contacts, with merchants and envoys traveling between the Islamic world and Christian Europe.
Exchange of Envoys: Both Muslims and Christians sent envoys to each other's courts, facilitating not only political and economic negotiations but also cultural and knowledge exchange.

Mutual Curiosity and Respect

Interest in Each Other's Cultures: These early contacts were characterized by a degree of mutual curiosity and respect, with each side seeking to understand the other's culture, religion, and political systems.
Documentation of Diplomatic Missions: Accounts of these missions, recorded by travelers and historians, provide insights into the perceptions and attitudes of both sides.

Impact on Perception and Knowledge

Shaping Perceptions: These early contacts played a significant role in shaping mutual perceptions between the Muslim and Christian worlds, influencing later diplomatic and cultural relations.
Transmission of Knowledge: Diplomatic missions facilitated the transmission of scientific, philosophical, and cultural knowledge between the Islamic world and Europe.

Challenges and Misunderstandings

Religious and Cultural Differences: Despite the diplomatic engagements, religious and cultural differences often led to misunderstandings and conflicts.
Impact of Crusades: The onset of the Crusades added a layer of complexity to these diplomatic relations, often overshadowing earlier peaceful interactions.

Legacy and Historical Significance

Foundation for Future Relations: These early contacts laid the groundwork for future diplomatic, trade, and cultural relations between the Muslim and Christian worlds.
Influence on Modern Diplomacy: The principles and practices established during these early interactions have had a lasting impact, influencing the norms and conduct of modern diplomacy.

Section 2: Alliances Against Common Enemies

Forming Strategic Partnerships Across Cultural Divides

This section explores the historical alliances formed between Muslim and Christian states against common enemies, highlighting how these alliances transcended religious and cultural boundaries for strategic purposes.

Context of Alliances

Shifting Political Landscapes: Throughout history, the political landscapes of both the Islamic and Christian worlds were fluid, with changing power dynamics often leading to unexpected alliances.
Pragmatism Over Religious Differences: These alliances often reflected pragmatic considerations, with political and territorial interests taking precedence over religious affiliations.

Notable Alliances

The Ayyubid Dynasty and Christian States: During the Crusades, the Ayyubid dynasty under Salah al-Din (Saladin) formed temporary alliances with some Christian states against mutual adversaries.
Ottoman-French Alliance: In the 16th century, the Ottoman Empire and France, under Francis I, formed an alliance against their common enemy, the Habsburg Empire, despite their religious differences.

Diplomatic Negotiations and Agreements

Complex Negotiations: Forming these alliances often involved complex diplomatic negotiations, balancing religious sensitivities with political and military objectives.
Treaties and Agreements: Formal treaties and agreements were sometimes drafted, outlining the terms of cooperation and mutual assistance.

Impact on Warfare and Politics

Joint Military Campaigns: These alliances sometimes led to joint military campaigns, where Muslim and Christian forces fought side by side against a common enemy.
Influence on Regional Politics: The alliances had significant impacts on regional politics, often altering the balance of power and influencing subsequent historical events.

Cultural and Social Implications

Exchange of Ideas and Technology: Alongside political and military cooperation, these alliances facilitated the exchange of ideas, technology, and culture.
Perceptions and Attitudes: The formation of such alliances challenged prevailing perceptions and attitudes within both Muslim and Christian societies, sometimes leading to internal dissent or criticism.

Legacy and Historical Interpretation

Reevaluation of Historical Narratives: Modern scholarship often reevaluates these alliances, offering a more nuanced understanding of historical relationships between the Islamic and Christian worlds.
Significance in Contemporary Diplomacy: The history of these alliances provides insights into contemporary diplomacy, demonstrating how common interests can bridge cultural and religious divides.

Section 3: Trade Agreements and Peace Treaties

Navigating Commerce and Conflict Resolution Across Cultures

This section delves into the history of trade agreements and peace treaties between Muslim and Christian states, illustrating how economic interests and the desire for peaceful coexistence often drove diplomatic engagements.

Economic Interdependence and Trade Agreements

Historical Trade Routes: Trade routes such as the Silk Road and maritime routes in the Mediterranean facilitated commerce between the Islamic world and Christian Europe.
Mutually Beneficial Agreements: Trade agreements were established for mutual economic benefit, allowing for the exchange of goods like spices, textiles, and precious metals.

Diplomatic Negotiations for Trade

Negotiating Trade Terms: Diplomatic missions often involved complex negotiations to establish favorable trade terms, including tariffs, trade rights, and protection of merchants.
Cultural and Linguistic Challenges: Negotiators had to navigate cultural and linguistic differences, often relying on translators and intermediaries.

Peace Treaties and Conflict Resolution

Ending Hostilities: Peace treaties were sometimes necessary to end hostilities or conflicts between Muslim and Christian states, setting terms for ceasefire, territorial disputes, and prisoner exchanges.
Diplomatic Rapprochement: These treaties often led to a rapprochement, paving the way for renewed or enhanced diplomatic relations.

Impact on Societies and Economies

Economic Growth and Prosperity: Trade agreements contributed to economic growth and prosperity in both the Islamic and Christian worlds.
Cultural Exchange: The movement of goods and people fostered cultural exchange, bringing new ideas, technologies, and artistic influences across borders.

Influential Treaties and Agreements

Notable Examples: Treaties like the Treaty of Jaffa between Crusaders and Muslims, and various agreements between the Ottoman Empire and European powers, were influential in shaping regional politics and trade dynamics.

Modern Interpretations and Legacy

Revisiting Historical Narratives: Contemporary scholarship reexamines these agreements and treaties, highlighting their significance in shaping intercultural relations.
Legacy in International Trade and Diplomacy: The principles and practices developed through these historical trade agreements and peace treaties continue to influence modern international trade and diplomatic protocols.

Section 4: Cultural Diplomacy and Exchange

Fostering Understanding and Exchange through Art, Science, and Philosophy

This section focuses on cultural diplomacy and exchange between the Muslim and Christian worlds, highlighting how art, science, and philosophy were instrumental in bridging cultures and enhancing mutual understanding.

Cultural Diplomacy in Historical Context

Role of Cultural Exchange: Cultural exchange served as a form of diplomacy, fostering understanding and respect between Muslim and Christian societies.
Artistic and Intellectual Exchanges: These exchanges often involved the sharing of artistic, scientific, and intellectual achievements, influencing thought and culture on both sides.

Artistic Influences and Collaborations

Islamic Art in Europe: Islamic art, with its distinctive styles and techniques, influenced European art, seen in architecture, decorative arts, and manuscripts.
European Art in the Muslim World: European artistic styles and motifs were also adopted in various Islamic regions, contributing to the evolution of local artistic traditions.

Scientific and Philosophical Dialogues

Transmission of Knowledge: The translation and study of Islamic scientific and philosophical works in Europe contributed to advancements in fields such as medicine, mathematics, and astronomy.
Collaborative Learning: Scholars from both cultures engaged in collaborative learning, attending each other's centers of learning and participating in joint intellectual endeavors.

Literature and Language

Literary Exchanges: The exchange of literature, including poetry, tales, and philosophical works, enriched the literary traditions of both cultures.
Language as a Bridge: The learning of languages, such as Arabic in Europe and Latin in the Islamic world, facilitated deeper understanding and appreciation of each other's culture.

Impact on Society and Worldview

Shaping Cultural Perceptions: These cultural exchanges played a significant role in shaping perceptions and attitudes in both societies, sometimes challenging existing stereotypes and prejudices.
Contribution to Renaissance and Enlightenment: The influx of Islamic knowledge and culture contributed to the cultural and intellectual ferment of the Renaissance and Enlightenment in Europe.

Modern Significance and Legacy

Appreciation of Shared Heritage: Modern scholarship and cultural initiatives increasingly recognize and celebrate the shared cultural heritage resulting from these historical exchanges.
Influence on Contemporary Cultural Diplomacy: The legacy of these exchanges informs contemporary cultural diplomacy, highlighting the value of cultural understanding in international relations.

Section 5: Diplomatic Missions and Ambassadors

Exploring the Role of Envoys in Bridging Cultures and Negotiating Peace

This section delves into the history and significance of diplomatic missions and ambassadors between Muslim and Christian states, highlighting their roles in negotiation, peacekeeping, and cultural exchange.

Early Diplomatic Envoys

Pioneering Diplomatic Contacts: From the early stages of Islamic expansion and throughout the Middle Ages, diplomatic envoys played crucial roles in establishing and maintaining relations between Muslim and Christian realms.
Notable Missions: Significant missions, such as those during the Crusades or between the Ottoman Empire and European states, set precedents for international diplomacy.

Functions of Diplomatic Missions

Negotiation and Treaty-Making: Envoys were essential in negotiating treaties, including peace accords, trade agreements, and military alliances.
Information Gathering: Diplomats often served as vital sources of information, observing political, military, and social conditions in the host country.

Cultural and Educational Roles

Cultural Exchange: Ambassadors and their entourages were conduits of cultural exchange, introducing their host countries to their own cultures, customs, and knowledge.
Educational Impact: These exchanges had educational impacts, with scholars and scientists often accompanying diplomatic missions, leading to the transfer of knowledge across borders.

Challenges and Diplomatic Protocol

Navigating Cultural Differences: Diplomats had to navigate significant cultural, religious, and linguistic differences, requiring skills in diplomacy and often relying on interpreters and local guides.
Development of Diplomatic Protocol: Over time, these interactions contributed to the development of diplomatic protocol, including the treatment and rights of envoys.

Influential Ambassadors and Envoys

Historical Figures: Certain ambassadors and envoys are remembered for their significant contributions to diplomacy, including their roles in major treaties and cultural exchanges.
Legacy in International Relations: The work of these early diplomats laid the foundations for modern international relations and diplomatic practices.

Modern Perspectives on Historical Diplomacy

Reassessment of Diplomatic History: Contemporary scholarship often reassesses the role and impact of these early diplomatic missions, offering new insights into their significance in historical international relations.
Influence on Modern Diplomacy: The principles and practices established by these early envoys continue to influence modern diplomatic relations, emphasizing the importance of dialogue and cultural understanding in international affairs.

Section 6: Espionage and Intelligence in Diplomatic Relations

The Covert Side of Diplomacy Between Islamic and Christian States

This section addresses the often-overlooked aspect of espionage and intelligence-gathering in the diplomatic relations between Muslim and Christian states, highlighting how espionage played a critical role in shaping strategies and policies.

Role of Espionage in Diplomacy

Covert Intelligence Gathering: While open diplomatic interactions were important, covert intelligence gathering was a common practice by both Muslim and Christian states to gain strategic advantages.
Use of Spies and Informants: Spies and informants were employed to infiltrate the courts and societies of opposing states, gathering information on military capabilities, political developments, and economic conditions.

Notable Instances of Espionage

Crusades and Reconnaissance: During the Crusades, both sides used espionage to gather information on troop movements, fortifications, and supply routes.
Ottoman Empire and European Courts: The Ottoman Empire was known for its sophisticated network of spies in various European courts, which played a significant role in its diplomatic and military strategies.

Impact on Diplomatic and Military Decisions

Informed Decision-Making: Intelligence gathered through espionage often informed diplomatic negotiations and military decisions, impacting the outcomes of conflicts and treaties.

Counterintelligence Efforts: The awareness of espionage activities led to counterintelligence efforts, with states attempting to protect their secrets and identify foreign spies.

Ethical and Moral Considerations

Deception and Trust: The use of espionage in diplomacy raised questions about deception and trust in international relations, impacting the perception and treatment of envoys and diplomats.
Moral Ambiguity: The moral ambiguity of espionage in the pursuit of state interests led to complex ethical debates, both historically and in contemporary discussions.

Techniques and Tools of Espionage

Evolution of Espionage Tactics: Espionage tactics evolved over time, from simple observation and eavesdropping to more sophisticated methods of surveillance and communication.
Role of Technology: Advances in technology, such as coded messages and disguised communications, played a role in the development of espionage techniques.

Legacy in Modern Espionage

Foundations of Modern Intelligence: The espionage activities of this period laid the groundwork for modern intelligence agencies and practices.
Continued Relevance in Diplomacy: The interplay between open diplomacy and covert intelligence gathering continues to be a relevant and dynamic aspect of international relations.

Section 7: Religious Diplomacy: Popes and Caliphs

Intersecting Religious Authority and International Relations

This section explores the unique role of religious leaders, particularly popes and caliphs, in diplomacy between Christian and Muslim states, highlighting how religious authority influenced political and diplomatic interactions.

Role of Religious Leaders in Diplomacy

Religious Leaders as Diplomatic Figures: Both popes and caliphs held significant religious authority, which they often leveraged in diplomatic affairs, influencing international relations from a religious perspective.
Spiritual and Temporal Power: Their roles embodied the intersection of spiritual and temporal power, making them key figures in diplomatic negotiations and peace initiatives.

Papal Diplomacy

Papal Envoys and Missions: Popes dispatched envoys and missions to Muslim rulers for various purposes, including attempts at peaceful resolution, religious dialogue, and, during the Crusades, calls for Christian mobilization.
Negotiations for Peace and Protection: In some cases, popes negotiated for the protection of Christian pilgrims and holy sites in Muslim-controlled territories.

Caliphal Diplomacy

Caliphs and Diplomatic Outreach: Caliphs engaged in diplomatic outreach to Christian states, sometimes to negotiate peace, form alliances, or assert their political and religious influence.
Interfaith Dialogues and Letters: Instances of interfaith dialogues and exchange of letters between caliphs and popes reflect efforts at mutual understanding, despite theological differences.

Influence on Political Events

Impact on Crusades and Conflicts: Religious diplomacy by popes and caliphs significantly impacted the course of events such as the Crusades and other conflicts.
Shaping of Borders and Alliances: Diplomatic efforts by these religious leaders also played a role in shaping borders and forming alliances.

Challenges and Limitations

Religious and Political Tensions: The intertwining of religious and political motives often led to tensions and complications in diplomatic relations.
Differing Perceptions and Goals: The differing religious and cultural perceptions, as well as the distinct goals of popes and caliphs, sometimes hindered effective diplomatic outcomes.

Legacy and Contemporary Relevance

Influence on Modern Religious Diplomacy: The legacy of these diplomatic interactions between popes and caliphs continues to influence modern concepts of religious diplomacy and interfaith dialogue.
Historical Understanding and Interpretation: Modern scholarship seeks to understand the complexities of these interactions, contributing to a nuanced interpretation of religious influence in historical diplomacy.

Section 8: Treaty of Westphalia and Its Impact

Shaping Modern Diplomacy and State Sovereignty

This section examines the Treaty of Westphalia's impact on international relations, including its influence on the development of modern diplomacy and its implications for relations between Islamic and Christian states.

Background and Context of the Treaty

End of the Thirty Years' War: The Treaty of Westphalia, signed in 1648, marked the end of the Thirty Years' War in Europe, a conflict that had significant religious, political, and territorial dimensions.
Framework for Peace: The treaty established a new framework for peace and stability in Europe, based on the principles of state sovereignty and non-interference.

Principles of the Treaty

Sovereignty and Equality of States: One of the key principles established by the Treaty of Westphalia was the concept of the sovereignty and legal equality of states, a foundational element of modern international law.
Balance of Power: The treaty also contributed to the concept of a balance of power in Europe, aiming to prevent the dominance of any single state.

Impact on Diplomacy

Shaping Modern Diplomatic Practices: The Treaty of Westphalia is often cited as a turning point in the history of diplomacy, leading to the establishment of permanent diplomatic missions and the professionalization of diplomacy.
Influence on International Relations Theory: The treaty's principles significantly influenced the development of international relations theory, particularly regarding statehood, sovereignty, and diplomatic engagement.

Implications for Islamic-Christian Relations

European State System: While the treaty primarily concerned European states, its principles indirectly impacted relations between Islamic and Christian states by solidifying the European state system.

Shift in Power Dynamics: The political reorganization in Europe affected the balance of power, which in turn influenced diplomatic and trade relations with Islamic states.

Contemporary Relevance

Enduring Legacy: The legacy of the Treaty of Westphalia continues to shape modern international relations, including the principles of state sovereignty and diplomatic immunity.
Debates on Westphalian Sovereignty: In contemporary times, the concept of Westphalian sovereignty is often debated, especially in the context of globalization, transnational issues, and interventionist policies.

Critiques and Modern Perspectives

Eurocentric Perspective: Some modern critiques of the treaty's legacy highlight its Eurocentric perspective and its limited application in non-European contexts.
Adaptation in a Globalized World: The principles established by the Treaty of Westphalia are continually being adapted to suit the realities of a globalized and interconnected world.

Section 9: Modern Diplomatic Relations and Their Roots

Tracing the Evolution of Contemporary Diplomatic Practices and Relations

This section explores the development of modern diplomatic relations, highlighting how historical interactions between Islamic and Christian states have influenced contemporary diplomatic practices and international norms.

Historical Foundations of Modern Diplomacy

Legacy of Early Diplomatic Contacts: The early diplomatic contacts between Islamic and Christian states laid the groundwork for several principles and practices in modern diplomacy, including the exchange of ambassadors, negotiation tactics, and treaty-making.
Influence of the Treaty of Westphalia: The principles established by the Treaty of Westphalia, particularly regarding state sovereignty and the balance of power, continue to underpin modern diplomatic relations.

Continuity and Change in Diplomatic Relations

Evolution of Statecraft: Over the centuries, statecraft and diplomatic relations have evolved, adapting to changes in political, social, and technological landscapes while retaining some core principles from earlier times.
Interplay of Culture and Diplomacy: The interplay of different cultural and religious backgrounds in diplomatic relations, a feature since the early contacts between Muslims and Christians, remains a significant aspect of international diplomacy.

Modern Diplomatic Institutions and Conventions

Establishment of International Organizations: The formation of international organizations, such as the United Nations, reflects the evolution of diplomatic relations and the collective effort to maintain peace and cooperation.
Development of International Law: Modern diplomatic relations are governed by a body of international law, which has its roots in historical treaties and agreements, including those between Islamic and Christian states.

Contemporary Challenges and Adaptations

Globalization and Multilateralism: In the face of globalization, diplomacy has adapted to include multilateral relations and address global issues like climate change, human rights, and international security.
Technology and Diplomacy: Advances in technology have transformed diplomatic communication and information exchange, necessitating adaptations in diplomatic protocol and practices.

Influence on Global Politics and Relations

Shaping International Policies: The history of diplomatic relations between Islamic and Christian states has influenced contemporary international policies and alliances.
Cross-Cultural Diplomacy: Today's diplomacy often involves navigating cross-cultural dynamics, a practice with deep historical roots in the interactions between diverse civilizations and cultures.

Reflecting on Historical Impact

Reassessing Historical Contributions: Modern scholarship increasingly recognizes the contributions of different cultures and civilizations, including the Islamic world, in shaping the evolution of diplomatic relations.
Learning from History: Understanding the historical evolution of diplomacy, including the role of Islamic-Christian interactions, provides valuable insights for managing contemporary international relations and conflicts.

Section 10: The Role of Diplomacy in Shaping Modern Europe

Assessing the Impact of Diplomatic Interactions on European Development

This final section of Chapter 14 examines the significant role that diplomacy, particularly in its interactions with the Islamic world, played in shaping the political, cultural, and intellectual landscape of modern Europe.

Influence on Political Structures and Alliances

Formation of State Alliances: Diplomatic interactions with Islamic states influenced the formation of political alliances within Europe, often driven by mutual interests or common threats.
Shaping of European Statehood: The principles of state sovereignty and diplomatic immunity, refined through interactions with Islamic states, contributed to the shaping of modern European statehood.

Cultural and Intellectual Exchange

Transmission of Knowledge: Diplomatic contacts facilitated the transfer of knowledge from the Islamic world to Europe, impacting European science, philosophy, and the arts.
Cultural Appreciation and Orientalism: While diplomatic relations led to a greater appreciation of Islamic culture, they also gave rise to Orientalism, which both romanticized and stereotyped the East.

Economic Impact and Trade Relations

Trade Agreements and Economic Growth: Diplomatic relations with Islamic states opened trade routes and markets, contributing to economic growth and the exchange of goods and ideas in Europe.

Development of Global Trade Networks: These interactions were instrumental in developing global trade networks, which played a key role in the economic expansion of Europe.

Impact on International Law and Diplomacy

Formation of Diplomatic Norms: The diplomatic engagements with Islamic states influenced the development of international law and the norms of diplomatic conduct, many of which are still in practice today.
Evolution of Diplomatic Institutions: The need to manage complex relations with Islamic states contributed to the evolution of diplomatic institutions and practices in Europe.

Religious and Ideological Dimensions

Religious Diplomacy: Relations with the Islamic world had religious dimensions, influencing the policies of both secular and religious authorities in Europe.
Ideological Exchanges: Diplomatic interactions also facilitated ideological exchanges, which impacted European thought, particularly during the Renaissance and Enlightenment.

Contemporary Relevance and Reflection

Lessons for Modern Diplomacy: The history of diplomatic relations between Europe and the Islamic world offers valuable lessons for contemporary diplomacy, especially in managing cross-cultural and interfaith relations.
Reassessing Historical Narratives: Modern scholarship continues to reassess these historical narratives, recognizing the complex interplay of diplomacy, culture, and politics in shaping modern Europe.

Chapter 15: America's Founding Ideologies and Islamic Influence

Section 1: Principles of American Democracy

Exploring the Roots of Democratic Ideals in Early America

This section delves into the foundational principles of American democracy, examining their origins and the potential influences of Islamic thought on these emerging ideas during the formation of the United States.

Foundational Democratic Principles

Liberty and Individual Rights: Central to American democracy is the emphasis on individual liberty and rights, principles enshrined in key documents like the Declaration of Independence and the Constitution.

Representative Government and Separation of Powers: The principles of representative government and the separation of powers were revolutionary ideas that formed the backbone of American political systems.

Influences on American Democratic Thought

European Enlightenment: American democratic ideals were significantly influenced by European Enlightenment thinkers, who advocated for reason, individual rights, and skepticism of traditional authority.

Native American Governance Models: The governance models of Native American tribes also provided a template for democratic organization, particularly in their emphasis on collective decision-making and consensus.

Potential Islamic Contributions

Historical Interactions with the Islamic World: While direct influences of Islamic thought on early American democracy are less documented, the intellectual exchanges between the Islamic world and Europe indirectly impacted the development of democratic ideas.

Principles of Islamic Governance: Islamic governance, with its emphasis on justice, consultation (Shura), and community welfare, shares some parallels with democratic principles.

Debate and Scholarly Perspectives

Assessing Islamic Influence: Scholars debate the extent of Islamic influence on American democracy, with some arguing for indirect influences through the transmission of ideas from the Islamic world to Europe.

Recognition of Diverse Influences: Contemporary scholarship increasingly acknowledges the diverse influences that shaped American democracy, moving beyond a solely Eurocentric perspective.

Legacy and Modern Interpretations

Enduring Democratic Ideals: The principles of American democracy continue to be central to the United States' political identity and discourse.
Relevance in Contemporary Debates: Understanding the origins and influences of these democratic principles is relevant in contemporary debates about governance, civil rights, and multiculturalism.

Section 2: Islamic Governance and Its Influence

Tracing the Impact of Islamic Political Thought on Early American Ideals

This section investigates the influence of Islamic governance principles on the founding ideologies of the United States, examining how Islamic political thought may have indirectly shaped some aspects of early American political systems.

Principles of Islamic Governance

Justice and Consultation: In Islamic governance, principles of justice ('Adl) and consultation (Shura) are fundamental, emphasizing the ruler's responsibility to the ruled and the importance of collective decision-making.
Rights and Responsibilities: Islamic law (Sharia) outlines specific rights and responsibilities for individuals and leaders, aiming to ensure a balanced and just society.

Potential Influences on American Founders

Indirect Transmission of Ideas: While direct influences of Islamic governance on American founding ideologies are not explicitly documented, the indirect transmission of Islamic political ideas through European enlightenment thought is plausible.
Exposure to Islamic Legal and Political Systems: Some founding fathers, including Thomas Jefferson, had exposure to Islamic legal and political systems, which may have provided them with a broader perspective on governance and law.

Comparative Analysis

Similarities in Principles: Certain principles, such as the emphasis on justice, the rule of law, and the welfare of the community, find echoes in both Islamic governance and American democratic ideals.

Differences in Context and Implementation: Despite these similarities, the context and implementation of these principles were distinct, reflecting the different cultural, religious, and historical backgrounds.

Scholarly Debates

Assessing the Extent of Influence: Scholars continue to debate the extent to which Islamic governance principles influenced the founding ideologies of the United States.
Recognition of Diverse Inspirations: Increasingly, there is a recognition of the diverse inspirations behind American political thought, including potential Islamic influences.

Legacy and Contemporary Relevance

Contribution to Political Pluralism: Understanding these potential influences contributes to a broader appreciation of the pluralistic roots of American political thought.
Relevance in Modern Governance: Examining the principles of Islamic governance and their potential impact on American democracy offers valuable insights for contemporary discussions on governance, pluralism, and intercultural dialogue.

Section 3: The Constitution: A Comparative Analysis

Examining the American Constitution in Light of Islamic Governance Principles

This section offers a comparative analysis of the United States Constitution and Islamic governance principles, exploring similarities, differences, and the potential indirect influences of Islamic political thought on this foundational American document.

Key Features of the U.S. Constitution

Framework of Governance: The U.S. Constitution established a framework for federal governance, delineating the powers of different branches of government and the rights of citizens.
Bill of Rights: The first ten amendments, known as the Bill of Rights, guarantee essential freedoms and protections for individuals, a cornerstone of American democracy.

Islamic Governance Principles

Sharia and Constitutionalism: In Islamic governance, Sharia (Islamic law) provides a comprehensive framework that covers aspects of public and private life, emphasizing justice, equity, and the welfare of the community.

Principles of Consultation and Accountability: Islamic political thought stresses the importance of consultation (Shura) in governance and the accountability of rulers to the people and to divine law.

Comparative Analysis

Similarities in Principles: Both the U.S. Constitution and Islamic governance principles emphasize the rule of law, rights and responsibilities, and checks on power. The concept of Shura in Islamic thought has parallels with the democratic principle of representation and accountability.

Differences in Foundations: While the U.S. Constitution is a secular document founded on Enlightenment principles, Islamic governance is rooted in religious law and principles.

Potential Indirect Influences

Transmission of Ideas through Enlightenment Thought: Ideas from Islamic governance may have indirectly influenced the framers of the Constitution through the broader intellectual exchange of the Enlightenment, which incorporated aspects of Islamic philosophy and legal thought.

Influence on Legal and Political Concepts: Some concepts in Islamic governance, such as contractual agreements and rights protection, may have parallels in the Constitution's approach to governance and individual rights.

Scholarly Perspectives and Debates

Extent of Influence: Scholars continue to explore the extent to which Islamic governance principles may have influenced the development of the U.S. Constitution, with varying conclusions.

Recognition of Diverse Intellectual Contributions: There is a growing recognition of the diverse intellectual contributions, including potential Islamic influences, that shaped the founding principles of the United States.

Contemporary Implications

Understanding Constitutional Origins: A comparative analysis contributes to a deeper understanding of the origins and foundations of the U.S. Constitution.
Interfaith and Intercultural Dialogue: Exploring these potential connections can foster interfaith and intercultural dialogue, highlighting shared values and principles in governance.

Section 4: Enlightenment Thinkers and Islamic Philosophy

Exploring the Intersection of Islamic Thought and Enlightenment Ideals in American Founding Principles

This section examines how Islamic philosophy may have indirectly influenced the ideas of Enlightenment thinkers who, in turn, shaped the ideologies of America's founding fathers.

Islamic Philosophy's Influence on the Enlightenment

Transmission of Knowledge: The transmission of Islamic philosophical works to Europe during the Middle Ages introduced European scholars to advanced concepts in science, philosophy, and governance.
Influence on Key Thinkers: Islamic philosophers like Averroes (Ibn Rushd) and Avicenna (Ibn Sina) influenced key Enlightenment thinkers, including Locke and Descartes, through their works on rationalism and empiricism.

Enlightenment Ideals in American Thought

Adoption of Enlightenment Principles: The founding fathers of the United States were significantly influenced by Enlightenment ideals, which emphasized reason, individual rights, and skepticism of traditional authority.
Formation of a New Governmental Philosophy: These ideals were instrumental in shaping the American approach to governance, emphasizing democratic principles, separation of powers, and the protection of individual liberties.

Indirect Islamic Contributions

Philosophical Underpinnings: While direct Islamic influences on American founding ideologies are less documented, the philosophical underpinnings provided by Islamic scholars to European Enlightenment thought likely had an indirect impact.

Shared Concepts of Justice and Reason: The emphasis on justice, reason, and ethical governance in Islamic philosophy resonates with the principles that informed America's founding documents and ideologies.

Debates and Interpretations

Extent of Islamic Influence: Scholars debate the extent and significance of Islamic philosophical influence on American founding principles, with some emphasizing direct Enlightenment influences and others acknowledging a broader intellectual heritage.
Recognition of Diverse Influences: Modern interpretations increasingly recognize the diverse intellectual influences, including potential Islamic contributions, that shaped the foundations of American democracy.

Contemporary Relevance

Broader Understanding of American Ideals: Exploring these connections contributes to a broader understanding of the origins and influences behind American democratic ideals.
Interfaith and Intercultural Understanding: Recognizing the interconnectedness of Islamic and Western philosophical traditions can foster greater interfaith and intercultural understanding in contemporary society.

Section 5: Religious Freedom and Pluralism

Understanding the Roots and Development of Religious Tolerance in American Ideology

This section explores the concept of religious freedom and pluralism in the United States, examining its origins and considering the potential influence of Islamic principles on these foundational aspects of American democracy.

American Principles of Religious Freedom

First Amendment Rights: The First Amendment to the U.S. Constitution guarantees freedom of religion, reflecting a core principle of American democracy that emerged as a reaction against religious persecution in Europe.
Historical Context: The establishment of religious freedom in the United States was groundbreaking, differing significantly from the religious homogeneity and state religions common in Europe at the time.

Islamic Principles of Religious Tolerance

Historical Precedent in Islamic Governance: Islamic governance, particularly during certain periods, demonstrated a degree of religious tolerance and pluralism, allowing for the practice of various religions under Islamic rule.
Dhimmi System: The dhimmi system in Islamic law provided protections for non-Muslims (such as Christians and Jews) living in Muslim-majority societies, although with certain conditions and taxes.

Potential Influences and Parallels

Indirect Influences on Enlightenment Thought: While direct influences of Islamic principles on American ideologies of religious freedom are not explicitly documented, the broader intellectual exchange during the Enlightenment period, which included aspects of Islamic thought, might have indirectly influenced these concepts.
Shared Values of Tolerance: Both Islamic governance and American democracy, in their ideal forms, emphasize the importance of tolerance and the protection of individual rights, including religious freedom.

Contemporary Debates and Interpretations

Debates on the Origins of Religious Freedom: Scholars debate the origins and influences of religious freedom in American ideology, with some highlighting the unique context of American history and others pointing to broader intellectual influences, including Islamic thought.
Recognition of Diverse Contributions: Contemporary scholarship increasingly acknowledges the contributions of various cultures and religions, including Islam, in shaping the concept of religious freedom.

Modern Implications

Relevance in Multicultural Societies: Understanding the historical roots and development of religious freedom is crucial in contemporary multicultural societies, particularly in addressing issues related to religious rights and interfaith relations.
Influence on Global Discourse: The American model of religious freedom and pluralism continues to influence global discourse on human rights and religious tolerance.

Section 6: Economic Theories and Islamic Principles

Examining the Intersection of Islamic Economic Concepts with American Founding Economic Ideals

This section explores the potential influence of Islamic economic principles on the economic theories that underpinned the founding of the United States, highlighting the similarities and differences between these systems.

Foundations of American Economic Thought

Capitalism and Free Market: The economic system of the early United States was heavily influenced by capitalist and free market principles, advocating for minimal government intervention in the economy.
Influence of European Enlightenment: Economic ideas from European Enlightenment thinkers like Adam Smith, who emphasized free trade and market-driven growth, were instrumental in shaping America's economic foundations.

Islamic Economic Principles

Economic Justice and Fairness: Islamic economic principles emphasize justice and fairness, advocating for the equitable distribution of wealth and the prohibition of exploitative practices.
Zakat and Charitable Giving: A key component of Islamic economics is the obligation of zakat, a form of almsgiving, and a general encouragement of charitable practices to support community welfare.

Potential Influences and Parallels

Indirect Influence through Enlightenment Thought: While direct Islamic influences on early American economic thought are not explicitly documented, Islamic economic principles may have indirectly influenced Enlightenment economists, whose ideas, in turn, influenced American economic foundations.
Similarities in Ethical Considerations: Both Islamic economic principles and some early American economic ideas share a concern for ethical considerations in economic activities, though their implementations differ.

Comparative Analysis

Differences in Economic Systems: The economic system in early America was largely capitalistic and market-driven, whereas Islamic economics places a stronger emphasis on social welfare and ethical constraints on economic activities.
Shared Concerns for Social Welfare: Despite these differences, both systems exhibit a concern for social welfare, though the mechanisms and philosophies behind this concern vary.

Modern Interpretations and Debates

Debating the Origins of American Economic Ideas: The extent of Islamic influence on American economic thought is subject to scholarly debate, with differing views on the transmission and adaptation of economic ideas across cultures.
Recognition of Diverse Economic Philosophies: Modern economic discussions increasingly recognize the diversity of economic philosophies and their contributions to contemporary economic thought.

Contemporary Relevance

Insights for Modern Economic Challenges: Exploring the potential intersections of Islamic economic principles with American economic thought provides insights into addressing modern economic challenges, such as income inequality and ethical business practices.
Global Economic Dialogue: Understanding these historical influences contributes to a more inclusive global economic dialogue, acknowledging the contributions of various cultural and intellectual traditions.

Section 7: The Role of Education and Scholarship

Exploring Educational Philosophies and the Exchange of Knowledge

This section investigates the role of education and scholarship in the founding ideologies of the United States, considering the potential influences of Islamic educational traditions on these aspects of early American society.

Educational Foundations in Early America

Emphasis on Literacy and Learning: The early American ethos placed a high value on literacy and education, viewing them as essential for informed citizenship and the functioning of a democratic society.

Establishment of Educational Institutions: Colleges and universities established during the colonial period and early years of the Republic were key in shaping American intellectual and political life.

Islamic Traditions of Learning and Scholarship

Centers of Learning in the Islamic World: During the Islamic Golden Age, centers of learning such as Al-Qarawiyyin and Al-Azhar universities were renowned for their contributions to science, philosophy, and the arts.
Islamic Emphasis on Knowledge: Islamic culture historically placed a high value on knowledge and learning, encompassing both religious and secular subjects.

Potential Influences on American Education

Indirect Transmission of Ideas: While direct influences of Islamic educational practices on early American education are not clearly documented, the broader intellectual exchange during the Enlightenment, which was influenced by Islamic scholarship, might have had an indirect impact.
Shared Values in Education: Both Islamic and early American educational traditions shared values such as the pursuit of knowledge, the development of individual potential, and the preparation of individuals for societal participation.

Comparative Perspectives

Differences in Educational Systems: Despite shared values, the educational systems in the Islamic world and early America had different foundations, with Islamic education being deeply intertwined with religious studies and American education being more secular.
Influence of Enlightenment Thinkers: Enlightenment thinkers, who were themselves influenced by Islamic scholarship, played a more direct role in shaping the educational ideals of early America.

Contemporary Relevance and Interpretations

Reevaluating Educational Roots: Modern scholarship increasingly explores the diverse influences on American educational foundations, including potential Islamic contributions.
Education as a Tool for Interfaith Understanding: Understanding these historical connections can enhance interfaith and intercultural dialogue in contemporary educational settings.

Section 8: Foreign Policy: Islamic Influence on Early American Relations

Analyzing the Impact of Islamic Principles on America's Formative Foreign Policy

This section examines how interactions with Islamic states and principles might have influenced the development of early American foreign policy, considering the historical context and the nature of these early international relations.

Early American Foreign Policy

Founding Principles: America's early foreign policy was characterized by principles of neutrality and non-entanglement, as advocated by figures like George Washington and Thomas Jefferson. First International Challenges: The young nation faced its first major international challenges with European powers and the Barbary States of North Africa, which were Islamic states.

Islamic States and American Diplomacy

Barbary Wars: The Barbary Wars were among America's first significant foreign conflicts, involving negotiations and conflicts with North African Islamic states over piracy and tribute. Negotiation and Treaty-Making: These interactions required diplomatic negotiations, leading to treaties that were among the United States' first international agreements.

Potential Islamic Influences

Exposure to Islamic Diplomacy: American diplomats' exposure to Islamic diplomatic practices and principles during these negotiations might have provided insights and experiences that shaped their approach to international relations.
Adaptation of Diplomatic Strategies: The need to navigate relations with Islamic states may have influenced the development of American diplomatic strategies, emphasizing negotiation and treaty-making.

Comparative Analysis

Shared Diplomatic Practices: While there were differences in context and religious backgrounds, there were also shared diplomatic practices, such as the use of envoys, the importance of formal agreements, and respect for sovereignty.
Differences in Approaches: American diplomatic approaches were influenced by Enlightenment ideals and a desire to establish a distinct national identity, which sometimes diverged from traditional Islamic diplomatic practices.

Contemporary Relevance and Legacy

Foundations of American Diplomacy: Understanding these early interactions with Islamic states provides insights into the foundations of American diplomacy and its evolution.
Interpreting Historical Interactions: Modern scholarship continues to interpret the nature and impact of early American interactions with Islamic states, contributing to a broader understanding of the origins of American foreign policy.

Section 9: Debates on Slavery and Human Rights

Exploring the Historical Context and Philosophical Discussions on Slavery and Human Rights in Early America

This section investigates the debates on slavery and human rights during the founding period of the United States, considering the potential influence of Islamic perspectives on these critical issues.

Context of Slavery in Early America

Prevalence of Slavery: Slavery was a deeply entrenched institution in early America, with significant economic, social, and political implications.
Contradictions with Democratic Ideals: The existence of slavery presented a stark contradiction with the emerging democratic ideals of liberty and equality espoused by the founding fathers.

Islamic Perspectives on Slavery

Slavery in Islamic Contexts: Slavery existed in various Islamic societies, but Islamic law included provisions for the humane treatment of slaves and their eventual emancipation.
Emphasis on Rights and Dignity: While Islamic law did not outright abolish slavery, it emphasized the rights and dignity of enslaved individuals, and encouraged manumission as a virtuous act.

Potential Influences and Parallels

Indirect Influence on Debates: While direct Islamic influences on the American debates about slavery are not explicitly documented, the broader ethical and philosophical discussions on human rights and dignity in Islamic thought might have indirectly influenced some American thinkers.

Shared Ethical Concerns: Both Islamic perspectives and the emerging American views on slavery grappled with ethical concerns about human dignity, rights, and the contradictions inherent in maintaining slavery in a society valuing freedom.

Debates and Philosophical Arguments

Abolitionist Movements: The growing abolitionist movement in America, influenced by Enlightenment ideals and religious convictions, argued against the institution of slavery on moral and ethical grounds.
Justifications and Compromises: Pro-slavery factions, on the other hand, developed a range of justifications for slavery, leading to compromises in early American legislation.

Modern Interpretations and Implications

Reassessing Historical Perspectives: Contemporary scholarship often reassesses these historical debates on slavery, including the potential influences of various cultural and religious perspectives.
Legacy in Human Rights Discourse: The evolution of these debates in early America has a lasting impact on the country's human rights discourse and policies.

Section 10: The Legacy of Islamic Thought in American Ideology

Assessing the Enduring Influences of Islamic Intellectual Traditions on American Founding Principles

This final section of Chapter 15 explores the extent to which Islamic intellectual traditions may have indirectly influenced the founding ideologies of the United States, and how this legacy continues to resonate in contemporary American thought.

Indirect Influences of Islamic Thought

Through the Lens of the Enlightenment: Islamic contributions to science, philosophy, and governance during the medieval period were transmitted to Europe and, subsequently, may have indirectly influenced American Enlightenment thinkers.
Shared Principles of Justice and Ethics: While the United States was founded on principles largely derived from European Enlightenment thought, some of these principles, such as justice, the rule of law, and ethical governance, have parallels in Islamic intellectual traditions.

Recognition of Diverse Intellectual Contributions

Broadening the Historical Narrative: Modern scholarship increasingly acknowledges the diverse intellectual contributions that shaped the founding principles of the United States, including potential influences from Islamic thought.
Incorporating Global Perspectives: This recognition contributes to a more inclusive understanding of American history, incorporating global perspectives and influences.

Contemporary Relevance

Interfaith Dialogue and Understanding: Acknowledging these historical connections can foster interfaith dialogue and understanding, highlighting shared values and principles across different cultures and religions.
Educational Implications: This broader understanding of America's intellectual heritage has implications for educational curricula, promoting a more comprehensive view of the nation's founding ideologies.

Challenges and Debates

Assessing the Degree of Influence: There is ongoing debate among scholars regarding the degree and significance of Islamic influence on early American ideologies, with some emphasizing direct Enlightenment influences and others acknowledging a broader range of inspirations.
Navigating Cultural and Religious Sensitivities: Discussions about the influence of Islamic thought in American ideology must navigate cultural and religious sensitivities, balancing recognition of contributions with historical accuracy.

Legacy in American Ideology

Influence on Democratic Principles: While the direct impact of Islamic thought on American democracy may be subtle, its legacy, as part of a broader pool of global intellectual traditions, contributes to the richness of American democratic principles.
Ongoing Influence in Public Discourse: The potential influences of Islamic thought, along with other global intellectual traditions, continue to be relevant in American public discourse, particularly in discussions around governance, ethics, and multiculturalism.

Chapter 16: The Ottoman Legacy in European Art and Culture

Section 1: Influence of Ottoman Art on European Styles

Tracing the Ottoman Aesthetic's Integration into European Artistic Traditions

This section explores the profound influence of Ottoman art on European styles, examining how elements of Ottoman aesthetic were integrated into European art and design, thus creating a unique cross-cultural dialogue.

Introduction to Ottoman Art

Distinctive Characteristics: Ottoman art is renowned for its rich decorative motifs, vibrant colors, intricate patterns, and integration of calligraphy. These elements reflect a blend of diverse cultural influences, including Persian, Arab, and Byzantine traditions.
Variety of Art Forms: Ottoman artistic expression spanned various forms, including ceramics, textiles, miniature paintings, and architectural designs.

Integration into European Art

Adoption of Motifs and Techniques: European artists and craftsmen, particularly during the Renaissance and Baroque periods, adopted and adapted various motifs and techniques from Ottoman art.
Influence in Decorative Arts: The impact was most evident in the decorative arts, such as ceramics, tapestries, and furniture, which often featured Ottoman-inspired designs.

Cultural Exchange through Trade and Diplomacy

Trade Routes: Trade routes between Europe and the Ottoman Empire facilitated the exchange of art and ideas. Luxury goods from the Ottoman Empire, such as silks and ceramics, were highly prized in Europe.
Diplomatic Gifts: Diplomatic exchanges often included gifts of artwork, which introduced European courts to Ottoman artistic styles.

Impact on European Artistic Styles

Orientalism in European Art: The fascination with Ottoman art contributed to the development of Orientalism in European art, characterized by the depiction and imitation of Eastern cultures and aesthetics.
Adaptation and Evolution: European artists did not merely copy Ottoman styles; instead, they adapted these influences, merging them with local traditions to create new, hybrid forms.

Case Studies of Influence

Architectural Elements: Elements of Ottoman architecture, like domes and ornamental tiles, influenced some European architectural designs.
Fashion and Textiles: Ottoman textiles and fashion had a significant impact on European clothing styles, introducing new fabrics and patterns.

Contemporary Relevance and Legacy

Enduring Influence in Modern Design: The influence of Ottoman art on European styles continues to be evident in contemporary design, where motifs and patterns originating from the Ottoman period are still used in various forms.
Appreciation of Cross-Cultural Artistic Exchange: Modern appreciation of this artistic exchange fosters a greater understanding of the shared cultural heritage between Europe and the Ottoman Empire.

Section 2: Architectural Exchange: Mosques and Cathedrals

Exploring the Mutual Influences of Islamic and Christian Architectural Traditions

This section delves into the architectural exchanges between the Ottoman Empire and Europe, focusing on how mosques and cathedrals influenced each other's design, style, and construction techniques.

Ottoman Influence on European Architecture

Adoption of Architectural Elements: European architecture, particularly in regions close to or under Ottoman influence, began to incorporate elements typical of Islamic architecture. This included the use of domes, minarets, and ornate tilework.
Examples of Influence: Notable examples include buildings in Spain, the Balkans, and parts of Eastern Europe, where Ottoman architectural elements are evident.

European Influence on Ottoman Architecture

Integration of European Styles: Conversely, Ottoman architecture, especially during its later periods, showed the influence of European styles. This was part of a broader trend of Westernization within the Ottoman Empire.
Blending of Architectures in the Ottoman Empire: European architectural styles were often blended with traditional Islamic elements, creating a unique fusion that reflected the multicultural nature of the Ottoman Empire.

Cultural and Religious Significance

Mosques and Cathedrals as Cultural Symbols: Both mosques and cathedrals were not just places of worship but also symbols of cultural and religious identity. Their architectural styles often reflected the prevailing cultural and religious attitudes.
Dialogue Through Design: The architectural exchanges between mosques and cathedrals represented a form of cultural dialogue, where each tradition learned from and influenced the other.

Technological and Artistic Exchanges

Advancements in Construction Techniques: The exchange was not just stylistic but also technological. European and Ottoman architects borrowed construction techniques and innovations from each other, advancing the field of architecture.
Artistic Collaboration: There were instances of architects and artisans from different cultural backgrounds collaborating on projects, combining their skills and aesthetics.

Legacy and Modern Interpretation

Enduring Influences: The mutual influences between Ottoman and European architecture have left a lasting legacy, visible in historic buildings across Europe and the former Ottoman territories.
Appreciation of Shared Architectural Heritage: In contemporary times, there is a growing appreciation of this shared architectural heritage, recognized for its artistic and historical value.

Section 3: Ottoman Contributions to European Music

Tracing the Influence of Ottoman Music on European Compositions and Styles

This section examines how Ottoman music, with its distinctive instruments and rhythms, influenced European musical traditions, contributing to a rich cross-cultural exchange in the realm of music.

Ottoman Musical Traditions

Unique Instruments and Scales: Ottoman music is characterized by unique instruments like the oud (a precursor to the lute) and distinctive musical scales, which differ from the typical Western scales.
Military Bands and Court Music: The Ottoman military bands, known as Janissary bands, were particularly influential. They introduced new rhythmic patterns and sounds, which were novel to European ears.

Influence on European Composers

Adoption of Ottoman Elements: Several European composers, especially from the 16th to the 18th centuries, were influenced by Ottoman music. They incorporated elements of its rhythm and instrumentation into their compositions.
Famous Examples: Composers like Mozart, Beethoven, and Haydn wrote pieces that reflected the influence of Ottoman music, sometimes explicitly referred to as "Turkish" in their titles or styles.

Cultural Exchange Through Music

Exposure Through Military Encounters: European exposure to Ottoman music often occurred during military encounters, where they experienced Janissary bands. These encounters sparked an interest in the exotic and distinct sounds of Ottoman music.
Integration in Operas and Orchestral Works: Elements of Ottoman music found their way into operas and orchestral works, contributing to the development of the "Turquerie" trend in European art and music.

Impact on European Musical Development

Broadening of Musical Horizons: The incorporation of Ottoman elements helped broaden the musical horizons of Europe, challenging composers to explore new sounds and rhythms.

Contribution to the Exoticism Trend: Ottoman influence contributed to the trend of exoticism in European music, where composers sought to evoke the allure of non-European cultures.

Contemporary Perspectives and Legacy

Recognition of Cross-Cultural Influences: Modern musicology increasingly recognizes the cross-cultural influences in music, including the contributions of Ottoman music to European compositions.
Enduring Influence in Modern Compositions: The legacy of these interactions can still be heard in some modern compositions, where the blending of Eastern and Western musical traditions continues.

Section 4: Fashion and Textiles: A Cross-Cultural Dialogue

The Interweaving of Ottoman and European Aesthetics in Textile and Fashion Design

This section explores the profound influence of Ottoman textiles and fashion on European styles, tracing how this exchange led to a rich blend of aesthetics and techniques in the realm of clothing and fabric design.

Ottoman Influence on European Textiles

Luxury Fabrics and Patterns: Ottoman textiles were renowned for their quality and intricate designs. Materials like silk, velvet, and brocade, often adorned with elaborate patterns, were highly sought after in Europe.
Trade and Transmission: The trade of textiles through routes connecting the Ottoman Empire and Europe facilitated the transmission of styles and techniques.

Adoption and Adaptation in Europe

Incorporation in European Fashion: European fashion, particularly from the 16th to the 18th centuries, saw the incorporation of Ottoman-inspired designs. This was evident in clothing, accessories, and interior fabrics.
Hybrid Styles: The interaction led to hybrid styles that combined European cuts and silhouettes with Ottoman patterns and ornamentation.

Cultural Exchange and Appreciation

Exotic Appeal: Ottoman textiles appealed to the European taste for the exotic, symbolizing luxury and sophistication.
Diplomatic Gifts and Royal Collections: Ottoman textiles were often part of diplomatic gifts and found their way into royal and aristocratic collections, further influencing European tastes.

Impact on European Textile Industry

Inspiration for Local Industries: The popularity of Ottoman textiles inspired European textile industries to produce similar fabrics and patterns, leading to innovations in weaving and dyeing techniques.
Influence on Design and Artistry: The artistic influence extended beyond textiles to other decorative arts in Europe, including tapestry and carpet making.

Contemporary Legacy and Relevance

Enduring Influence in Fashion and Design: The influence of Ottoman textiles and fashion continues in modern fashion and textile design, with designers often drawing inspiration from these historical styles.
Recognition of Cross-Cultural Artistic Exchange: The blend of Ottoman and European elements in textiles is recognized as a significant example of cross-cultural artistic exchange, contributing to a richer understanding of global art and design history.

Section 5: Culinary Influences and Shared Tastes

Exploring the Fusion of Ottoman and European Culinary Traditions

This section delves into how the Ottoman Empire's rich culinary traditions influenced European cuisine, leading to a delightful fusion of flavors and culinary practices that enriched the gastronomic landscape of Europe.

Ottoman Culinary Traditions

Diverse Influences: Ottoman cuisine, reflecting the empire's vast geography and cultural diversity, incorporated elements from Middle Eastern, Central Asian, and Balkan culinary traditions.
Rich Flavors and Ingredients: Characterized by the use of spices, herbs, and a variety of meats and vegetables, Ottoman dishes offered a distinct palette of flavors.

Transmission to Europe

Trade and Exchange: The spice trade and political interactions between the Ottoman Empire and Europe facilitated the transmission of ingredients, dishes, and cooking techniques.
Culinary Exchange Through Conquest and Diplomacy: Regions under Ottoman influence, such as the Balkans and parts of Eastern Europe, experienced a direct impact on their culinary practices, which later spread to other parts of Europe.

Influence on European Cuisine

Adoption of Ingredients and Techniques: European cuisine adopted various ingredients like coffee, aubergines, and yoghurt, and cooking techniques from the Ottoman culinary repertoire.
Fusion Dishes: This exchange led to the creation of fusion dishes that blended Ottoman and European flavors, evident in the cuisines of countries like Hungary, Greece, and Bulgaria.

Coffee Culture

Introduction of Coffee: One of the most significant impacts was the introduction of coffee and the coffeehouse culture, which originated in the Ottoman Empire and spread to Europe, becoming a central aspect of social life.
Evolution of Coffee Culture: The European adaptation of coffee led to the establishment of cafes, which became hubs of intellectual and social activity.

Legacy in Modern European Cuisine

Enduring Influences: The influence of Ottoman cuisine is still evident in various European culinary traditions, contributing to the continent's rich gastronomic diversity.
Appreciation of Culinary Heritage: Modern culinary trends often revisit these historical influences, celebrating the shared heritage and continued fusion of Ottoman and European tastes.

Section 6: Literature and Poetry: Echoes of the East

The Influence of Ottoman Themes and Styles in European Literary Works

This section examines how Ottoman literature and poetry, with their distinctive themes and styles, resonated within European literary circles, influencing various aspects of European literary traditions.

Ottoman Literary Contributions

Rich Literary Tradition: The Ottoman Empire boasted a rich literary tradition, encompassing a wide range of genres including poetry, travel literature, and historical narratives.
Distinctive Features: Ottoman literature was characterized by its lyrical quality, elaborate metaphors, and often, a blend of mystical and secular themes.

Transmission to Europe

Cultural Interactions: Interactions through trade, diplomacy, and military encounters provided Europeans with access to Ottoman literary works, either in their original form or through translations.
Admiration and Curiosity: European intellectuals and writers were often intrigued by the exoticism and rich imagery found in Ottoman literature, which differed markedly from their own literary traditions.

Influence on European Writers

Incorporation of Ottoman Themes: European writers incorporated themes and motifs from Ottoman literature into their own works, often as a means of adding exotic flair or exploring novel literary expressions.
Orientalist Perspectives: Some European literary works adopted Orientalist perspectives, portraying the Ottoman world in a romanticized and sometimes stereotypical manner.

Impact on Poetry and Narrative Forms

Adaptation in Poetry: European poets adapted forms and stylistic elements from Ottoman poetry, experimenting with new rhythms, structures, and themes.
Influence on Narrative Literature: In narrative literature, European authors sometimes set their stories in Ottoman lands or used Ottoman characters, reflecting the cultural fascination with the East.

Case Studies of Influence

Famous Works and Authors: Notable European authors, such as Lord Byron and Victor Hugo, were influenced by Ottoman literature, as evidenced in some of their works that reflect themes or settings related to the Ottoman Empire.

Contemporary Legacy and Relevance

Enduring Influence in Literature: The influence of Ottoman literature on European works contributed to the rich tapestry of European literary history, with echoes of this influence still perceptible in modern literature.
Appreciation of Cross-Cultural Literary Exchange: Modern literary studies increasingly acknowledge and appreciate the cross-cultural exchanges between Ottoman and European literature, recognizing their contribution to the development of a more diverse and inclusive literary canon.

Section 7: Ottoman Themes in European Painting

Capturing the Essence of the East in European Artistic Expression

This section explores how European painting was influenced by Ottoman themes, focusing on the ways in which European artists captured and interpreted the visual and cultural aspects of the Ottoman Empire in their work.

Fascination with the Ottoman Empire

Exotic Appeal: The Ottoman Empire, with its rich culture, diverse people, and grandeur, held an exotic appeal for many European artists. This fascination was often reflected in their paintings, which depicted Ottoman life, architecture, and landscapes.
Orientalist Movement: The interest in Ottoman themes was part of the broader Orientalist movement in European art, where artists sought to represent the East with a mix of admiration, fantasy, and sometimes stereotypical portrayals.

Representation in European Painting

Scenes of Daily Life: European paintings often featured scenes of daily life in the Ottoman Empire, showcasing bazaars, harems, and street scenes, aiming to capture the vibrancy and uniqueness of Ottoman society.
Historical and Military Themes: Some paintings depicted historical or military events involving the Ottoman Empire, reflecting the ongoing interactions and conflicts between Europe and the Ottomans.

Artistic Interpretation and Style

Romanticized Imagery: While striving for realism, many European artists romanticized their depictions of the Ottoman world, emphasizing its perceived exoticness and splendor.
Influence on Artistic Techniques: The color palette, attire, and architecture of the Ottoman Empire influenced the techniques and styles of European painters, leading to richer and more varied compositions.

Notable European Artists and Works

Influential Artists: Artists such as Jean-Léon Gérôme, Eugène Delacroix, and Gustav Bauernfeind were known for their Ottoman-themed works, which played a significant role in shaping Western perceptions of the East.
Iconic Paintings: Some iconic paintings became emblematic of the European fascination with the Ottoman world, capturing the imagination of audiences both then and now.

Contemporary Perspectives and Legacy

Reassessment of Orientalist Art: Contemporary art history reassesses Orientalist art, including paintings with Ottoman themes, critiquing its perspectives while also acknowledging its artistic merit and influence.
Enduring Influence in Modern Art: The legacy of this fascination with the Ottoman Empire continues to influence modern artists, who explore these themes with a more nuanced and critical approach.

Section 8: Artistic Techniques and Innovations

Exploring the Exchange of Artistic Skills and Methods Between the Ottoman Empire and Europe

This section highlights how the Ottoman Empire contributed to European art through the exchange of artistic techniques and innovations, enriching the artistic practices of both cultures.

Ottoman Artistic Techniques

Calligraphy and Ornamentation: Ottoman art was renowned for its exquisite calligraphy and intricate ornamentation, which influenced European decorative arts.
Miniature Painting: The tradition of miniature painting in the Ottoman Empire, known for its detailed and vibrant depictions, offered a different perspective to European artists accustomed to larger canvases.

Influence on European Artistic Practices

Adoption of New Techniques: European artists adopted various Ottoman techniques, particularly in the realms of textile design, ceramics, and decorative arts.
Innovation in Color and Pattern: The rich color schemes and complex patterns characteristic of Ottoman art inspired European artists to experiment with new palettes and designs.

Technological Exchange

Ceramics and Pottery: The Ottoman influence was particularly significant in ceramics and pottery, where European craftsmen adopted techniques like Iznik tilework.
Textile Production: Techniques in textile production and dyeing, influenced by Ottoman practices, led to advancements in European textile arts.

Cross-Cultural Workshops and Artisans

Collaboration and Exchange: Artisans from the Ottoman Empire and Europe sometimes worked together in shared workshops, leading to a fruitful exchange of ideas and techniques.
Migration of Artisans: The migration of skilled artisans between the Ottoman Empire and Europe facilitated the transmission of artistic knowledge and skills.

Impact on European Art Movements

Inspiration for New Movements: The introduction of Ottoman artistic techniques contributed to the development of new art movements in Europe, influencing styles and themes.
Blending of Artistic Traditions: The blend of Ottoman and European artistic traditions created a unique cultural synergy, reflected in the artworks of the period.

Legacy and Modern Interpretation

Enduring Influence on Art and Design: The influence of Ottoman artistic techniques continues to be felt in modern art and design, with contemporary artists and designers drawing inspiration from this rich heritage.
Recognition of Cross-Cultural Artistic Contributions: Modern art history increasingly acknowledges the cross-cultural artistic contributions between the Ottoman Empire and Europe, appreciating the shared artistic heritage.

Section 9: The Role of Patronage in Artistic Exchange

Understanding the Impact of Patronage on the Cross-Cultural Flow of Art

This section delves into how patronage, both in the Ottoman Empire and Europe, played a pivotal role in facilitating the exchange of artistic ideas and styles, significantly influencing the development of art in both regions.

Patronage in the Ottoman Empire

Royal and Aristocratic Support: Ottoman sultans and high-ranking officials were major patrons of the arts, commissioning works that showcased the empire's power and cultural achievements.
Development of Distinct Styles: Patronage by the Ottoman elite led to the development of distinct artistic styles in various fields, including architecture, textiles, and miniature painting.

European Patronage and Its Influence

Royal and Noble Patrons: In Europe, kings, queens, and nobility played a similar role, commissioning works of art that reflected their status and tastes.
Art as a Diplomatic Tool: Art commissioned by European patrons was sometimes used as a diplomatic tool, with gifts of artwork being exchanged between European and Ottoman courts.

Cross-Cultural Artistic Commissions

Commissioning of Foreign Artists: There were instances where European patrons commissioned works from Ottoman artists and vice versa, leading to a direct exchange of artistic techniques and styles.
Influence on Artistic Trends: These cross-cultural commissions influenced artistic trends in both the Ottoman Empire and Europe, fostering a greater appreciation for each other's artistic traditions.

Impact of Patronage on Artistic Exchange

Facilitating Artistic Collaboration: Patronage facilitated collaboration between artists from different cultural backgrounds, encouraging the blending of styles and techniques.
Preservation and Dissemination of Art: The works commissioned by patrons played a crucial role in preserving and disseminating artistic traditions, contributing to their longevity and influence.

Legacy of Patronage in Art

Enduring Impact on Artistic Heritage: The legacy of patronage in the Ottoman Empire and Europe is evident in the rich artistic heritage that continues to be celebrated and studied today. Recognition of Shared Cultural Influences: Modern understanding of art history recognizes the role of patronage in fostering shared cultural influences between the Ottoman Empire and Europe.

Section 10: Enduring Influences in Modern Art and Design

Tracing the Ottoman Empire's Lasting Impact on Contemporary Artistic Practices

This final section of Chapter 16 examines how the Ottoman Empire's artistic legacy continues to influence modern art and design, reflecting a lasting cultural exchange that transcends time and geography.

Ongoing Influence in Modern Art

Incorporation of Ottoman Motifs: Modern artists and designers continue to incorporate motifs and stylistic elements from Ottoman art, such as intricate patterns and vibrant color palettes, into their work.
Inspiration for Contemporary Creations: The aesthetic richness of Ottoman art provides inspiration for contemporary creations in various media, including painting, sculpture, and digital art.

Influence on Design and Decor

Textiles and Fashion: Ottoman-inspired designs are evident in modern textiles and fashion, where traditional patterns are reimagined in contemporary clothing and home décor.
Interior Design and Architecture: Elements of Ottoman architecture, such as domes, arches, and tilework, find their way into modern interior design and architectural projects.

Cultural Resonance in Modern Times

Appreciation of Cultural Diversity: The ongoing influence of Ottoman art in modern times is a testament to the appreciation of cultural diversity in art and design.
Cross-Cultural Artistic Dialogues: Contemporary artists and designers often engage in cross-cultural dialogues, exploring and reinterpreting Ottoman artistic heritage in a modern context.

Educational and Scholarly Interest

Academic Study and Exhibitions: The Ottoman Empire's art and culture remain subjects of academic study and are featured in exhibitions around the world, highlighting their historical significance and contemporary relevance.
Workshops and Collaborative Projects: Workshops and collaborative projects focusing on Ottoman art techniques foster an understanding and appreciation of this rich artistic tradition.

Legacy in Global Art and Design

Influence Beyond Borders: The Ottoman Empire's artistic influence extends beyond its historical borders, contributing to a global artistic language that is inclusive of various cultural traditions.
Role in Contemporary Creative Expression: The legacy of Ottoman art in modern art and design underscores the role of historical artistic traditions in shaping contemporary creative expression.

Chapter 17: Legal Systems: Islamic Law and Western Jurisprudence

Section 1: Foundations of Islamic Law (Sharia)

Exploring the Origins, Principles, and Structure of Islamic Legal Systems

This section provides an overview of the foundations of Islamic law, known as Sharia, detailing its origins, key principles, and the structure that underpins Islamic legal systems.

Origins of Islamic Law

Rooted in Religious Texts: Sharia is rooted in the Quran, the holy book of Islam, and the Hadith, which are collections of sayings and actions of the Prophet Muhammad. These texts provide the primary sources of Islamic law.
Development Over Centuries: The development of Sharia was a complex process involving interpretation (ijtihad) by religious scholars (ulama) over centuries, leading to the formation of various schools of Islamic jurisprudence (madhabs).

Principles of Sharia

Comprehensive Legal and Ethical System: Sharia covers not only legal aspects but also ethical, moral, and social guidelines for Muslims. It encompasses a wide range of topics, including family life, finance, ritual practices, and criminal law.
Balance of Justice and Mercy: Sharia aims to balance justice with mercy, emphasizing fairness and compassion in its application.

Structure of Islamic Legal Systems

Division into Branches: Sharia is typically divided into branches such as ibadat (acts of worship) and mu'amalat (social transactions), each covering different aspects of life.
Role of Jurists and Scholars: Islamic jurists and scholars play a key role in interpreting Sharia and issuing legal opinions (fatwas) based on their understanding of religious texts.

Schools of Islamic Jurisprudence

Major Schools: The major schools of Islamic jurisprudence, including Hanafi, Maliki, Shafi'i, and Hanbali in Sunni Islam, and Jafari in Shia Islam, differ in their methodologies of interpretation but share core principles.
Regional Variations: The practice and interpretation of Sharia can vary significantly across different regions and cultures, reflecting the diversity within the Muslim world.

Modern Context of Sharia

Contemporary Application: In the modern context, the application of Sharia varies widely among Muslim-majority countries, with some implementing it as state law and others using it as a reference for personal law matters.
Debates and Reforms: Contemporary debates around Sharia involve issues of interpretation, human rights, and its role in modern legal systems, with ongoing efforts in some regions to reform Islamic law to address contemporary challenges.

Section 2: Influence of Islamic Jurisprudence on European Legal Thought

Tracing the Impact of Islamic Legal Traditions on the Development of European Law

This section explores how Islamic jurisprudence, with its rich traditions and principles, influenced the development of legal thought in Europe, particularly during key historical periods of intellectual exchange.

Transmission of Islamic Legal Concepts to Europe

Medieval Interactions: During the Middle Ages, especially through the translation movement in places like Spain and Sicily, European scholars gained access to Islamic legal texts and commentaries.
Role of Islamic Spain (Al-Andalus): Islamic Spain served as a crucial bridge for the transmission of Islamic jurisprudence to Europe, where scholars translated and studied Arabic works on law and philosophy.

Influence on European Legal Systems

Adoption of Concepts and Principles: European legal systems, particularly in the areas of commercial and maritime law, adopted various concepts and principles from Islamic jurisprudence.
Impact on Legal Institutions: The organization of legal institutions, procedures for legal testimony, and the formulation of legal documents in Europe were influenced by Islamic practices.

Case Studies of Influence

Commercial Law: Islamic commercial law, with its advanced understanding of contracts, partnerships, and financial transactions, influenced the development of similar legal frameworks in European mercantile centers.
Maritime Law: The principles of Islamic maritime law, as seen in documents like the "Kitab al-Muqaddimah" (The Book of Introduction) of Ibn Khaldun, impacted the evolution of maritime law in Mediterranean Europe.

Islamic Contributions to Legal Scholarship

Methodologies of Legal Reasoning: Islamic jurisprudence's methodologies of legal reasoning, such as analogy (qiyas) and consensus (ijma), contributed to the evolution of legal scholarship in Europe.
Preservation and Expansion of Legal Knowledge: Islamic scholars preserved and expanded upon ancient legal knowledge, including Greek and Roman law, which was later transmitted to European scholars.

Modern Relevance and Legacy

Recognition of Shared Legal Heritage: Modern legal scholarship increasingly acknowledges the shared heritage between Islamic and European legal traditions, recognizing the contributions of Islamic jurisprudence to European law.
Influence in Contemporary Legal Studies: Understanding the influence of Islamic jurisprudence aids in a more comprehensive view of the history and development of European legal systems.

Section 3: Comparative Study of Legal Principles

Analyzing the Parallels and Divergences Between Islamic and Western Legal Systems

This section offers a comparative analysis of the fundamental legal principles in Islamic law and Western jurisprudence, highlighting both the commonalities and differences in their approaches to law and justice.

Foundational Principles of Islamic Law

Rooted in Divine Commands: Islamic law is based on divine commands as revealed in the Quran and exemplified in the Hadith, with a strong emphasis on moral and ethical guidelines.
Holistic Approach: Sharia encompasses a comprehensive approach to law, blending religious, ethical, and legal aspects to govern all facets of a Muslim's life.

Western Legal Traditions

Roots in Roman and Common Law: Western legal systems have their roots in Roman law and, in the case of common law countries, medieval English law. These systems are characterized by their reliance on statutes and legal precedents.
Secular Foundation: Unlike Islamic law, Western legal systems are generally secular, separating religious considerations from legal judgments.

Comparative Analysis

Approach to Justice: Both Islamic law and Western jurisprudence aim to achieve justice, but their approaches differ, with Islamic law intertwining religious and moral principles, while Western law focuses more on secular and procedural aspects.
Sources of Law: While Islamic law relies heavily on religious texts and scholarly interpretation, Western law derives its principles from statutory enactments and judicial decisions.

Commonalities and Differences

Common Legal Concepts: There are shared concepts, such as the importance of contracts, property rights, and personal responsibility, in both legal traditions.
Divergences in Implementation: The implementation and interpretation of these concepts differ significantly, reflecting the diverse cultural, religious, and historical contexts of Islamic and Western societies.

Case Studies in Comparative Law

Family Law: Family law offers a clear example of divergence, with Islamic law providing specific religious guidelines on marriage, divorce, and inheritance, while Western law approaches these issues from a secular perspective.
Commercial Law: In commercial law, despite different foundations, there are parallels in the recognition of contracts and business ethics.

Implications for Modern Legal Practice

Cross-Cultural Legal Understanding: Understanding the similarities and differences between Islamic and Western legal systems is crucial in today's globalized world, where legal practitioners increasingly encounter cross-cultural legal issues.
Influence on International Law: The comparative study of these legal systems contributes to a richer understanding of international law and its development.

Section 4: The Concept of Justice in Islam and the West

Comparing the Philosophical and Practical Approaches to Justice

This section examines how the concept of justice is approached and interpreted in Islamic law compared to Western jurisprudence, highlighting the philosophical underpinnings and practical applications in both legal systems.

Justice in Islamic Law

Divine Origin: In Islamic law, justice is seen as a divine command, rooted in the principles laid out in the Quran and Hadith. It is considered a fundamental objective of Sharia to establish justice in society.
Holistic Approach: Justice in Islamic law encompasses not only legal justice but also social and economic equity, emphasizing the welfare and rights of individuals and communities.

Justice in Western Jurisprudence

Secular and Rational Basis: In Western legal systems, justice is often based on secular and rational principles, derived from a combination of legal precedents, statutory law, and philosophical ideas of fairness and equality.
Rule of Law: Western concepts of justice emphasize the rule of law, where justice is achieved through the consistent and impartial application of established laws.

Comparative Perspectives

Balance of Individual and Community Rights: Both Islamic law and Western jurisprudence strive to balance individual rights with the needs of the community, though the methods and emphasis can differ significantly.
Retributive vs. Restorative Justice: Islamic law often incorporates elements of restorative justice, focusing on reconciliation and restitution, whereas Western law tends to emphasize retributive justice, focusing on punishment and deterrence.

Case Studies and Examples

Criminal Justice: In the criminal justice arena, the differences in the approach to justice can be seen in the handling of crimes and penalties, with Islamic law sometimes prescribing specific punishments based on religious texts.
Social and Economic Justice: Islamic law's approach to social and economic justice, such as the distribution of wealth through mechanisms like Zakat (almsgiving), contrasts with Western legal systems that typically address these issues through secular social welfare policies.

Modern Challenges and Debates

Adaptation to Contemporary Needs: Both legal systems face challenges in adapting their concepts of justice to contemporary global issues, including human rights, international conflicts, and economic disparities.
Interlegal Dialogue: The interaction between Islamic and Western legal systems in a globalized world necessitates a dialogue that respects the principles of justice in both traditions while addressing common challenges.

Section 5: Contract Law and Commercial Ethics

Exploring the Foundations and Ethical Dimensions of Contract Law in Islamic and Western Legal Traditions

This section delves into the principles of contract law and commercial ethics in both Islamic law and Western jurisprudence, examining how each system approaches contracts and the ethical considerations involved in commercial transactions.

Contract Law in Islamic Jurisprudence

Rooted in Religious Principles: Islamic contract law is deeply rooted in religious principles, emphasizing fairness, mutual consent, and the avoidance of unjust enrichment or exploitation. Prohibitions and Requirements: Sharia prohibits certain types of contracts, such as those involving excessive uncertainty (gharar) or usury (riba), and prescribes specific requirements for valid contracts, including clear terms and mutual consent.

Western Approaches to Contract Law

Secular Legal Frameworks: In contrast, Western contract law operates within a secular legal framework, primarily concerned with the enforcement of agreements and the resolution of disputes.
Focus on Autonomy and Enforcement: Western legal systems typically emphasize the autonomy of contracting parties and the enforceability of contracts, with less explicit focus on the ethical dimensions of transactions.

Comparative Analysis

Common Legal Foundations: Both Islamic and Western legal systems recognize the importance of contracts in commercial transactions and the need for clear terms, mutual consent, and remedy for breach.
Divergent Ethical Perspectives: The two systems diverge in their ethical perspectives, with Islamic law placing greater emphasis on the moral and ethical dimensions of contracts, reflecting its religious underpinnings.

Case Studies and Applications

Islamic Finance: Islamic finance provides a practical example of how Islamic contract law is applied, with financial products designed to comply with Sharia principles.

International Business Transactions: In international business transactions, the interaction of Islamic and Western contract law principles can present unique challenges and opportunities for harmonization.

Impact on Global Commerce

Influence on International Trade: The principles of Islamic contract law have influenced international trade, particularly in regions with significant Muslim populations, necessitating an understanding of these principles in global commerce.
Ethical Considerations in Business: Both systems contribute to the ongoing dialogue on the role of ethics in business, with potential learnings for creating more equitable and sustainable commercial practices.

Section 6: Rights and Responsibilities of Citizens

Contrasting the Approaches to Civil Rights and Obligations in Islamic and Western Legal Systems

This section explores how Islamic law and Western jurisprudence define and enforce the rights and responsibilities of citizens, highlighting the similarities and differences in their approaches to civil liberties and societal duties.

Citizen Rights in Islamic Law

Rights Defined by Religious Doctrine: In Islamic law, the rights and responsibilities of citizens are often defined by religious doctrine, covering aspects of life ranging from family and social obligations to economic and political rights.
Protection of Individual Rights: Sharia emphasizes the protection of individual rights, including the right to life, property, and dignity, while also stressing communal responsibilities and moral behavior.

Citizen Rights in Western Jurisprudence

Secular and Constitutional Basis: In Western legal systems, citizens' rights are typically grounded in secular, constitutional frameworks, focusing on individual liberties, equality before the law, and the protection of personal freedoms.
Evolution Through Legal Precedents: The rights and responsibilities of citizens in Western law have evolved over time, influenced by legal precedents, societal changes, and philosophical thought on human rights.

Comparative Perspectives

Approach to Individual Rights: Both Islamic law and Western jurisprudence value the protection of individual rights, but their approaches differ, with Islamic law intertwining rights with religious obligations and Western law emphasizing secular freedoms.
Balance of Rights and Duties: Both systems seek to balance individual rights with societal duties, though the emphasis and interpretation of these duties vary.

Case Studies and Examples

Family Law: In areas like family law, the rights and responsibilities of citizens under Islamic and Western legal systems show marked differences, reflecting divergent cultural and religious values.
Political Participation: The approach to citizens' rights in political participation also differs, with Islamic law often placing these rights within a religious context, while Western law frames them in terms of secular democracy and civil liberties.

Contemporary Challenges and Debates

Adapting to Modern Contexts: Both Islamic and Western legal systems face challenges in adapting their approaches to citizens' rights to contemporary global issues, including gender equality, freedom of expression, and minority rights.
Interlegal Dialogue: In an increasingly interconnected world, the dialogue between Islamic and Western legal systems on citizens' rights and responsibilities is crucial for addressing global challenges and fostering mutual understanding.

Section 7: Criminal Law: Punishments and Procedures

Comparing the Administration of Criminal Justice in Islamic and Western Legal Frameworks

This section delves into the differences and similarities in how criminal law, including the nature of punishments and legal procedures, is administered in Islamic law compared to Western jurisprudence.

Criminal Law in Islamic Jurisprudence

Based on Religious Texts: In Islamic law, criminal offenses and punishments are often derived from the Quran and Hadith, with some crimes, known as hudud, having fixed punishments prescribed by religious texts.

Emphasis on Moral Rectitude: Islamic criminal law places a strong emphasis on moral rectitude and social order, with the aim of preserving religious and ethical norms.

Western Approaches to Criminal Law

Secular Legal Systems: Western criminal law operates within a secular framework, focusing on the protection of individual rights, public order, and societal norms.
Variety of Punishments: Unlike the fixed punishments in Islamic law, Western criminal law offers a range of punishments, often determined by the severity of the crime, the circumstances, and legal precedents.

Comparative Analysis

Nature of Punishments: Islamic law is known for certain severe punishments for specific crimes, which can differ markedly from the punishments in Western legal systems.
Procedural Differences: There are significant procedural differences in how criminal trials are conducted, with Islamic law placing specific requirements on evidence and testimony, while Western law follows a more adversarial or inquisitorial process.

Human Rights Perspectives

Contemporary Debates: The application of criminal law in Islamic contexts, especially concerning hudud punishments, has been a subject of debate from a human rights perspective.
Reform and Modernization: Some Muslim-majority countries have undertaken efforts to reform their criminal justice systems to align with international human rights standards.

Case Studies and Applications

Examples from Muslim-Majority Countries: Case studies from various Muslim-majority countries show how Islamic criminal law is applied and how it interacts with modern legal and human rights norms.
Comparison with Western Criminal Cases: Comparative studies of criminal cases in Western contexts provide insights into the differing principles and practices in criminal justice.

Implications for Global Legal Practices

Cross-Cultural Legal Understanding: An understanding of the differences in criminal law is essential in a globalized world, especially for international legal cooperation and human rights advocacy.

Challenges in International Law: These differences pose challenges in the realms of international law and criminal justice, necessitating dialogue and mutual understanding between different legal traditions.

Section 8: The Evolution of International Law

Tracing the Development of International Legal Principles from Islamic and Western Perspectives

This section examines how international law has evolved, considering the contributions and influences of both Islamic law and Western jurisprudence, and how these distinct legal traditions have shaped modern international legal norms.

Islamic Contributions to International Law

Early Foundations: Islamic legal traditions, dating back to the early Islamic caliphates, included principles relating to war, peace, diplomacy, and the treatment of non-combatants, which contributed to early concepts of international law.

Treaties and Diplomacy: Islamic rulers historically engaged in treaty-making and diplomatic relations with other states, including non-Muslim states, establishing precedents for international agreements and diplomatic immunity.

Western Influence on International Law

European Developments: In Europe, the Peace of Westphalia in 1648 and subsequent treaties laid the groundwork for modern concepts of state sovereignty and non-interference, which are central to contemporary international law.

Codification and Expansion: Over the centuries, Western legal scholars, such as Hugo Grotius, contributed to the codification and expansion of international law, incorporating principles of natural law and state relations.

Comparative Perspectives

Shared Principles: Both Islamic and Western legal traditions share certain principles in international law, such as the sanctity of treaties and the conduct of warfare, though their applications and interpretations may differ.

Differences in Approach: Islamic law traditionally integrated international law within a religious framework, while Western jurisprudence developed international law along secular lines, focusing on state-to-state relations.

Modern International Law

Convergence of Traditions: Modern international law represents a convergence of various legal traditions, including Islamic and Western, especially in areas like human rights, humanitarian law, and the laws of war.
Influence of Globalization: With globalization, there has been an increasing need to harmonize different legal approaches to address global issues, leading to a more inclusive international legal framework.

Challenges and Contemporary Debates

Balancing Diverse Legal Traditions: One of the challenges in the evolution of international law is balancing the diverse legal and cultural traditions that contribute to it.
Addressing Contemporary Issues: Contemporary issues such as international terrorism, human trafficking, and environmental protection require an evolving approach to international law that respects different legal perspectives.

Section 9: Contemporary Legal Challenges and Islamic Perspectives

Navigating Modern Legal Issues Through the Lens of Islamic Jurisprudence

This section explores how Islamic perspectives can contribute to addressing contemporary legal challenges, examining the relevance and application of Islamic legal principles in the modern world.

Contemporary Issues in a Globalized World

Human Rights: One of the significant challenges is the integration of human rights norms, where Islamic law's approach to rights and freedoms can sometimes differ from Western human rights paradigms.
International Conflicts and Terrorism: Islamic jurisprudence offers perspectives on the laws of war and peace, which can be pivotal in addressing issues related to international conflicts and terrorism.

Islamic Law and Modern Governance

Democratic Governance: The application of Islamic principles in the context of modern democratic governance is a subject of ongoing debate, particularly in Muslim-majority countries grappling with issues of political freedom and civil rights.

Economic Justice: Islamic economic principles, such as the prohibition of usury (riba) and the promotion of equitable wealth distribution, provide an alternative framework for addressing economic disparities and financial ethics.

Environmental Law and Ethics

Stewardship of the Earth: Islamic law emphasizes the stewardship of the earth (khalifah), offering ethical directives for environmental conservation and sustainable development, which are increasingly relevant in the face of global environmental challenges.

Technology and Cyber Law

Adapting to Technological Advances: The rapid advancement of technology presents new legal challenges, from data privacy to cybercrime, where Islamic legal principles may offer guiding ethics and moral considerations.

Islamic Perspectives on Family and Personal Law

Marriage, Divorce, and Inheritance: Islamic law provides detailed regulations for personal status matters, such as marriage, divorce, and inheritance. The integration and application of these principles in multicultural societies present both challenges and opportunities for legal harmonization.

Challenges of Interpretation and Reform

Diverse Interpretations: The diverse interpretations of Sharia among Muslim scholars and communities lead to varying applications in different contexts, affecting its role in modern legal challenges.
Reform Movements: There are ongoing reform movements within Islamic jurisprudence, seeking to reconcile traditional Islamic principles with contemporary needs and international norms.

Contributions to Global Legal Discourse

Ethical and Moral Dimensions: Islamic perspectives contribute to the global legal discourse by offering ethical and moral dimensions to legal issues, emphasizing social justice, communal welfare, and moral responsibility.
Dialogue and Mutual Understanding: Engaging with Islamic legal perspectives can foster greater dialogue and mutual understanding in addressing global legal challenges.

Section 10: Legacy of Islamic Law in Modern Legal Systems

Assessing the Enduring Influence of Islamic Jurisprudence in Contemporary Legal Frameworks

This final section of Chapter 17 explores the lasting impact of Islamic law on modern legal systems, both in Muslim-majority countries and in the global legal landscape, highlighting how its principles continue to shape legal practices and concepts today.

Islamic Law in Muslim-Majority Countries

Foundational Role: In many Muslim-majority countries, Islamic law serves as a foundational legal framework, particularly in matters of personal law, such as marriage, divorce, and inheritance.
Constitutional Incorporation: Some countries have incorporated principles of Sharia into their constitutions, establishing it as a source, or the primary source, of legislation.

Influence on National Legal Systems

Hybrid Legal Systems: Many Muslim-majority countries operate hybrid legal systems, where Islamic law coexists with civil law or common law systems, leading to unique legal amalgamations.
Judicial Interpretation: Courts in these countries often interpret civil and criminal laws through the lens of Islamic principles, blending traditional jurisprudence with contemporary legal needs.

Impact on International Law

Contributions to Human Rights Discourse: Islamic legal principles contribute to international human rights discourse, offering perspectives on issues like social justice, women's rights, and economic equity.
Influence in International Bodies: Muslim-majority countries, through their participation in international bodies, bring Islamic legal perspectives to discussions on global legal standards and treaties.

Islamic Law and Western Legal Systems

Interactions in Multicultural Societies: In Western countries with significant Muslim populations, Islamic legal principles, particularly in family law, interact with domestic legal systems, leading to discussions on legal pluralism and accommodation.

Comparative Law Studies: Islamic law has become an important area of study in comparative law, contributing to a more diverse and inclusive understanding of global legal traditions.

Modern Interpretations and Reforms

Contemporary Interpretation: There is an ongoing effort among modern Islamic scholars to interpret Islamic law in ways that address contemporary challenges while remaining faithful to its principles.
Reform Movements: Reform movements within Islamic jurisprudence seek to harmonize traditional Islamic principles with modern legal practices and human rights norms.

Legacy and Future Outlook

Enduring Influence: The legacy of Islamic law is enduring, continuing to influence legal practices and concepts in various parts of the world.
Dynamic and Evolving Tradition: As a dynamic and evolving tradition, Islamic law is likely to continue playing a significant role in shaping legal systems and contributing to global legal discourse.

Chapter 18: Medicine: Islamic Knowledge and European Enlightenment

Section 1: Islamic Medical Practices and Their Transmission to Europe

Exploring the Impact of Islamic Medicine on European Medical Knowledge and Practices

This section examines how medical knowledge from the Islamic world during the medieval period significantly influenced European medicine during the Renaissance and Enlightenment, contributing to the development of modern medical science.

Foundations of Islamic Medicine

Integration of Diverse Traditions: Islamic medicine integrated knowledge from Greek, Persian, and Indian medical traditions, synthesizing and expanding upon them.
Prominent Medical Scholars: Renowned Islamic scholars like Avicenna (Ibn Sina) and Al-Razi (Rhazes) made groundbreaking contributions to medicine, writing extensively on various medical topics.

Transmission to Europe

Translation Movement: Many Islamic medical texts were translated into Latin during the Middle Ages, particularly in places like Spain and Sicily, facilitating their dissemination in Europe.
Centers of Learning: Islamic centers of learning, such as those in Baghdad, Cairo, and Cordoba, attracted European scholars, who brought back medical knowledge to their homelands.

Influence on European Medicine

Adoption of Techniques and Concepts: European medicine adopted various techniques and concepts from Islamic medicine, including pharmacology, diagnostics, and surgical practices.
Medical Texts and Treatises: Works like Avicenna's "The Canon of Medicine" and Al-Razi's "Comprehensive Book" became standard texts in European medical schools.

Impact on Medical Practices

Clinical Practices and Observations: Islamic medicine's emphasis on clinical practices, direct observation, and empirical evidence influenced European medical approaches, laying the groundwork for more scientific methodologies.
Pharmacology and Drug Compounding: The advanced Islamic knowledge of pharmacology, including the preparation and use of compounds, significantly impacted European pharmacy.

Legacy in Modern Medicine

Enduring Principles: Many principles and techniques from Islamic medicine continue to influence modern medical practices, particularly in areas like holistic patient care and the ethical practice of medicine.
Recognition and Integration: The historical impact of Islamic medicine is increasingly recognized in the field of medical history, underscoring the interconnected nature of global medical developments.

Section 2: Key Islamic Physicians and Their Contributions

Highlighting the Pioneering Figures in Islamic Medicine and Their Enduring Legacy

This section focuses on some of the most influential Islamic physicians whose work and discoveries had a profound impact on the development of medical science, both in the Islamic world and in Europe.

Avicenna (Ibn Sina)

The Canon of Medicine: Avicenna's most famous work, "The Canon of Medicine" (Al-Qanun fi al-Tibb), was a comprehensive medical encyclopedia that synthesized and expanded upon existing medical knowledge.
Legacy: This work remained a standard medical text in Europe for several centuries, influencing the practice and teaching of medicine.

Al-Razi (Rhazes)

Pioneering Clinical Observations: Al-Razi is known for his detailed clinical observations and for writing the comprehensive medical book "Al-Hawi" (The Comprehensive Book).
Contributions to Pediatrics and Smallpox: He made significant contributions to pediatrics and was among the first to differentiate smallpox from measles, improving diagnostic accuracy.

Al-Zahrawi (Abulcasis)

Surgical Innovations: Known as the father of modern surgery, Al-Zahrawi's 30-volume medical encyclopedia, "Al-Tasrif," included detailed descriptions of surgical instruments and techniques.
Influence on European Surgery: His work profoundly influenced the development of surgery in Europe and introduced several surgical tools still in use today.

Ibn al-Nafis

Discovery of Pulmonary Circulation: Ibn al-Nafis is credited with the first accurate description of pulmonary circulation, a discovery that predated the European descriptions by centuries.
Impact on Cardiology: His work laid the foundations for the later development of cardiology and the understanding of the circulatory system.

Ibn Zuhr (Avenzoar)

Advancements in Experimental Medicine: Ibn Zuhr is known for his work in experimental medicine and for being among the first to conduct animal testing to understand surgical procedures.
Influence on European Medicine: His practical approach to medicine and emphasis on empirical evidence influenced European medical practices.

Legacy and Modern Recognition

Enduring Contributions: The contributions of these and other Islamic physicians continue to be recognized for their foundational role in the development of various medical fields.
Integration in Medical History: The recognition of these scholars in the broader narrative of medical history highlights the interconnected nature of scientific progress across different cultures.

Section 3: The Impact of Islamic Texts on European Medicine

Exploring How Islamic Medical Literature Shaped European Medical Knowledge and Practices

This section discusses the significant impact of Islamic medical texts on European medicine, detailing how these works introduced advanced concepts and practices that were instrumental in the development of medical science during the Renaissance and Enlightenment.

Translation and Transmission

Translation Movement: Islamic medical texts were translated into Latin and other European languages during the Middle Ages, particularly in centers of learning such as Toledo and Sicily.
Key Translated Works: Works like Avicenna's "The Canon of Medicine" and Al-Razi's "The Comprehensive Book" were among the texts that were widely translated and disseminated in Europe.

Influence on European Medical Education

Standard Medical Curriculum: Islamic medical texts became part of the standard curriculum in many European medical schools, teaching generations of European physicians.
Introduction of New Medical Concepts: These texts introduced European scholars to advanced medical concepts, including detailed anatomical knowledge, diagnostic techniques, and pharmacological formulations.

Advancements in Various Medical Fields

Diagnostics and Treatments: Islamic texts provided detailed descriptions of diseases and their treatments, influencing European approaches to diagnostics and therapeutics.
Pharmacology and Drug Compilation: The sophisticated understanding of pharmacology in Islamic texts, including the preparation and properties of drugs, greatly enriched European pharmacy.

Integration of Philosophical and Ethical Considerations

Holistic Approach to Medicine: Islamic medical literature often integrated philosophical and ethical considerations into medical practice, an approach that influenced European medicine's understanding of the physician's role and medical ethics.

Impact on Surgical Practices

Surgical Techniques and Instruments: Texts like Al-Zahrawi's "Al-Tasrif" introduced European surgeons to a variety of surgical techniques and instruments, some of which laid the groundwork for modern surgical practices.

Enduring Legacy in Modern Medicine

Foundation for Later Advancements: The knowledge disseminated through these texts formed a foundation for later advancements during the European Renaissance and Enlightenment.
Recognition in Medical History: The impact of Islamic medical texts is increasingly recognized in the history of medicine, acknowledging the contributions of Islamic scholars to the evolution of medical science.

Section 4: Innovations in Surgery and Pharmacology

Highlighting the Contributions of Islamic Medicine to Surgical and Pharmacological Advancements

This section delves into the significant innovations in surgery and pharmacology made by Islamic medical practitioners, which were instrumental in shaping these fields during the European Renaissance and beyond.

Advancements in Surgery

Pioneering Surgical Techniques: Islamic physicians like Al-Zahrawi (Abulcasis) introduced and refined various surgical techniques, including those for treating wounds, fractures, and specific surgical conditions.
Development of Surgical Instruments: Al-Zahrawi's work, "Al-Tasrif," described over 200 surgical instruments, many of which were innovative for their time and some of which laid the groundwork for modern surgical tools.

Pharmacological Contributions

Pharmacy as a Science: Islamic medicine treated pharmacy as a distinct science. Scholars like Ibn Sina (Avicenna) and Al-Razi (Rhazes) compiled extensive knowledge on the preparation and properties of drugs.
Formulation of Medicines: Islamic physicians were adept at formulating medicines, including pills, syrups, and ointments, using complex methods of extraction, distillation, and combination of various ingredients.

Influence on European Medicine

Dissemination Through Texts: Islamic medical texts that were translated into Latin provided a wealth of knowledge on these subjects, influencing European medical practices and teachings.
Improvement of European Surgical Practices: European surgeons adopted and further developed the surgical techniques and instruments described in Islamic texts, improving the overall practice of surgery in Europe.

Integration of Empirical Observations

Clinical Approach: Islamic medical practitioners emphasized empirical observation and clinical experience in both surgery and pharmacology, an approach that contributed to the development of more scientific methods in medicine.

Legacy in Modern Medical Practice

Continued Relevance of Techniques and Formulations: Some of the surgical techniques and pharmacological formulations from Islamic medicine continue to be relevant and are recognized as important contributions to modern medicine.
Recognition in Medical History: The contributions of Islamic medicine to surgery and pharmacology are increasingly acknowledged in the history of medicine, highlighting the interconnected nature of medical advancements across cultures.

Section 5: Public Health and Hospital Systems

Examining the Influence of Islamic Practices on the Development of Public Health and Hospital Systems in Europe

This section focuses on how Islamic innovations in public health and the establishment of hospitals influenced similar developments in Europe, contributing significantly to the evolution of healthcare systems.

Public Health Initiatives in the Islamic World

Preventive Healthcare: Islamic medical practice emphasized preventive healthcare, including personal hygiene, dietary regulations, and environmental sanitation, rooted in both religious and medical recommendations.
Community Health Measures: Muslim-majority cities implemented public health measures such as waste disposal and water management to prevent diseases, setting early examples of community health initiatives.

Development of Hospitals

Bimaristans (Hospitals): The Islamic world saw the establishment of bimaristans, or hospitals, which were among the first to offer care to all, regardless of their ability to pay.
Advanced Hospital Facilities: These hospitals were advanced for their time, offering specialized wards, lecture halls, libraries, and even provisions for mental health care.

Influence on European Healthcare

Introduction of Hospital Concepts: The concept and structure of Islamic hospitals influenced the development of similar institutions in Europe, particularly during the Crusades when European knights encountered these facilities.
Adoption of Public Health Practices: European cities gradually adopted Islamic practices of public health, especially as they faced outbreaks of diseases like the plague.

Integration of Medical Education

Teaching Hospitals: Islamic hospitals often functioned as centers of medical education, integrating patient care with medical training and research. This model influenced the establishment of teaching hospitals in Europe.

Legacy in Modern Healthcare Systems

Foundations of Modern Hospitals: The foundations laid by Islamic healthcare systems contributed significantly to the modern concept and functioning of hospitals.

Continued Relevance in Public Health: The emphasis on public health measures in the Islamic world remains relevant today, especially in the context of global health challenges.

Recognition and Influence

Acknowledgment in Medical History: The influence of Islamic practices on European healthcare systems is increasingly recognized in medical history, acknowledging the contributions of the Islamic world to global healthcare developments.
Impact on Healthcare Policies: The principles of comprehensive care and public health initiatives from Islamic practices continue to influence healthcare policies and practices in various parts of the world.

Section 6: Anatomy and Physiology: A Comparative Study

Exploring the Contributions of Islamic Scholars to Anatomy and Physiology and Their Influence on European Medical Understanding

This section examines the advancements in the study of anatomy and physiology made by Islamic scholars and how these contributions significantly influenced the field of medicine in Europe, particularly during the Renaissance.

Advancements in Islamic Anatomy and Physiology

Detailed Studies: Islamic scholars conducted detailed studies of the human body, contributing to a more comprehensive understanding of anatomy and physiology. Their work was often based on dissections and observations, albeit limited compared to later European practices.
Notable Contributions: Scholars like Ibn al-Nafis made groundbreaking discoveries, including the first accurate description of pulmonary circulation, which challenged earlier understandings based on Galenic physiology.

Transmission to Europe

Translations of Islamic Texts: Key medical texts from the Islamic world, including those containing anatomical and physiological knowledge, were translated into Latin and other European languages, particularly during the 12th and 13th centuries.
Influence on European Scholars: These texts influenced European medical scholars, who began to explore human anatomy and physiology more rigorously, leading to a renaissance in anatomical studies.

Impact on European Medicine

Shifting from Galenic Views: The influence of Islamic scholarship helped shift European medicine away from Galenic views, which were often based on animal dissections, towards a more accurate understanding of human anatomy.
Foundations for Future Discoveries: The work of Islamic scholars laid the groundwork for later European anatomical discoveries, such as those by Andreas Vesalius, which revolutionized the study of human anatomy.

Integration of Empirical Observations

Empirical Approach: Both Islamic and European scholars eventually adopted a more empirical approach to studying the human body, emphasizing direct observation and dissection, although this was more pronounced in Europe post-Renaissance.

Legacy and Modern Recognition

Enduring Impact on Medical Science: The contributions of Islamic scholars to the fields of anatomy and physiology have a lasting impact, forming an essential part of the historical foundation of medical science.
Recognition in Medical History: Modern medical history increasingly acknowledges these contributions, highlighting the role of Islamic scholars in shaping our understanding of the human body.

Section 7: Medical Ethics in Islamic and Western Traditions

Analyzing the Philosophical and Practical Approaches to Medical Ethics in Islamic and Western Medicine

This section explores the approaches to medical ethics in Islamic and Western medical traditions, focusing on the principles and practices that guide ethical decision-making in healthcare.

Medical Ethics in Islamic Tradition

Rooted in Religious Principles: Islamic medical ethics are deeply rooted in religious principles, derived from the Quran and Hadith. They emphasize compassion, beneficence, and the sanctity of life.

Patient Care and Rights: Islamic ethics place a strong emphasis on patient care, advocating for the rights and dignity of patients, including the provision of care regardless of the patient's background.

Medical Ethics in Western Tradition

Secular Ethical Frameworks: In contrast, Western medical ethics are generally based on secular principles, drawing from philosophical concepts such as autonomy, justice, beneficence, and non-maleficence.
Development of Bioethics: The field of bioethics in Western medicine has evolved to address ethical challenges arising from technological advances and diverse societal values.

Comparative Perspectives

Shared Ethical Concerns: Both Islamic and Western medical ethics share concerns for patient welfare, informed consent, and the ethical use of medical knowledge.
Differences in Ethical Reasoning: The ethical reasoning in Islamic medical ethics is often intertwined with religious teachings, while Western medical ethics tends to rely on secular and philosophical reasoning.

Case Studies and Applications

End-of-Life Care: Islamic and Western traditions approach end-of-life care differently, particularly in matters of life-sustaining treatments and palliative care.
Medical Research and Trials: Ethical considerations in medical research, including patient consent and the use of new treatments, are addressed differently in Islamic and Western contexts.

Contemporary Challenges and Debates

Navigating Modern Medical Advances: Both traditions face challenges in applying ethical principles to modern medical advances, such as genetic engineering, cloning, and organ transplantation.
Cultural and Religious Sensitivities: In increasingly multicultural societies, healthcare providers must navigate a range of ethical perspectives, balancing religious and cultural sensitivities with medical practice.

Impact on Global Medical Ethics

Influence on International Guidelines: Islamic medical ethics contribute to international discussions on medical ethics, offering perspectives that may differ from dominant Western paradigms.
Enhancing Cross-Cultural Understanding: Understanding the nuances of medical ethics in both Islamic and Western traditions enhances cross-cultural understanding and improves patient care in a globalized world.

Section 8: The Role of Medical Schools and Universities

Tracing the Development and Influence of Medical Education in Islamic and Western Traditions

This section examines the establishment and evolution of medical schools and universities in the Islamic world and their impact on the development of medical education in Europe, highlighting the exchange of knowledge and practices.

Medical Education in the Islamic World

Early Medical Institutions: The Islamic world was home to some of the earliest medical schools and universities, where medicine was taught as a structured discipline. Notable examples include the Al-Qarawiyyin University in Fez and Al-Azhar University in Cairo.
Comprehensive Curriculum: These institutions offered a comprehensive curriculum, including the study of various Islamic medical texts, practical training, and often, an emphasis on holistic patient care.

Transmission of Medical Knowledge to Europe

Translation of Islamic Texts: Many foundational texts used in Islamic medical schools were translated into Latin, becoming part of the medical curriculum in European universities.
Influence on European Medical Education: The methods of teaching and the structure of medical courses in Islamic institutions influenced the development of medical education in European universities, particularly during the Renaissance.

Collaboration and Exchange

Cross-Cultural Exchange: The interaction between Islamic and European scholars in medical schools and universities facilitated the exchange of medical knowledge and practices.

Contribution to the European Renaissance: The knowledge and methodologies from Islamic medical education played a significant role in shaping the medical Renaissance in Europe.

Modern Medical Education

Legacy in Contemporary Institutions: The legacy of early Islamic medical education is evident in the structure and curriculum of modern medical schools, both in the Islamic world and globally. Recognition of Historical Contributions: The historical contributions of Islamic medical schools to the field of medical education are increasingly recognized and appreciated.

Challenges and Adaptations

Adapting to Modern Medical Advances: Medical schools in both Islamic and Western traditions continue to adapt their curricula and methodologies to keep pace with rapid medical and technological advances.
Integrating Traditional and Modern Practices: There is an ongoing effort to integrate traditional medical knowledge from Islamic history with contemporary medical practices and ethical considerations.

Section 9: Disease and Epidemics: Cross-Cultural Responses

Analyzing the Approaches of Islamic and Western Medicine to Disease Control and Epidemic Management

This section explores how Islamic and Western medical traditions have historically approached the challenges posed by diseases and epidemics, offering insights into the cross-cultural management of public health crises.

Islamic Medicine and Epidemic Management

Holistic Health Measures: Islamic medicine emphasized holistic health measures, including personal hygiene, quarantine, and dietary regulations, which were integral to managing epidemics.
Historical Responses to Epidemics: During times of epidemics, Islamic scholars and physicians advocated for measures such as isolation and care for the sick, based on both medical knowledge and religious teachings.

Western Medicine and Disease Control

Development of Public Health Systems: In the Western tradition, the response to epidemics over time led to the development of more organized public health systems, especially after experiencing major outbreaks like the Black Death.
Scientific Advancements: Western medicine, particularly from the Enlightenment onwards, made significant advancements in understanding the causes and spread of diseases, leading to more effective control measures.

Comparative Analysis

Approaches to Quarantine and Isolation: Both Islamic and Western medical traditions recognized the importance of quarantine and isolation in controlling the spread of infectious diseases, although the implementation and understanding of these measures evolved differently.
Role of Religion and Ethics: Islamic responses to epidemics often integrated religious and ethical considerations, while Western approaches increasingly relied on scientific and secular principles.

Case Studies of Historical Epidemics

Plague and Smallpox: The response to historical epidemics like the plague and smallpox provides a window into how Islamic and Western medical traditions dealt with public health crises, including the development of early forms of inoculation and vaccination.

Modern Implications and Legacy

Influence on Contemporary Public Health: The historical approaches to disease control in both traditions have influenced contemporary public health strategies, particularly in dealing with modern pandemics.
Cross-Cultural Lessons: Understanding the historical responses of Islamic and Western medicine to epidemics offers valuable lessons for current and future public health challenges, emphasizing the need for a holistic and collaborative approach.

Section 10: The Lasting Influence of Islamic Medicine

Assessing the Enduring Legacy of Islamic Medical Knowledge and Practices

This final section of Chapter 18 highlights the enduring impact of Islamic medicine on the contemporary medical field, acknowledging its contributions to various aspects of modern medical science and practice.

Foundational Contributions

Comprehensive Medical Texts: Islamic medical scholars like Avicenna and Al-Razi authored texts that served as fundamental references in medicine for centuries, both in the Islamic world and in Europe.
Innovations in Various Fields: Contributions in areas such as pharmacology, surgery, and anatomy by Islamic scholars laid the groundwork for future advancements in these fields.

Influence on European Medicine

Introduction of New Concepts and Techniques: The translation and study of Islamic medical texts during the Middle Ages introduced Europe to a range of new medical concepts and techniques.
Shaping Medical Education: The structure and content of Islamic medical education influenced the development of European medical schools, shaping the curriculum and teaching methods.

Integration of Ethical Practices

Holistic and Ethical Approach: The holistic and ethical approach to medicine in Islamic traditions, which emphasized patient care and moral responsibility, influenced the evolution of medical ethics and patient management in Western medicine.

Modern Medical Practices

Continued Relevance of Principles: Many principles and practices from Islamic medicine, such as the emphasis on preventative care and holistic treatment, continue to find relevance in modern medical practices.
Integration in Contemporary Healthcare: Elements of Islamic medicine, including herbal remedies and holistic approaches, are increasingly integrated into contemporary healthcare, particularly in alternative and complementary medicine.

Recognition and Revival

Increasing Acknowledgment: The historical contributions of Islamic medicine are increasingly acknowledged in the field of medical history and education, with a growing appreciation of its role in the development of modern medicine.
Revival of Interest: There is a revival of interest in the study of Islamic medical texts and practices, both for historical understanding and for exploring their potential applications in contemporary medicine.

Legacy and Future Directions

Enduring Legacy: The legacy of Islamic medicine is enduring, continuing to influence medical thought and practice across the world.
Cross-Cultural Medical Dialogue: The contributions of Islamic medicine foster a cross-cultural medical dialogue, enriching the global medical community's understanding and approach to healthcare.

Chapter 19: Gender and Society: Women in Islamic and Western Worlds

Section 1: Women's Roles in Islamic Societies

Understanding the Historical and Contemporary Roles of Women in Islamic Cultures

This section explores the roles and statuses of women in Islamic societies, both historically and in the contemporary context, examining the complexities and diversities of their experiences across different cultural and geographical landscapes.

Historical Perspectives

Early Islamic Era: During the early Islamic era, women played significant roles in society, including as scholars, business owners, and leaders. The teachings of Islam initially brought several rights to women, including property rights, inheritance, and consent in marriage.
Varied Historical Roles: The role of women in Islamic societies varied over time and across regions, influenced by cultural, political, and social factors.

Cultural and Regional Variations

Diversity Across the Islamic World: The experience of women in Islamic societies varies widely, influenced by local cultures, traditions, and interpretations of Islamic law.
Contemporary Variations: In contemporary Muslim-majority countries, women's roles range from active participation in public life and politics to more traditional and domestic roles.

Islamic Law and Women's Rights

Sharia and Women's Rights: Islamic law (Sharia) provides guidelines on women's rights and duties, but interpretations and applications vary significantly across different Islamic schools of thought and countries.
Impact on Personal Status Laws: Personal status laws, which govern matters such as marriage, divorce, and inheritance, often reflect Islamic principles and affect the legal rights of women in many Muslim-majority countries.

Modern Challenges and Reform Movements

Gender Equality Movements: There are ongoing movements and efforts within Islamic societies to address gender equality, challenge discriminatory practices, and reinterpret Islamic texts concerning women's rights.
Education and Employment: Increasing access to education and employment opportunities for women in many Muslim-majority countries reflects a shift towards greater gender equality.

Contemporary Debates and Perspectives

Balancing Tradition and Modernity: Contemporary debates in Islamic societies often revolve around balancing traditional interpretations of Islam with modern concepts of gender equality and women's rights.
Global and Local Influences: Globalization and international human rights discourse influence the discussion on women's roles in Islamic societies, interacting with local cultural and religious norms.

Section 2: Comparative Analysis of Women's Rights and Status

Exploring the Evolution and Status of Women's Rights in Islamic and Western Contexts

This section provides a comparative analysis of the evolution, current status, and challenges related to women's rights in Islamic and Western societies, highlighting the diversity of experiences and the impact of cultural, religious, and legal factors.

Women's Rights in Islamic Societies

Historical Advancements: In the early Islamic era, women were granted rights that were revolutionary for the time, including property ownership, inheritance rights, and marital consent.
Contemporary Variability: Today, the status and rights of women in Islamic societies vary widely, influenced by local cultural practices, the interpretation of Islamic law, and socioeconomic factors.

Women's Rights in Western Societies

Historical Struggles for Equality: In Western societies, women's rights have evolved significantly, particularly over the past two centuries, with movements for suffrage, equal pay, and reproductive rights.
Current Challenges: Despite advancements, challenges remain in Western societies, including gender pay gaps, underrepresentation in leadership positions, and issues related to reproductive rights.

Comparative Perspectives

Legal Frameworks: The legal frameworks governing women's rights differ, with Islamic societies often referencing Sharia in personal status laws, while Western societies rely on secular legal systems.
Cultural and Religious Influences: Both Islamic and Western contexts are influenced by cultural and religious norms, which shape attitudes towards women's roles and rights.

Shared Challenges and Achievements

Global Gender Equality Movements: Women in both Islamic and Western societies participate in global movements advocating for gender equality, challenging traditional norms and stereotypes.
Achievements in Education and Employment: Significant achievements have been made in areas like education and employment for women, although disparities and challenges persist.

Contemporary Debates and Dynamics

Interplay of Tradition and Modernity: Debates in both Islamic and Western societies often center around the interplay of traditional norms and modern concepts of gender equality.
Impact of Globalization: Globalization and international human rights discourse influence the discussion and evolution of women's rights, leading to both advancements and resistance based on local cultural and religious values.

Section 3: Influence of Islamic Feminine Ideals on Europe

Examining the Impact of Islamic Conceptions of Womanhood on European Cultural and Social Norms

This section explores how Islamic feminine ideals, as conveyed through cultural, intellectual, and trade exchanges, influenced perceptions and representations of women in Europe, particularly during the Middle Ages and the Renaissance.

Islamic Feminine Ideals

Cultural Portrayals: In Islamic societies, women were often portrayed in literature and art as figures of wisdom, virtue, and influence, reflecting a complex view of womanhood.
Role Models: Historical figures in Islamic history, such as scholars, poets, and rulers, served as role models, demonstrating the diverse roles women could occupy.

Transmission to Europe

Cultural and Intellectual Exchange: Through interactions during the Crusades, trade, and the translation of Arabic texts into European languages, European societies were exposed to Islamic conceptions of femininity.
Influence of Islamic Literature and Art: Islamic literature and art, with their depictions of women, provided alternative perspectives on womanhood that differed from existing European norms.

Impact on European Perceptions of Women

Renaissance Art and Literature: Islamic influences can be seen in European Renaissance art and literature, where portrayals of women began to reflect a mix of traditional European and Islamic traits.
Altered Social Norms: These exchanges contributed to gradually altering social norms and perceptions of women in Europe, influencing their roles and rights over time.

Examples of Influence

Courtly Love and Chivalry: The Islamic influence on the concepts of courtly love and chivalry in medieval Europe led to a more nuanced portrayal of women in European literature and social practices.
Feminine Archetypes: European literature and poetry began to incorporate feminine archetypes that mirrored those in Islamic texts, portraying women as more complex and multifaceted.

Contemporary Relevance and Legacy

Ongoing Influence in Cultural Expressions: The influence of Islamic feminine ideals on European culture has a lasting legacy, evident in various cultural expressions and literary works.
Recognition in Historical Studies: The role of Islamic culture in shaping European perceptions of women is increasingly recognized in historical and cultural studies, highlighting the interconnectedness of Eastern and Western traditions.

Section 4: Prominent Women Figures in Islamic History

Highlighting the Impact and Contributions of Notable Women in Islamic History

This section focuses on the lives and achievements of prominent women figures in Islamic history, illustrating their significant roles and contributions in various fields such as scholarship, politics, and the arts.

Influential Women in Early Islamic Society

Khadijah bint Khuwaylid: As the first wife of the Prophet Muhammad, Khadijah was a successful businesswoman and a key supporter of the early Islamic community.
Aisha bint Abi Bakr: A scholar, political figure, and wife of the Prophet Muhammad, Aisha was known for her intelligence and is credited with narrating many Hadiths, contributing greatly to Islamic jurisprudence.

Women Scholars and Educators

Fatima al-Fihri: Founder of the Al-Qarawiyyin Mosque and University in Fez, Morocco, in the 9th century, recognized as one of the world's oldest universities.
Rabia al-Adawiyya: A prominent Sufi mystic and poet, known for her devotional poetry and the emphasis on love in her spiritual teachings.

Women Rulers and Political Leaders

Shajarat al-Durr: An Egyptian sultana who played a crucial role in the politics of the Mamluk Sultanate in the 13th century.
Razia Sultana: The first and only female monarch of the Delhi Sultanate in India, known for her administrative skills and efforts to promote education.

Artistic and Literary Contributions

Wallada bint al-Mustakfi: A renowned poetess of Al-Andalus, known for her bold and eloquent poetry.
Lubna of Cordoba: A writer, librarian, and mathematician in the Caliphate of Cordoba, remembered for her intellect and contributions to the preservation of knowledge.

Contemporary Recognition and Legacy

Revisiting Historical Narratives: Recent scholarship has begun to revisit and highlight the roles of women in Islamic history, recognizing their contributions and challenging traditional narratives.
Inspiration for Modern Women: These historical figures continue to serve as inspirations for women in Muslim-majority countries and beyond, exemplifying women's capabilities and achievements in various domains.

Section 5: The Renaissance and Changing Roles of Women

Exploring the Transformation of Women's Roles and Status During the Renaissance in Europe

This section examines how the Renaissance period in Europe served as a pivotal time for the transformation of women's roles, marking significant changes in their societal status, educational opportunities, and cultural representations.

Background of the Renaissance

Period of Rebirth: The Renaissance, spanning roughly from the 14th to the 17th century, was a period of cultural, artistic, and intellectual "rebirth" in Europe, following the Middle Ages.
Humanism and Individualism: Central to the Renaissance was the rise of humanism and individualism, which began to challenge traditional roles and views of women in society.

Changing Roles of Women

Increased Educational Opportunities: The Renaissance saw a gradual increase in educational opportunities for women, particularly among the upper classes, leading to a rise in female literacy and learning.
Women in Art and Literature: Women became more prominently featured in art and literature, not only as subjects but also as creators and patrons.

Notable Women Figures of the Renaissance

Isabella d'Este: Known as the "First Lady of the Renaissance," Isabella d'Este was a patron of the arts and an influential political figure in Italy.
Christine de Pizan: A French-Italian medieval author, she is best known for her works advocating for women's education and challenging misogynistic views.

Societal Impact

Shift in Gender Dynamics: The Renaissance contributed to a shift in gender dynamics, with women starting to assert more agency and influence in various spheres of life.
Contrasting Experiences: Despite these advancements, the experiences of women during the Renaissance varied greatly, with many still confined to traditional roles and limited by societal norms.

Legacy and Modern Perspectives

Foundations for Future Movements: The Renaissance laid important foundations for future movements toward gender equality and women's rights.
Reevaluation of Women's Contributions: Modern scholarship continues to reevaluate and recognize the contributions of women during the Renaissance, highlighting their impact on art, politics, and society.

Section 6: Education and Literacy for Women

Evaluating the Progress and Challenges in Women's Education and Literacy Across Cultures

This section explores the evolution of education and literacy for women in both Islamic and Western contexts, discussing historical developments, modern achievements, and ongoing challenges.

Education and Literacy in Islamic Societies

Early Islamic Emphasis: Early Islamic societies placed a significant emphasis on education, and this included women. Women scholars and educators played important roles in Islamic history. Contemporary Variability: In modern Islamic societies, there is considerable variability in women's access to education, ranging from high literacy rates and strong female representation in universities to regions where educational opportunities for women are limited.

Progress in Western Societies

Historical Barriers: Historically in Western societies, women faced significant barriers to education, with limited access to formal schooling and higher education until the 19th and 20th centuries.
Modern Achievements: Significant strides have been made in recent decades, with women achieving high levels of literacy and outnumbering men in higher education enrollment in many Western countries.

Challenges and Socio-Cultural Factors

Socio-Cultural Barriers: In both Islamic and Western contexts, socio-cultural factors, including traditional gender roles and economic barriers, continue to impact women's educational opportunities.
Gender Gaps in Specific Fields: Despite overall progress, gender gaps remain in specific fields, particularly in STEM (Science, Technology, Engineering, and Mathematics) and leadership positions in academia.

Governmental and NGO Initiatives

Policy Interventions: Various governments and non-governmental organizations (NGOs) have implemented policies and programs to promote female education and literacy, particularly in regions where disparities are most significant.
International Efforts: International efforts, such as the United Nations' Sustainable Development Goals, emphasize the importance of gender equality in education.

Impact on Society and Development

Empowerment and Economic Growth: Educating women is widely recognized as key to empowering them and contributing to broader economic and social development.

Changing Norms: The increasing education and literacy levels of women are contributing to changing societal norms and expectations regarding gender roles and equality.

Section 7: Marriage, Family, and Social Norms

Analyzing the Role and Evolution of Marriage and Family Structures in Islamic and Western Cultures

This section examines the cultural, legal, and social aspects of marriage and family life for women in Islamic and Western societies, highlighting how these norms have evolved and continue to influence gender roles and family dynamics.

Marriage and Family in Islamic Societies

Islamic Legal Framework: In Islamic law, marriage is both a social contract and a religious covenant, with specific rights and duties outlined for both spouses.
Polygamy and Divorce: While polygamy is permitted in some Islamic societies under specific conditions, it is increasingly rare. Divorce rights, traditionally favoring men, have seen reforms in various Muslim-majority countries.
Family Structure and Dynamics: Family life in Islamic societies often emphasizes strong kinship bonds, with extended family playing a significant role in social and economic support.

Marriage and Family in Western Societies

Shift Towards Nuclear Family: Western societies have seen a shift towards nuclear family structures, with increasing emphasis on individual choice in marriage and child-rearing.
Legal and Social Changes: Legal reforms in Western countries have addressed issues such as marital rights, divorce, and domestic violence, reflecting changing social norms about gender equality.
Diverse Family Models: There is increasing recognition and acceptance of diverse family models, including single-parent households, blended families, and same-sex partnerships.

Comparative Cultural Perspectives

Cultural and Religious Influences: Both Islamic and Western societies are influenced by cultural and religious values that shape marriage and family norms, though the specific practices and expectations vary widely.
Evolving Gender Roles: In both contexts, gender roles within marriage and family are evolving, with women increasingly participating in public and professional life.

Contemporary Challenges and Debates

Balancing Tradition and Modernity: Debates in both Islamic and Western societies often center around balancing traditional norms with contemporary views on marriage, family, and gender roles.
Impact of Globalization and Migration: Globalization and migration are influencing and changing traditional marriage and family structures, leading to new challenges and adaptations.

Implications for Women's Status and Rights

Empowerment and Autonomy: Changes in marriage and family norms are closely linked to the broader empowerment and autonomy of women, impacting their roles both within the family and in society at large.
Legal and Policy Reforms: Ongoing legal and policy reforms in both Islamic and Western societies aim to address gender inequalities and protect the rights of women within marriage and family life.

Section 8: Women in Politics and Leadership

Examining the Evolution and Current Status of Women's Participation in Politics and Leadership Roles

This section explores the presence and role of women in political and leadership positions in both Islamic and Western societies, discussing historical progress, contemporary achievements, and ongoing challenges.

Women in Politics in Islamic Societies

Historical Precedents: Islamic history has examples of women in leadership roles, such as rulers and queens, although these instances were relatively rare.
Contemporary Scenario: In modern Islamic societies, the participation of women in politics varies widely. Some countries have seen significant progress, with women serving in parliament, ministerial positions, and other leadership roles, while in others, women's political participation remains limited.

Women in Western Political Arenas

Suffrage Movements: The struggle for women's suffrage in the 19th and 20th centuries was a pivotal moment in Western history, leading to women gaining the right to vote and hold office in many countries.

Modern Representation: While there has been significant progress, women in Western societies are still underrepresented in political leadership roles. Efforts continue to increase female representation and address systemic barriers.

Challenges and Barriers

Cultural and Social Norms: In both Islamic and Western contexts, cultural and social norms can pose barriers to women's full participation in politics and leadership.

Structural and Institutional Hurdles: Women face various structural and institutional hurdles, such as gender bias and lack of mentorship and support networks.

Impact of Women Leaders

Role Models and Policy Impact: Female leaders serve as role models and can influence policies, particularly those affecting women and families. Their presence in leadership positions challenges stereotypes and promotes gender equality.

Diversity in Decision-Making: The inclusion of women in political leadership contributes to diversity in decision-making processes and can lead to more inclusive and representative governance.

Efforts to Increase Participation

Quotas and Legal Reforms: Some countries have implemented quotas and legal reforms to increase women's political representation. These measures have had varying levels of success in different contexts.

Advocacy and Grassroots Movements: Advocacy groups and grassroots movements continue to play a crucial role in promoting women's political participation and leadership across the globe.

Section 9: Feminism and Women's Movements: A Historical Perspective

Tracing the Evolution and Impact of Feminist Movements Across Cultures

This section provides an overview of the historical development and impact of feminism and women's movements in both Islamic and Western contexts, highlighting their achievements, challenges, and the diversity of perspectives within these movements.

Feminism in Western Societies

Origins and Waves: Feminism in Western societies has evolved through several 'waves,' beginning with the first wave in the late 19th and early 20th centuries, focusing primarily on suffrage and legal rights.
Expansion of Issues: Subsequent waves expanded to include broader issues such as reproductive rights, sexuality, workplace equality, and combating systemic gender-based discrimination.

Women's Movements in Islamic Societies

Historical Context: Women's movements in Islamic societies have a complex history, intertwined with national, cultural, and religious identities.
Contemporary Feminism: Modern feminist movements in these societies often focus on issues like legal rights, education, and political participation, balancing calls for gender equality with cultural and religious values.

Diverse Feminist Ideologies

Variations in Feminist Thought: Feminist ideologies vary widely, with different movements emphasizing various aspects such as economic equality, social justice, or cultural and religious identity.
Intersectional Feminism: The concept of intersectional feminism, which considers overlapping identities and experiences, has gained prominence, acknowledging the diverse experiences of women based on race, class, ethnicity, religion, and other factors.

Achievements and Impact

Legislative and Social Changes: Feminist movements have been instrumental in achieving significant legislative and social changes, advancing women's rights, and challenging traditional gender norms.

Global Women's Movements: The globalization of women's movements has led to increased awareness and solidarity across borders, though challenges remain in addressing the unique needs and struggles of women in different cultural contexts.

Challenges and Criticism

Resistance and Backlash: Both in Islamic and Western societies, feminist movements have faced resistance and backlash, sometimes characterized as a threat to traditional values or national identity.
Internal Debates: Within feminism, debates continue over strategies, goals, and inclusivity, reflecting the movement's diversity and the complexity of addressing gender issues globally.

Section 10: Ongoing Challenges and Progress

Assessing the Current Landscape of Women's Rights and Gender Equality

This final section of Chapter 19 looks at the ongoing challenges and progress in the realm of women's rights and gender equality in both Islamic and Western societies, highlighting the continuing efforts and evolving dynamics in the struggle for gender parity.

Continued Struggles for Equality

Workplace and Economic Disparities: Women in many societies continue to face disparities in the workplace, including wage gaps, underrepresentation in leadership positions, and barriers to certain professions.
Social and Cultural Barriers: Social and cultural norms can still limit women's rights and opportunities, with issues like gender-based violence and restrictive practices persisting in various forms across cultures.

Advancements in Legal Rights

Legal Reforms: There have been significant legal reforms in several countries, aimed at improving women's rights in areas such as property ownership, marital rights, and protection against violence.
International Agreements and Protocols: Global agreements, such as the Convention on the Elimination of all Forms of Discrimination Against Women (CEDAW), have played a role in promoting gender equality and women's rights internationally.

Impact of Education and Advocacy

Role of Education: Increased access to education for women has been a key driver of change, empowering women to seek greater opportunities and challenge traditional roles.
Advocacy and Activism: Women's advocacy groups and activists continue to be at the forefront of pushing for change, raising awareness, and advocating for policy reforms.

Challenges in Political Representation

Political Participation: While there has been progress, women are still underrepresented in political leadership and decision-making roles in many countries.
Efforts to Increase Representation: Initiatives like gender quotas in politics and campaigns to encourage women's participation in governance are ongoing in various regions.

Cultural and Religious Dialogues

Balancing Tradition and Modernity: In many societies, there is a continuous dialogue between traditional cultural and religious values and modern concepts of gender equality and women's rights.
Intersecting Identities: The intersection of gender with other identities such as race, class, and religion adds layers of complexity to the pursuit of gender equality.

Future Outlook

Continued Advocacy and Reform: The future of gender equality and women's rights will likely involve continued advocacy, reform efforts, and societal shifts in attitudes.
Global and Local Dynamics: The interplay between global movements and local cultural contexts will continue to shape the path toward gender parity in different societies.

Chapter 20: Misconceptions and Legacy: Islam in Western Consciousness

Section 1: Common Misconceptions About Islam in the West

Addressing the Prevailing Misunderstandings and Stereotypes of Islam in Western Societies

This section explores the common misconceptions about Islam prevalent in Western societies, aiming to clarify misunderstandings and provide a more nuanced understanding of the Islamic faith and its followers.

Stereotypes and Generalizations

Monolithic Perception: A prevalent misconception in the West is viewing Islam and Muslims as a monolithic entity, ignoring the vast diversity in practices, beliefs, and cultures among Muslim communities worldwide.
Association with Extremism: There is a tendency to associate Islam with extremism and terrorism, overshadowing the peaceful practices and teachings of the majority of Muslims.

Misunderstanding Islamic Principles

Sharia Law: Sharia, or Islamic law, is often misunderstood in the West, with misconceptions about its nature, scope, and application in various Muslim-majority countries.
Jihad Misinterpreted: The concept of Jihad is frequently misinterpreted as a call for violent extremism, whereas in Islam, it primarily refers to a spiritual struggle against sin.

Cultural and Social Misconceptions

Women's Rights: There are widespread misconceptions about women's rights in Islam, often focusing solely on restrictive practices in certain countries rather than the diverse experiences of Muslim women globally.
Lifestyle and Practices: Common misunderstandings also exist regarding Muslim lifestyles, dietary habits, and social practices, often based on stereotypes rather than factual understanding.

Impact of Media and Politics

Media Representation: The portrayal of Islam in Western media often contributes to these misconceptions, emphasizing negative aspects and incidents while underrepresenting positive contributions and diversity.
Political Rhetoric: Political rhetoric in some Western countries can perpetuate misunderstandings and fear of Islam, leading to prejudice and discrimination.

Efforts to Address Misconceptions

Interfaith Dialogue: Interfaith and intercultural dialogues play a crucial role in addressing misconceptions, promoting mutual understanding and respect.
Educational Initiatives: Educational initiatives that provide accurate information about Islam and its teachings can help counter stereotypes and foster a more informed perspective.

Section 2: Historical Roots of Islamophobia

Exploring the Origins and Evolution of Islamophobia in Western Societies

This section delves into the historical development of Islamophobia in Western consciousness, tracing its origins and how historical events have shaped current perceptions and attitudes towards Islam and Muslims.

Early Encounters and Conflicts

Medieval Perceptions: Islamophobia can be traced back to the early medieval period, where the rise of Islam was seen as a threat to Christendom. This period was marked by religious conflicts, including the Crusades.
Stereotypes in Literature and Art: Medieval European literature and art often depicted Muslims in a negative light, reinforcing stereotypes and fears.

Colonialism and Imperialism

Orientalism: During the era of colonialism and imperialism, the Western portrayal of the 'Orient' was often characterized by exoticism and patronization, a concept Edward Said termed "Orientalism."
Cultural and Religious Superiority: The colonial mindset often positioned Western culture and Christianity as superior to Islamic culture and religion, reinforcing negative stereotypes and prejudices.

Modern Developments

20th Century Conflicts: Political and military conflicts in the 20th century, including the Arab-Israeli conflict and the Iranian Revolution, contributed to the resurgence of Islamophobia in the West.
Post-9/11 Era: The events of September 11, 2001, had a significant impact, leading to an increase in Islamophobia, often associating Islam and Muslims with terrorism.

Influence of Media and Politics

Media Portrayal: Western media has played a role in perpetuating Islamophobia, often highlighting extremist actions while neglecting the peaceful majority.
Political Exploitation: Some political leaders and groups in the West have exploited fears of Islam for political gain, further entrenching Islamophobic sentiments.

Challenges in Addressing Islamophobia

Lack of Understanding: A lack of understanding and knowledge about Islam among many in the West contributes to the persistence of Islamophobia.
Social and Institutional Biases: Islamophobia is not just a social issue but is also embedded in institutional policies and practices, making it a complex problem to address.

Efforts to Combat Islamophobia

Educational Initiatives: Educational programs aimed at providing accurate information about Islam and promoting cultural understanding are crucial in combating Islamophobia.
Interfaith and Intercultural Dialogue: Efforts to promote dialogue and interaction between Muslims and non-Muslims can help break down stereotypes and build mutual respect and understanding.

Section 3: The Crusades and Their Long-Term Impact on Perceptions

Assessing How the Crusades Shaped Western Views of Islam and Muslims

This section examines the long-term impact of the Crusades on Western perceptions of Islam and Muslims, exploring how these historical military campaigns have influenced contemporary attitudes and misunderstandings.

Historical Context of the Crusades

Religious and Military Campaigns: The Crusades, occurring from the late 11th to the late 13th centuries, were a series of religious and military campaigns launched by Christian Europe against Muslim powers in the Near East.
Motivations and Objectives: Initially aimed at reclaiming Jerusalem and the Holy Land, the Crusades were driven by a mix of religious fervor, political ambition, and economic interests.

Perceptions and Narratives

Demonization of Muslims: During the Crusades, Muslims were often portrayed as infidels and enemies of Christianity, creating a narrative of religious and cultural conflict.
Stereotypes in Literature and Art: Medieval European literature and art reflected and reinforced these negative perceptions, depicting Muslims in a stereotypical and often dehumanizing manner.

Legacy and Impact on Western Consciousness

Enduring Stereotypes: The stereotypes and perceptions formed during the Crusades have had a lasting impact, influencing Western views of Islam and Muslims for centuries.
Contribution to Islamophobia: The historical narrative of the Crusades contributed to the development and persistence of Islamophobia in Western societies.

Contemporary Relevance

Modern Interpretations: The Crusades are sometimes invoked in contemporary political and religious discourse, often to justify or criticize modern conflicts involving Muslim and Western countries.
Misunderstandings and Appropriations: Misunderstandings of the historical context and significance of the Crusades continue, with some groups appropriating crusader imagery and rhetoric for nationalist or anti-Islamic purposes.

Efforts to Recontextualize

Historical Reevaluation: Scholars and historians are reevaluating the Crusades, emphasizing their complex motivations and consequences, and the mutual influences between Christian and Muslim civilizations.

Educational Initiatives: Educational initiatives that present a more nuanced understanding of the Crusades can help dispel long-standing myths and foster a more informed perspective on historical Christian-Muslim relations.

Section 4: Orientalism and Representation in Literature and Art

Understanding the Influence of Orientalism on Western Perceptions of Islam

This section delves into the concept of Orientalism and its impact on Western representations of Islam and the Muslim world in literature, art, and academic discourse.

Concept of Orientalism

Definition and Origins: Orientalism, a term popularized by Edward Said in his 1978 book, refers to the Western depiction and study of Eastern societies, including the Islamic world, characterized by stereotypes and a colonialist viewpoint.
Perpetuation of Stereotypes: Orientalism often involves portraying Eastern cultures as exotic, backward, uncivilized, and at times, dangerous, reinforcing a binary view of the East versus the West.

Representation in Literature

Exoticism and Romanticism: Western literature has frequently depicted the Islamic world through a lens of exoticism and romanticism, focusing on themes like harems, deserts, and fantastical tales, while often ignoring the complex realities of these societies.
Impact of Literary Works: Works such as "The Arabian Nights" and writings by authors like Rudyard Kipling played a significant role in shaping Western perceptions of the Islamic world.

Orientalism in Art

Visual Depictions: In art, Orientalism led to a genre that depicted the East as a place of mystery, sensuality, and decadence. These depictions were more about Western fantasies than accurate representations of Eastern societies.
Influence on European Art Movements: Orientalist art influenced various European art movements and continues to be a subject of interest and critique in the art world.

Academic Study and Critique

Orientalist Scholarship: Academic studies on the East, under the Orientalist framework, often lacked genuine understanding and respect for the cultures being studied, leading to biased and one-sided interpretations.
Critique and Reassessment: Edward Said's critique of Orientalism sparked a reevaluation of how the Islamic world is studied and represented in Western academia, literature, and art, advocating for a more balanced and respectful approach.

Contemporary Implications

Influence on Modern Perceptions: The legacy of Orientalism continues to influence contemporary Western perceptions of Islam and the Muslim world.
Efforts to Counter Orientalist Narratives: There is an ongoing effort in media, academia, and art to counter Orientalist narratives and promote a more accurate and nuanced understanding of Islamic cultures.

Section 5: Impact of Colonialism on Islamic-Western Relations

Examining the Long-Term Effects of Colonialism on the Dynamics Between the Islamic World and the West

This section explores how Western colonialism has shaped perceptions and relations between Islamic societies and Western countries, influencing contemporary attitudes, geopolitical dynamics, and mutual understanding.

Colonial Expansion and Control

Era of Colonialism: From the 18th to the early 20th century, Western powers colonized large parts of the Islamic world, including regions in the Middle East, North Africa, and South Asia.
Political and Economic Domination: Colonial rule often involved political control, economic exploitation, and cultural imposition, leading to lasting impacts on the colonized societies.

Perceptions and Stereotypes

Orientalist Views: Colonialism reinforced Orientalist views, where Western perspectives on Islamic societies were often characterized by superiority and a lack of genuine understanding.

Resistance and Liberation Movements: The struggle against colonial rule in many Muslim-majority countries fostered a sense of national and religious identity, sometimes leading to anti-Western sentiments.

Post-Colonial Legacy

Continued Political and Economic Influence: Even after the end of formal colonialism, Western countries have continued to exert significant political and economic influence in former colonies. Cultural and Psychological Impact: The colonial era left a deep cultural and psychological impact on the societies it dominated, affecting their internal dynamics and external relations.

Contemporary Relations

Geopolitical Dynamics: The legacy of colonialism plays a role in contemporary geopolitical dynamics, influencing international relations and conflicts in regions with a history of Western colonization.
Migration and Multiculturalism: Post-colonial migration has led to significant Muslim populations in Western countries, contributing to multicultural societies but also sometimes leading to cultural tensions.

Efforts to Address Colonial Legacy

Revisiting History: There is an increasing effort to critically reassess and understand the history of colonialism and its impacts on both the Islamic world and Western societies.
Building Mutual Understanding: Initiatives aimed at building mutual understanding and respect between Western and Islamic societies are crucial for overcoming the long-term effects of colonialism.

Section 6: Islam in Contemporary Western Media and Education

Evaluating the Representation and Understanding of Islam in Modern Western Media and Educational Systems

This section explores the portrayal of Islam in contemporary Western media, the coverage of Islamic topics in Western education, and the implications of these representations for mutual understanding between Islamic and Western societies.

Portrayal in Western Media

Stereotypical and One-Dimensional: The portrayal of Islam and Muslims in Western media is often criticized for being stereotypical, focusing predominantly on negative aspects such as extremism and terrorism.
Lack of Context and Nuance: Media coverage frequently lacks context and nuance, leading to a skewed understanding of Islam and its diverse practices and beliefs.

Coverage in Western Education

Educational Curriculum: The way Islam is taught in Western educational systems varies, with some curricula offering a comprehensive and balanced view, while others provide limited or biased perspectives.
Importance of Accurate Education: Accurate and inclusive education about Islam is crucial for fostering understanding and countering misconceptions among young generations in the West.

Impact of Media and Education on Perceptions

Influencing Public Opinion: Media and educational portrayals significantly influence public opinion and attitudes toward Islam and Muslims in Western societies.
Contributing to Islamophobia: Misrepresentations and lack of understanding can contribute to Islamophobia, affecting the experiences of Muslim communities in the West.

Efforts to Improve Representation

Media Initiatives: There are initiatives within Western media to improve the representation of Islam, including more nuanced reporting and including Muslim voices in media narratives.
Educational Reforms: Efforts are being made to reform educational curricula to provide a more accurate and comprehensive understanding of Islamic history, culture, and beliefs.

Role of Muslim Communities

Active Engagement: Muslim communities in the West are actively engaging in media and education, seeking to present a more authentic and diverse picture of Islam.
Cultural and Interfaith Programs: Cultural programs and interfaith dialogue initiatives help bridge gaps in understanding and challenge prevailing stereotypes.

Section 7: Interfaith Dialogue and Understanding

Exploring the Role and Impact of Interfaith Dialogue in Bridging the Gap Between Islamic and Western Societies

This section delves into the importance of interfaith dialogue as a tool for fostering mutual understanding and respect between Islamic and Western societies, examining successful initiatives and the challenges they face.

Need for Interfaith Dialogue

Breaking Down Barriers: Interfaith dialogue is crucial for breaking down barriers of misunderstanding and mistrust between Islamic and Western communities.
Addressing Misconceptions: Such dialogues provide a platform to address common misconceptions about Islam in the West and clarify religious beliefs and practices.

Forms of Interfaith Initiatives

Organizational Efforts: Various religious and secular organizations facilitate interfaith dialogues, conferences, and educational programs to promote understanding.
Grassroots Movements: Grassroots interfaith efforts, often led by community groups, play a significant role in fostering local-level engagement and empathy.

Successful Interfaith Dialogue Models

Shared Values and Common Ground: Effective interfaith dialogues often focus on finding shared values and common ground, such as a commitment to peace, justice, and community service.
Personal Stories and Experiences: Sharing personal stories and experiences can humanize communities and break down stereotypes.

Challenges and Limitations

Prejudices and Biases: Overcoming deeply ingrained prejudices and biases on both sides can be a significant challenge in interfaith dialogues.
Political and Social Contexts: The broader political and social context, including ongoing conflicts and geopolitical tensions, can impact the effectiveness of interfaith efforts.

Impact on Societal Attitudes

Building Trust and Cooperation: Successful interfaith dialogues can build trust and cooperation between communities, leading to more harmonious societal relationships.
Influence on Policy and Media: These dialogues can also influence broader policy and media narratives by demonstrating the benefits of religious and cultural pluralism.

Future Prospects

Expanding Reach and Inclusivity: There is potential for expanding the reach and inclusivity of interfaith dialogues, involving more diverse groups and perspectives.
Sustained Engagement: Ongoing and sustained engagement is key to the long-term success of interfaith understanding and cooperation.

Section 8: Islam's Contribution to Modern Science and Technology

Acknowledging the Historical and Contemporary Contributions of Islamic Scholars to Science and Technology

This section highlights the significant contributions made by Islamic scholars to the fields of science and technology, both historically and in contemporary times, and their impact on Western scientific advancements.

Historical Contributions

Golden Age of Islamic Science: During the Islamic Golden Age (8th to 14th centuries), Muslim scholars made groundbreaking advancements in various fields, including mathematics, astronomy, medicine, and engineering.
Key Figures and Inventions: Notable figures such as Al-Khwarizmi, Ibn Al-Haytham, and Avicenna contributed foundational knowledge and inventions that influenced subsequent scientific developments in Europe and beyond.

Mathematics and Astronomy

Algebra and Algorithms: Al-Khwarizmi's work in mathematics laid the foundation for algebra and introduced algorithms, profoundly impacting mathematical sciences.
Astronomical Observations: Islamic astronomers made significant contributions to the understanding of celestial movements, star charts, and the development of astronomical instruments.

Medicine and Pharmacology

Medical Texts and Practices: Islamic medical texts, particularly Avicenna's "The Canon of Medicine," were used in European universities for centuries and introduced innovative practices in surgery, diagnostics, and pharmacology.

Engineering and Technology

Architectural and Engineering Marvels: Islamic architecture and engineering, including sophisticated irrigation systems and architectural techniques, influenced European designs.
Innovations in Optics: Ibn Al-Haytham's work on optics laid the groundwork for the development of modern optics and the scientific method.

Contemporary Contributions

Modern Scientists and Innovators: Contemporary Muslim scientists and technologists continue to contribute to various fields, including information technology, medicine, and environmental science.
Global Collaboration: Many Muslim scientists collaborate with international teams, contributing to global scientific advancements and technological innovations.

Recognition and Legacy

Integrating into Educational Curricula: Efforts are being made to integrate these contributions into educational curricula, providing a more comprehensive understanding of the history of science and technology.
Bridging Cultural Divides: Acknowledging the contributions of Islamic scholars to science and technology can help bridge cultural divides and challenge stereotypes about the Islamic world.

Section 9: Contemporary Political Dynamics and Islamic Influence

Exploring the Interplay Between Islamic Thought and Modern Western Political Ideas

This section examines how Islamic thought has influenced contemporary political dynamics in the West, looking at both the historical interplay and modern intersections of Islamic and Western political ideologies.

Historical Interactions

Influence on Political Thought: Throughout history, Islamic political philosophy and governance models have interacted with Western political thought, influencing figures such as Thomas Aquinas and influencing the development of concepts such as natural law.
Exchange During the Golden Age: The exchange of ideas during the Islamic Golden Age had a significant impact on the development of political ideas during the European Renaissance and Enlightenment.

Contemporary Context

Muslim Populations in Western Democracies: The presence of significant Muslim populations in Western democracies has led to the incorporation of Islamic perspectives in political discourse and policymaking.
Integration of Islamic Values: In some Western countries, there has been an effort to integrate Islamic values and perspectives into broader societal frameworks, balancing cultural diversity with national political identities.

Political Movements and Ideologies

Islamic Political Movements: Islamic political movements, both moderate and radical, have had a varying impact on Western politics, influencing foreign policy, security measures, and intercultural relations.
Influence on Social Justice Movements: Islamic principles of social justice have found resonance in various global social justice movements, contributing to discussions on economic inequality, human rights, and environmental issues.

Challenges and Debates

Misunderstandings and Fear: Misunderstandings and fear of Islamic political ideologies can lead to tensions and conflicts, both within nations and internationally.
Balancing Religious and Secular Values: Western societies often grapple with balancing religious values, including Islamic ones, with secular governance and legal systems.

Prospects for Future Engagement

Dialogue and Policy Engagement: Encouraging dialogue and policy engagement between Islamic thinkers and Western policymakers can foster mutual understanding and better incorporation of diverse perspectives in political processes.

Educational Initiatives: Educational initiatives aimed at understanding Islamic political thought and its historical contributions can play a significant role in dispelling misconceptions and promoting informed discussions.

Section 10: Reassessing the Islamic Legacy in Western Civilization

Reflecting on the Historical and Cultural Contributions of Islam to Western Society

This final section of Chapter 20 explores the process of reassessing and recognizing the significant contributions of Islamic civilization to various aspects of Western culture, history, and knowledge.

Influence on Western Intellectual Traditions

Foundations of Knowledge: Islamic scholars and thinkers played a crucial role in preserving and expanding the knowledge of ancient civilizations, including Greek and Roman works, which later became foundational to Western intellectual traditions during the Renaissance.
Advancements in Science and Philosophy: The Islamic Golden Age saw significant advancements in areas like mathematics, astronomy, medicine, and philosophy, which were transmitted to Europe and influenced Western scientific and philosophical developments.

Cultural and Artistic Exchange

Architectural Influences: Islamic architectural styles and innovations had a notable influence on European architecture, visible in various historical buildings and urban designs.
Artistic and Literary Impact: The interaction between Islamic and Western artists and writers over centuries has enriched Western art and literature, introducing new themes, styles, and techniques.

Modern Recognition and Integration

Educational Curricula: There is a growing movement to include the contributions of Islamic civilization more comprehensively in Western educational curricula, providing a more balanced and inclusive historical perspective.
Cultural Appreciation: In contemporary Western societies, there is increasing appreciation and recognition of Islamic art, culture, and philosophy, both in academic circles and popular culture.

Challenges in Reassessment

Overcoming Stereotypes: Efforts to reassess the Islamic legacy in Western civilization often face challenges due to longstanding stereotypes and misconceptions about Islam.
Political and Social Contexts: The current political and social climate can impact how Islamic contributions are perceived and valued in Western societies.

Future Directions

Continued Scholarship and Dialogue: Ongoing scholarship and intercultural dialogue are crucial for deepening understanding and appreciation of the Islamic legacy in Western civilization.
Building Bridges: Recognizing and celebrating the contributions of Islamic civilization can serve as a bridge for greater understanding and cooperation between Western and Islamic societies.

Appendices

Appendix A: Timeline of Key Events

From the Crusades to the European Renaissance: Significant Historical Events
1096-1099: First Crusade – Capture of Jerusalem by Christian forces.
1126: Birth of Averroes (Ibn Rushd), influential Islamic philosopher.
1138: Birth of Maimonides, a prominent Jewish philosopher and scholar.
1147-1149: Second Crusade – launched by European powers.
1187: Saladin's capture of Jerusalem, leading to the Third Crusade.
1189-1192: Third Crusade – led by Richard the Lionheart.
1204: Fourth Crusade – Sack of Constantinople.
1215: Magna Carta signed in England, foundational to Western legal tradition.
1220: Birth of Thomas Aquinas, influential Christian theologian.
1248-1254: Seventh Crusade – led by Louis IX of France.
1258: Mongol siege and sack of Baghdad, end of the Abbasid Caliphate.
1270: Eighth Crusade – led by Louis IX.
1291: Fall of Acre, end of Crusader presence in the Holy Land.
1309-1377: Avignon Papacy, period of Papal residence outside Rome.
1325-1354: Travels of Ibn Battuta through Islamic world and beyond.
1347-1351: Black Death (Bubonic Plague) in Europe.
1380: Completion of Chaucer's "The Canterbury Tales."

1397: Establishment of the Medici Bank in Florence.

1401: Conquest of Damascus by Timur (Tamerlane).

1439: Fall of the Byzantine Empire, rise of the Ottoman Empire.

1453: Ottoman conquest of Constantinople.

1456: Invention of the Gutenberg Printing Press.

1478: Spanish Inquisition established.

1480: Ivan III of Russia stops paying tribute to the Golden Horde.

1482: First European slave-trading post established in West Africa.

1492: Columbus' first voyage to the Americas.

1492: Completion of the Reconquista and expulsion of Jews from Spain.

1494: Treaty of Tordesillas between Spain and Portugal.

1497-1498: Vasco da Gama's voyage to India.

1498: Execution of Girolamo Savonarola in Florence.

1500: Discovery of Brazil by Portuguese explorer Pedro Álvares Cabral.

1501: Safavid dynasty established in Persia (Iran).

1502: First African slaves brought to the Americas.

1517: Martin Luther's Ninety-Five Theses, start of the Protestant Reformation.

1520-1566: Reign of Suleiman the Magnificent, Ottoman Sultan.

1521: Fall of the Aztec Empire to Spanish conquistadors.

1522: Magellan-Elcano expedition completes first circumnavigation of the globe.

1529: First Siege of Vienna by the Ottomans.

1533: Henry VIII declares himself head of the Church of England.

1543: Copernicus publishes his heliocentric theory.

1555: Peace of Augsburg, allowing for Lutheran and Catholic states within the Holy Roman Empire.

1565: Foundation of the Spanish colony of the Philippines.

1571: Battle of Lepanto, naval clash between Ottoman Empire and Holy League.

1588: Defeat of the Spanish Armada by the English navy.

1596: Birth of René Descartes, French philosopher and mathematician.

1600: Execution of Giordano Bruno by the Roman Inquisition.

1602: Dutch East India Company established.

1605: Gunpowder Plot in England.

1607: Foundation of Jamestown, the first permanent English settlement in the Americas.

1611: Publication of the King James Bible.

1618-1648: Thirty Years' War in Europe.

1620: Mayflower Pilgrims arrive in North America.

1632: Birth of Isaac Newton, English mathematician and scientist.

1637: Rene Descartes' publication of "Discourse on the Method."

1644: End of the Ming Dynasty and rise of the Qing Dynasty in China.

1648: Peace of Westphalia, end of the Thirty Years' War.

1653: Oliver Cromwell becomes Lord Protector of England, Scotland, and Ireland.

1665: Great Plague of London.

1683: Second Siege of Vienna, marking the Ottoman Empire's westernmost advance.

1701: Act of Settlement passed in England, affecting the succession of the British throne.

1707: Act of Union unites England and Scotland into Great Britain.

1712: Thomas Newcomen invents the first practical steam engine.

1721: Peter the Great declared Emperor of Russia, modernizing the Russian Empire.

1732: First performance of George Frideric Handel's "Water Music" in London.

1751-1772: Publication of Diderot's Encyclopédie, a symbol of the Enlightenment.

1756-1763: Seven Years' War, a global conflict involving most European powers.

1769: James Watt patents his steam engine, a key moment in the Industrial Revolution.

1776: American Declaration of Independence.

1789: French Revolution begins with the storming of the Bastille.

1796: Edward Jenner's smallpox vaccine, the world's first vaccine.

1798: Napoleon's Egyptian campaign, a significant cultural and military encounter between the Islamic world and Europe.

1804: Haiti declares independence from France, the first successful slave revolt.

1805: Battle of Trafalgar, a naval battle during the Napoleonic Wars.

1815: Battle of Waterloo, Napoleon's final defeat.

1820: Missouri Compromise in the United States over slavery.

1830: July Revolution in France, leading to the establishment of the July Monarchy.

1839-1842: First Opium War between Britain and China.

1848: Publication of the Communist Manifesto by Karl Marx and Friedrich Engels.

1854-1856: Crimean War, a conflict involving Russia, the Ottoman Empire, France, and Britain.

1861-1865: American Civil War.

1863: Emancipation Proclamation issued by Abraham Lincoln.

1869: Completion of the Suez Canal, connecting the Mediterranean and Red Seas.

1871: Unification of Germany under Prussian leadership.

1885: Berlin Conference, division of Africa among European powers.

1893: New Zealand becomes the first country to grant women the right to vote.

1898: United States victory in the Spanish-American War, marking its emergence as a global power.

1903: Wright brothers' first powered flight.

1914-1918: World War I.

1917: Russian Revolution leads to the creation of the Soviet Union.

1919: Treaty of Versailles, officially ending World War I.

1924: Abolition of the Ottoman Caliphate.

1928: Discovery of penicillin by Alexander Fleming.

1929: Stock Market Crash, beginning of the Great Depression.

1933: Rise of Adolf Hitler and the Nazi Party in Germany.

1939-1945: World War II.

1945: United Nations founded.

1947: Partition of India and Pakistan.

1948: Establishment of the state of Israel.

1948: Creation of the State of Israel, followed by the Arab-Israeli War.

1949: Formation of NATO (North Atlantic Treaty Organization).

1949: Chinese Communist Revolution, establishment of the People's Republic of China.

1950-1953: Korean War.

1952: Egyptian Revolution and the end of the monarchy.

1953: Iranian coup d'état orchestrated by the CIA and MI6.

1954: Algerian War of Independence begins.

1955: Bandung Conference, a major milestone in the Non-Aligned Movement.

1956: Suez Crisis.

1957: Launch of Sputnik 1, beginning of the Space Race.

1958: Creation of the European Economic Community (EEC).

1959: Cuban Revolution.

1960: Formation of OPEC (Organization of Petroleum Exporting Countries).

1961: Berlin Wall construction begins.

1962: Cuban Missile Crisis.

1963: Assassination of U.S. President John F. Kennedy.

1964: Civil Rights Act passed in the United States.

1966: Cultural Revolution begins in China.

1967: Six-Day War in the Middle East.

1968: Prague Spring and subsequent Soviet invasion of Czechoslovakia.

1969: Apollo 11 Moon Landing.

1971: Bangladesh Liberation War.

1973: Yom Kippur War.

1974: Turkish invasion of Cyprus.

1975-1990: Lebanese Civil War.

1978-1979: Iranian Revolution.

1979: Soviet-Afghan War begins.

1980-1988: Iran-Iraq War.

1981: Assassination of Egyptian President Anwar Sadat.

1982: Falklands War between Argentina and the United Kingdom.

1983: United States invasion of Grenada.

1987: First Intifada begins in the Palestinian Territories.

1989: Fall of the Berlin Wall.

1990-1991: Persian Gulf War.

1991: Dissolution of the Soviet Union.

1992-1995: Bosnian War.

1993: Oslo Accords signed between Israel and the Palestine Liberation Organization.

1994: Rwandan Genocide.

1995: Dayton Agreement ends the Bosnian War.

1998: Good Friday Agreement in Northern Ireland.

1999: NATO bombing of Yugoslavia during the Kosovo War.

2001: September 11 attacks in the United States, leading to the War on Terror.

2001: U.S. invasion of Afghanistan.

2003: U.S. invasion of Iraq.

2004: Madrid train bombings.

2005: July London bombings.

2007: Global Financial Crisis begins.

2010: Arab Spring begins.

2011: Syrian Civil War begins.

2011: U.S. Navy SEALs kill Osama bin Laden in Pakistan.

2014: Rise of ISIS and the Caliphate declaration.

2014: Russia's annexation of Crimea.

2015: Iran Nuclear Deal signed.

2015: Syrian refugee crisis peaks.

2016: Brexit referendum in the United Kingdom.

2016: Election of Donald Trump as U.S. President.

2017: Rohingya refugee crisis in Myanmar.

2018: U.S. embassy moves to Jerusalem, sparking protests.

2019: Hong Kong protests against extradition bill.

2020: COVID-19 pandemic begins, leading to global health and economic crisis.

2020: U.S.-Taliban peace deal signed.

2021: U.S. withdrawal from Afghanistan and Taliban takeover.

2021: Israel-Hamas conflict escalates in May.

2022: Russian invasion of Ukraine.

Appendix B: Biographies of Key Figures

Short Biographies of Influential Figures in Islamic, European, and American Contexts

Saladin (1137-1193): Kurdish Muslim leader who recaptured Jerusalem during the Crusades and is renowned for his leadership and chivalry.

Thomas Aquinas (1225-1274): Influential Christian theologian and philosopher in the Catholic Church, known for synthesizing Aristotelian philosophy with Christian doctrine.

Marco Polo (1254-1324): Venetian merchant and explorer who traveled through Asia along the Silk Road and provided detailed accounts of his experiences.

Ibn Khaldun (1332-1406): A pioneering historian and philosopher from North Africa, known for his work on the philosophy of history and social sciences.

Joan of Arc (1412-1431): French heroine and military leader during the Hundred Years' War, later canonized as a saint.

Christopher Columbus (1451-1506): Italian explorer funded by Spain, whose transatlantic voyages opened the way for European exploration and conquest of the Americas.

Martin Luther (1483-1546): German professor of theology, composer, priest, and monk who was a seminal figure in the Protestant Reformation.

Suleiman the Magnificent (1494-1566): The longest-reigning Sultan of the Ottoman Empire, under whose rule the empire reached its zenith.

Galileo Galilei (1564-1642): Italian astronomer, physicist, and engineer, known for his contributions to the scientific revolution, particularly his support for Copernican heliocentrism.

Isaac Newton (1643-1727): English mathematician, physicist, astronomer, and author, widely recognized as one of the greatest mathematicians and physicists in history.

Napoleon Bonaparte (1769-1821): French military leader and emperor who rose to prominence during the French Revolution and led several successful campaigns during the Napoleonic Wars.

Simón Bolívar (1783-1830): Venezuelan military and political leader who played a key role in Latin America's successful struggle for independence from the Spanish Empire.

Florence Nightingale (1820-1910): English social reformer and statistician, and the founder of modern nursing.

Mahatma Gandhi (1869-1948): Leader of the Indian independence movement against British rule, employing nonviolent civil disobedience.

Albert Einstein (1879-1955): Theoretical physicist who developed the theory of relativity, one of the two pillars of modern physics.

Winston Churchill (1874-1965): British politician, army officer, and writer who was Prime Minister of the United Kingdom during World War II.

Nelson Mandela (1918-2013): South African anti-apartheid revolutionary, political leader, and philanthropist who served as President of South Africa.

Malcolm X (1925-1965): American Muslim minister and human rights activist who was a prominent figure in the civil rights movement.

Martin Luther King Jr. (1929-1968): American Baptist minister and activist who became the most visible spokesperson and leader in the civil rights movement.

Stephen Hawking (1942-2018): English theoretical physicist, cosmologist, and author, known for his work on black holes and relativity.

(This appendix provides brief biographies of key historical figures mentioned in the book. Further detailed biographies and their contributions can be found in the main text and referenced materials.)

Appendix C: Maps and Geographic Overviews

Historical Maps and Geographic Elements Pertinent to the Book's Narratives

Map of the Crusader States: A detailed map showing the Crusader states established in the Levant, their borders, and key battle sites during the Crusades.

Ottoman Empire at its Zenith: A map depicting the territorial extent of the Ottoman Empire at its peak under Suleiman the Magnificent, including its control in Europe, Asia, and Africa.

Trade Routes in the Medieval Islamic World: A map illustrating the major trade routes, including the Silk Road and maritime routes, that were under Islamic influence or control.

Voyages of Exploration: Maps showing the routes taken by explorers like Christopher Columbus, Vasco da Gama, and Ferdinand Magellan, highlighting the European exploration of the Americas and the route to Asia.

The Spread of the Black Death: A map depicting the spread of the Black Death (Bubonic Plague) across Europe and parts of Asia in the 14th century.

Reconquista and Spanish Empire: A map showing the Iberian Peninsula during the Reconquista and the subsequent establishment of the Spanish Empire, including its American colonies.

Europe During the Reformation: A map illustrating the religious divisions in Europe during the Reformation, showing Protestant and Catholic regions.

The Islamic Golden Age: A map Indicating the major centers of learning, cultural and scientific development during the Islamic Golden Age.

European Colonialism in the Islamic World: Maps showcasing European colonial territories in the Islamic world, highlighting regions under British, French, Dutch, and other European powers.

Major Battles and Campaigns of World War I and II: Maps showing the key battles and campaigns in the Middle East and North Africa during both World Wars.

The Middle East Post-World War II: A map detailing the new national borders, state formations, and conflict zones in the Middle East after World War II, including the creation of Israel and subsequent wars.

The Cold War in the Middle East: A geopolitical map illustrating the influence of the USA and USSR in the Middle East during the Cold War era.

Modern Trade and Oil Routes: A contemporary map showing major oil-producing regions in the Middle East and significant trade routes, including oil shipment paths.

Global Muslim Population Distribution: A map indicating the distribution of the Muslim population globally, highlighting regions with significant Muslim communities.

(These maps above provide geographical context to the historical and contemporary narratives discussed in the book, allowing readers to search for them online and visualize the spatial dynamics of key events and trends.)

Appendix D: Comparative Study of Religious Texts

Selected Excerpts from the Quran, Bible, and Torah

This appendix presents selected excerpts from the Quran, Bible, and Torah, providing a comparative perspective on key themes and teachings that have influenced the events and ideologies discussed in the book.

1. The Concept of Monotheism

Quran: "Say, 'He is Allah, [who is] One.'" (Surah Al-Ikhlas, 112:1)
Bible: "Hear, O Israel: The Lord our God, the Lord is one." (Deuteronomy 6:4)
Torah: "Hear, O Israel: The Lord our God, the Lord is one." (Deuteronomy 6:4)

2. Justice and Equality

Quran: "O you who have believed, be persistently standing firm in justice, witnesses for Allah, even if it be against yourselves or parents and relatives." (Surah An-Nisa, 4:135)
Bible: "Learn to do right; seek justice. Defend the oppressed. Take up the cause of the fatherless; plead the case of the widow." (Isaiah 1:17)
Torah: "Justice, justice shall you pursue, that you may live, and inherit the land which the Lord your God gives you." (Deuteronomy 16:20)

3. Compassion and Mercy

Quran: "And We have not sent you, [O Muhammad], except as a mercy to the worlds." (Surah Al-Anbiya, 21:107)
Bible: "Blessed are the merciful, for they will be shown mercy." (Matthew 5:7)
Torah: "He has told you, O man, what is good; and what does the Lord require of you but to do justice, and to love kindness, and to walk humbly with your God?" (Micah 6:8)

4. Stewardship of the Earth

Quran: "It is He who has made you successors upon the earth." (Surah Fatir, 35:39)
Bible: "The earth is the Lord's, and everything in it, the world, and all who live in it." (Psalm 24:1)
Torah: "The land shall not be sold in perpetuity, for the land is Mine; for you are strangers and sojourners with Me." (Leviticus 25:23)

5. The Value of Knowledge

Quran: "Read in the name of your Lord who created." (Surah Al-Alaq, 96:1)
Bible: "An intelligent heart acquires knowledge, and the ear of the wise seeks knowledge." (Proverbs 18:15)
Torah: "For the Lord gives wisdom; from his mouth come knowledge and understanding." (Proverbs 2:6)

(These excerpts provide a glimpse into the commonalities and unique aspects of the teachings in the Quran, Bible, and Torah. They are intended to offer a comparative perspective and encourage further exploration and understanding of these religious texts.)

Appendix E: Glossary of Terms

Definitions of Specific Terms, Phrases, and Concepts

This glossary explains specific terms, phrases, and concepts related to Islamic, Christian, and Jewish cultures and histories, as well as general historical and political terminology used in the book.

Caliphate: An Islamic state led by a caliph, who is considered a political and religious successor to the Prophet Muhammad.

Crusades: Military campaigns sanctioned by the Latin Church during the medieval period, aimed primarily at reclaiming Jerusalem and the Holy Land from Muslim rule.

Fatwa: A ruling on a point of Islamic law given by a recognized authority.

Hijra: The migration of the Prophet Muhammad and his followers from Mecca to Medina in 622 AD, marking the start of the Islamic calendar.

Jihad: An Arabic word meaning "struggle" or "striving," often used to describe a spiritual, moral, or physical struggle for Islam.

Madrasa: An educational institution in the Islamic world, traditionally focused on teaching Islamic subjects.

Reconquista: The period in the history of the Iberian Peninsula of about 780 years between the Umayyad conquest of Hispania in 711 and the fall of the Nasrid kingdom of Granada to the expanding Christian kingdoms in 1492.

Sharia: Islamic law derived from the Quran and the Hadiths.

Sufism: Mystical Islamic belief and practice in which Muslims seek to find the truth of divine love and knowledge through direct personal experience of God.

Sunni and Shia: The two major denominations of Islam. The split originated from a dispute over who should succeed the Prophet Muhammad as leader of the Islamic community after his death.

Zionism: A movement for the re-establishment and the development and protection of a Jewish nation in what is now Israel.

Orientalism: A term used to describe the representation of the Eastern world in a stereotyped way that is regarded as embodying a colonialist attitude.

Renaissance: A period in European history, covering the span between the 14th and 17th centuries, marking the transition from the Middle Ages to Modernity.

Humanism: A Renaissance cultural movement that turned away from medieval scholasticism and revived interest in ancient Greek and Roman thought.

Enlightenment: An intellectual and philosophical movement that dominated the world of ideas in Europe during the 17th and 18th centuries, centering on the ideas of reason, liberty, and the scientific method.

Appendix F: Annotated Bibliography

Detailed Bibliography of Sources and Further Readings

This annotated bibliography lists books, academic articles, and primary historical documents, offering readers more in-depth information on the topics covered in the book.

"The Crusades Through Arab Eyes" by Amin Maalouf

Synopsis: Maalouf offers a perspective on the Crusades from the Arab viewpoint, challenging traditional Western narratives.
Importance: Provides a nuanced understanding of the Crusades' impact on the Islamic world.

"A History of Islamic Societies" by Ira M. Lapidus

Synopsis: An extensive overview of Islamic societies and cultures from their beginnings to the present.
Importance: Useful for understanding the broad historical context of Islamic civilizations.

"The Ornament of the World" by Maria Rosa Menocal

Synopsis: Explores the rich cultural and religious coexistence in medieval Spain under Muslim rule.
Importance: Highlights a period of fruitful interaction between Muslim, Christian, and Jewish cultures.

"The Muqaddimah" by Ibn Khaldun

Synopsis: A 14th-century historical work that lays the foundations for several fields of knowledge, including sociology and historiography.
Importance: Offers insights into medieval Islamic thought and its influence on later intellectual developments.

"The Influence of Islam on Medieval Europe" by W. Montgomery Watt

Synopsis: Discusses the various ways in which Islamic civilization influenced medieval Europe.
Importance: Helps understand the transfer of knowledge and culture from the Islamic world to Europe.

"Destiny Disrupted: A History of the World Through Islamic Eyes" by Tamim Ansary

Synopsis: Presents world history from a perspective centered on the Islamic world.
Importance: Offers an alternative to Eurocentric historical narratives.

"Islam and the West" by Bernard Lewis

Synopsis: Explores the historical interactions between Islamic civilizations and Western societies.
Importance: A key text for understanding the complex relationship between these two cultures.

"The Arab Uprisings: What Everyone Needs to Know" by James L. Gelvin

Synopsis: Provides an accessible overview of the causes and consequences of the Arab Spring.
Importance: Essential for understanding recent political developments in the Islamic world.

"Lost Islamic History: Reclaiming Muslim Civilization from the Past" by Firas Alkhateeb

Synopsis: A concise history of the rise and fall of Islamic civilizations over the centuries.
Importance: Helps contextualize modern issues in the Islamic world within their historical backdrop.

Primary Sources Collection

A collection of translated primary sources, including excerpts from the Quran, Hadith, medieval texts on the Crusades, and historical treaties.
Importance: Offers direct insights into historical events and ideologies from original texts.

(This bibliography provides a starting point for readers interested in further exploring the rich and complex history of Islamic, European, and American interactions. Each source is selected for its relevance and contribution to the understanding of the topics discussed in the book.)

Appendix G: Collection of Artistic Works

Reproductions of Art, Architecture, and Music

This appendix showcases a collection of artistic works that illustrate the cultural exchanges and influences between Islamic and Western civilizations, as discussed throughout the book.

1. Islamic Art

Examples: Illuminated manuscripts, calligraphy, ceramics, and architectural elements like tilework from Islamic palaces and mosques.
Significance: Demonstrates the intricacy and beauty of Islamic artistic traditions and their influence on European art.

2. European Art Influenced by the Islamic World

Examples: Paintings and architecture from the Renaissance and later periods that show Orientalist themes or Islamic architectural influences.
Significance: Highlights how Islamic art and architecture captivated and influenced European artists and architects.

3. Music and Poetry

Examples: Selections of Andalusian music, which blends Islamic, Christian, and Jewish traditions, and poetry from figures like Rumi, Hafez, and Dante Alighieri.
Significance: Showcases the rich intercultural exchange in the realm of music and literature.

4. Architectural Works

Examples: Photographs and diagrams of significant Islamic architectural sites like the Alhambra, the Great Mosque of Córdoba, and European buildings with Islamic influences.
Significance: Provides visual examples of how Islamic architecture has been both distinct and influential.

5. Ottoman Miniature Paintings

Examples: Miniatures depicting various aspects of Ottoman life, culture, and history.
Significance: Offers insights into the artistic expression and historical perspectives within the Ottoman Empire.

6. Modern Artistic Expressions

Examples: Contemporary artworks by artists from Islamic backgrounds or inspired by Islamic art, showcasing how these traditions continue to influence modern art.
Significance: Demonstrates the ongoing dialogue and fusion between Islamic and Western artistic traditions.

(This collection of artistic works provides visual and auditory complements to the themes discussed in the book, enriching the reader's understanding of the cultural interplay between Islamic and Western civilizations.)

Appendix H: Diplomatic Correspondence and Treaties

Translations and Summaries of Key Diplomatic Documents

This appendix provides translations and summaries of significant diplomatic correspondences, treaties, and agreements between Islamic states and European powers, offering insights into the political and diplomatic relationships throughout history.

1. Treaty of Hudaybiyyah (628 AD)

Context: Agreement between the Islamic community of Medina and the Quraysh tribe of Mecca.
Significance: Regarded as a pivotal event in Islamic history, showcasing early Islamic diplomatic principles.

2. The Treaty of Umar (7th Century)

Context: Terms offered by the second Caliph, Umar, to the Christians of Jerusalem upon its conquest.
Significance: An early example of Islamic governance and protection of non-Muslim religious rights.

3. The Pact of Toledo (1085)

Context: Agreement following the Christian conquest of Toledo, Spain.
Significance: Illustrates the treatment of Muslim minorities in reconquered Christian territories.

4. Peace Treaty of Al-Hudaybiyah (628 AD)

Context: A peace agreement between the Islamic prophet Muhammad and the Quraysh tribe of Mecca.
Significance: Seen as a victory for the Muslims due to its favorable terms and the ensuing period of peace.

5. Letters between Sultan Mehmed II and Various European Leaders

Context: Diplomatic correspondences during the Ottoman conquests.
Significance: Reflects the complex interplay between the Ottoman Empire and European powers.

6. Treaty of Karlowitz (1699)

Context: Ended the Great Turkish War between the Ottoman Empire and the Holy League.
Significance: Marked a turning point in Ottoman-European relations, with significant territorial losses for the Ottomans.

7. Sykes-Picot Agreement (1916)

Context: A secret agreement between the UK and France, with assent from Russia, on the division of the Ottoman Empire's territory.
Significance: Played a major role in shaping the modern Middle East.

8. The Balfour Declaration (1917)

Context: A letter from the British Foreign Secretary Arthur Balfour expressing support for a "national home for the Jewish people" in Palestine.
Significance: Significant for its impact on the Israeli-Palestinian conflict.

9. Camp David Accords (1978)

Context: Peace agreement between Egypt and Israel, brokered by U.S. President Jimmy Carter.
Significance: The first peace agreement between Israel and an Arab country.

10. Iran Nuclear Deal (2015)

Context: An agreement on Iran's nuclear program reached in Vienna between Iran and the P5+1.

Significance: Represents a significant diplomatic effort in the context of Middle Eastern politics and nuclear non-proliferation.

(These documents provide historical and contemporary insights into the diplomatic interactions between Islamic states and European powers, illustrating the complexities and dynamics of these relationships.)

Appendix I: Scientific and Philosophical Texts

Excerpts from Significant Works by Islamic and European Scholars

This appendix presents excerpts from influential scientific and philosophical works by Islamic and European scholars, demonstrating the exchange of knowledge and ideas across cultures.

1. "The Canon of Medicine" by Avicenna (Ibn Sina)

Content: A comprehensive medical encyclopedia that was a standard medical text in the Islamic world and Europe for centuries.
Excerpt: Sections on the theory of medicine, including the principles of treatment and the categorization of illnesses.

2. "The Book of Healing" by Avicenna (Ibn Sina)

Content: A vast philosophical and scientific encyclopedia covering various subjects, including logic, natural sciences, and psychology.
Excerpt: Discussions on metaphysics and the nature of knowledge.

3. "Almagest" by Ptolemy

Content: An astronomical treatise that was foundational in the field for many centuries.
Excerpt: Descriptions of the geocentric model and the movements of celestial bodies.

4. "The Incoherence of the Philosophers" by Al-Ghazali

Content: A critique of the philosophical works of Avicenna and other philosophers.
Excerpt: Arguments on causality and the limits of philosophical speculation.

5. "The Guide for the Perplexed" by Maimonides

Content: A philosophical work addressing the conflict between philosophy and religious teachings.
Excerpt: Analysis of prophetic knowledge and the nature of God.

6. "The Divine Comedy" by Dante Alighieri

Content: An epic poem that is a cornerstone of Italian literature, describing Dante's journey through Hell, Purgatory, and Heaven.
Excerpt: Passages that reflect the influence of Islamic thought, particularly in the depiction of the afterlife.

7. "Principia Mathematica" by Isaac Newton

Content: A work laying the groundwork for classical mechanics.
Excerpt: Formulations of the laws of motion and universal gravitation.

8. "Dialogue Concerning the Two Chief World Systems" by Galileo Galilei

Content: A defense of the Copernican theory of heliocentrism.
Excerpt: Arguments supporting the heliocentric model over the geocentric model.

9. "The Alhambra" by Washington Irving

Content: A collection of essays, verbal sketches, and stories inspired by the Moorish palace in Granada, Spain.
Excerpt: Descriptions that capture the interplay of Islamic and Western cultures.

10. "The Muqaddimah" by Ibn Khaldun

Content: An introduction to history that is considered the first work on the philosophy of history and sociology.
Excerpt: Analysis of the rise and fall of civilizations and the factors influencing them.

(These texts and excerpts provide insights into the intellectual legacy and cross-cultural exchanges between Islamic and European scholars, reflecting the rich history of shared knowledge and ideas.)

Appendix J: Discussion and Study Guide

Questions and Topics for Further Exploration

This appendix offers a discussion and study guide with questions and topics designed to deepen understanding and facilitate conversation about the themes presented in the book. It's suitable for educational settings, book clubs, or individual study.

1. The Crusades' Impact on Islamic and Western Relations

Discuss the long-term effects of the Crusades on Islamic and Western societies. How have these historical events shaped contemporary perceptions?

2. Islamic Contributions to Science and Philosophy

Explore the contributions of Islamic scholars during the Golden Age of Islam. How did these advancements influence European Renaissance?

3. The Role of Trade in Cultural Exchange

Examine the impact of trade routes, such as the Silk Road, on the exchange of ideas, goods, and culture between the Islamic world and Europe.

4. Comparative Religious Studies

Compare and contrast key teachings in Islam, Christianity, and Judaism. How have these religions influenced each other historically?

5. Women's Roles in Islamic and Western Societies

Analyze the changing roles and statuses of women in both Islamic and Western contexts. How have these changes reflected broader societal transformations?

6. The Effects of Colonialism

Discuss the impact of European colonialism on Islamic societies. How does this history affect modern political and social dynamics?

7. Modern Political Dynamics

Evaluate the influence of Islamic political thought on contemporary Western political ideas and vice versa.

8. Islamophobia and Its Historical Roots

Explore the origins and development of Islamophobia in Western societies. What steps can be taken to address these misconceptions?

9. Artistic and Literary Influences

Discuss examples of Islamic influences in Western art and literature, and vice versa. How do these influences reflect cultural exchange and appreciation?

10. Future of Islamic-Western Relations

Speculate on the future of Islamic-Western relations. What trends or current events might shape this relationship in the coming decades?

(This guide is intended to provoke thought and discussion, encouraging readers to engage more deeply with the book's content and to consider its relevance in the context of current global affairs.)

Table of Contents

Preface   3
    In the Shadows of History: Zionism, Islam, and the Western World   3
Chapter 1: The Crusades: Europe's Clash with Islam   **4**
    Section 1: Historical Background of the Crusades   4
    Section 2: European Motivations and Goals   6
    Section 3: Key Battles and Turning Points   7
    Section 4: Impact on European Mindset   8
    Section 5: Lessons Learned and Missed Opportunities   10
    Section 6: Trade and Cultural Exchanges   11
    Section 7: The Role of the Church   13
    Section 8: Muslim Perspective and Response   14
    Section 9: Legacy of the Crusades   15
Chapter 2: Ottoman Dominance and European Navigation   **18**
    Section 1: The Ottoman Empire's Rise   18
    Section 2: Control Over Trade Routes   20
    Section 3: The Quest for Alternative Routes   21
    Section 4: Economic Implications   22
    Section 5: Cultural and Knowledge Exchange   24
    Section 6: The Spice Trade and Its Lures   25
    Section 7: The Economic Implications   26
    Section 8: Cultural and Knowledge Exchange   27
    Section 9: The Impact of Islamic Naval Power   29
    Section 10: Resource Exploitation and Trade Dynamics   30
Chapter 3: The Reconquista and the New World   **31**
    Section 1: Background and Overview of the Reconquista   31
    Section 2: Christian and Muslim Dynamics in Iberia   33
    Section 3: The Fall of Granada and Its Aftermath   34
    Section 4: Financing and Motivation for Exploration   35
    Section 5: The Legacy of Iberian Rule in the Americas   37
    Section 6: The Transfer of Military Tactics and Governance   38
    Section 7: Religious Missionaries: Converting the New World   40
    Section 8: Religious Tolerance and Persecution   41
    Section 9: Economic Exploitation and Trade Dynamics   42
    Section 10: The Persistence of Indigenous Cultures   44
Chapter 4: Protestant Reformation: A New Religious Landscape   **45**
    Section 1: Martin Luther's 95 Theses and Its Impact   45
    Section 2: John Calvin's Teachings and Influence   46
    Section 3: The Spread of Protestantism in Europe   48

Section 4: Protestantism vs. Catholicism: A New Divide   49

Section 5: Religious Wars and Persecution   51

Section 6: The Role of Printing and Mass Communication   52

Section 7: Protestant Ethics and the Spirit of Capitalism   53

Section 8: The Reformation and European Exploration   55

Section 9: The Reformation and the Shaping of American Ideologies   56

Section 10: Modern Reflections on Interreligious Dynamics   57

Chapter 5: Islamic Finance and European Economy   **59**

Section 1: Islamic Principles of Finance   59

Section 2: Influence on European Banking and Commerce   60

Section 3: The Venetian Connection: Trade and Exchange   61

Section 4: Development of Joint-Stock Companies   62

Section 5: The Impact on Global Trade Networks   64

Section 6: Economic Competition and Cooperation   65

Section 7: Financing the Voyages of Discovery   66

Section 8: Islamic Influence on European Market Practices   68

Section 9: Shifts in Global Economic Power   69

Section 10: Long-Term Impacts on Western Financial Systems   70

Chapter 6: Philosophical and Cultural Exchange   **72**

Section 1: Islamic Philosophy and European Enlightenment   72

Section 2: Transmission of Knowledge: From Al-Andalus to Europe   73

Section 3: Influence of Islamic Scholars on European Thinkers   74

Section 4: The Renaissance and Arabic Texts   76

Section 5: Medicine, Mathematics, and Astronomy   77

Section 6: Islamic Art and Architecture's Influence   78

Section 7: The Role of Translation Movements   80

Section 8: The Impact on European Education Systems   81

Section 9: Intellectual Debates and Exchanges   82

Section 10: Enduring Legacies in Western Thought   84

Chapter 7: Voyages to the Americas: An Islamic Echo   **85**

Section 1: Early European Expeditions and Their Motives   85

Section 3: The Quest for Alternative Trade Routes   88

Section 4: Columbus and the Drive Westward   89

Section 5: Interactions with Indigenous Peoples   91

Section 6: The Role of Religion in Colonization   92

Section 7: European Settlement Strategies   93

Section 8: The Impact of Islamic Naval Power   95

Section 9: Resource Exploitation and Trade Dynamics   96

Section 10: The Transformation of the New World   98

Chapter 8: The Jewish Community: Between Worlds   **99**

Section 1: Jewish Life in Islamic and Christian Lands   99

Section 2: Expulsion from Spain and Its Consequences   100

Section 3: Jewish Diaspora and Their Role in Exploration   102

Section 4: Contributions to Nautical Science and Cartography   103

Section 5: Financing Voyages: The Jewish Contribution   104

Section 6: The Jewish Experience in the New World   106

Section 7: Religious Tolerance and Persecution   107

Section 8: Intellectual Exchange Among Jews, Christians, and Muslims   108

Section 9: Influence on Early American Settlements   110

Section 10: Legacy of Jewish Communities in Western Development   111

Chapter 9: The Ottomans: Europe's Eastern Neighbor   **112**

Section 1: Rise and Expansion of the Ottoman Empire   112

Section 2: Ottoman Influence on European Politics and Warfare   114

Section 3: Trade and Diplomacy Between Ottomans and Europeans   115

Section 4: Ottoman Naval Power and Mediterranean Dynamics   117

Section 5: Cultural and Artistic Exchange   118

Section 6: The Siege of Vienna and Its Aftermath   120

Section 7: European Perceptions of the Ottomans   121

Section 8: Ottoman Legacy in European Architecture and Art   122

Section 9: Ottoman Decline and European Ascendancy   124

Section 10: Lasting Impacts on European Identity   125

Chapter 10: Comparative Religious Studies: Islam, Christianity, Judaism   **126**

Section 1: Fundamental Beliefs of Islam, Christianity, and Judaism   126

Section 2: Theological Similarities and Differences   128

Section 3: Historical Intersections and Conflicts   129

Section 4: Influence of Religious Thought on Governance   130

Section 5: The Role of Religion in Exploration and Colonization   132

Section 6: Religious Tolerance and Persecution Across Cultures   133

Section 7: Mysticism and Philosophical Thought   135

Section 8: Religious Reforms and Their Impacts   136

Section 9: Scriptural Interpretations and Their Influence   137

Section 10: Modern Reflections on Interreligious Dynamics   139

Chapter 11: Military Strategies: From Crusades to Colonial Wars   **140**

Section 1: Crusades as a Prelude to Modern Warfare   140

Section 2: Islamic Military Tactics and European Adaptations   141

Section 3: Naval Battles and Technological Advances   143

Section 4: The Role of Fortifications: From Castles to Colonial Forts   144

Section 5: European Conquests in the New World   146

Section 6: Guerrilla Warfare and Indigenous Resistance   147

Section 7: Arms Trade and Military Alliances   149

Section 8: The Impact of Gunpowder   150

Section 9: Siege Warfare: A Comparative Study   151

Section 10: Military Legacy in Modern Warfare ... 153

Chapter 12: Cultural Assimilation and Resistance in the New World ... **155**

Section 1: Indigenous Cultures and European Settlers ... 155

Section 2: Models of Cultural Assimilation ... 156

Section 3: Resistance and Revolt Against Colonizers ... 157

Section 4: The Role of Religion in Cultural Exchange ... 159

Section 5: Syncretism: Blending of Cultures and Beliefs ... 160

Section 6: Language and Literature as Tools of Assimilation ... 162

Section 7: Education and Indoctrination Strategies ... 163

Section 8: Economic Exploitation and Its Cultural Effects ... 164

Section 9: The Persistence of Indigenous Cultures ... 166

Section 10: Long-Term Cultural Impacts of Colonization ... 167

Chapter 13: European Enlightenment and Islamic Legacy ... **169**

Section 1: Defining the European Enlightenment ... 169

Section 2: Islamic Contributions to European Thought ... 170

Section 3: Philosophers Influenced by Islamic Works ... 172

Section 4: Enlightenment Ideals and Islamic Philosophy ... 173

Section 5: Scientific Revolution: An Intersection of Cultures ... 175

Section 6: The Role of Rationalism and Empiricism ... 177

Section 7: Political Theories and Islamic Governance ... 178

Section 8: Social Contract Theory and Islamic Law ... 179

Section 9: Enlightenment in Art and Architecture ... 181

Section 10: The Enlightenment's Legacy in Modern Western Thought ... 182

Chapter 14: Diplomacy and Alliances: East Meets West ... **184**

Section 1: Early Diplomatic Contacts Between Muslims and Christians ... 184

Section 3: Trade Agreements and Peace Treaties ... 187

Section 4: Cultural Diplomacy and Exchange ... 188

Section 5: Diplomatic Missions and Ambassadors ... 189

Section 6: Espionage and Intelligence in Diplomatic Relations ... 191

Section 7: Religious Diplomacy: Popes and Caliphs ... 192

Section 8: Treaty of Westphalia and Its Impact ... 194

Section 9: Modern Diplomatic Relations and Their Roots ... 195

Section 10: The Role of Diplomacy in Shaping Modern Europe ... 197

Chapter 15: America's Founding Ideologies and Islamic Influence ... **198**

Section 1: Principles of American Democracy ... 198

Section 2: Islamic Governance and Its Influence ... 200

Section 3: The Constitution: A Comparative Analysis ... 201

Section 4: Enlightenment Thinkers and Islamic Philosophy ... 203

Section 5: Religious Freedom and Pluralism ... 204

Section 6: Economic Theories and Islamic Principles ... 206

Section 7: The Role of Education and Scholarship ... 207

Section 8: Foreign Policy: Islamic Influence on Early American Relations   209

Section 9: Debates on Slavery and Human Rights   210

Section 10: The Legacy of Islamic Thought in American Ideology   211

Chapter 16: The Ottoman Legacy in European Art and Culture   **213**

Section 1: Influence of Ottoman Art on European Styles   213

Section 2: Architectural Exchange: Mosques and Cathedrals   214

Section 3: Ottoman Contributions to European Music   216

Section 4: Fashion and Textiles: A Cross-Cultural Dialogue   217

Section 5: Culinary Influences and Shared Tastes   218

Section 6: Literature and Poetry: Echoes of the East   219

Section 7: Ottoman Themes in European Painting   221

Section 8: Artistic Techniques and Innovations   222

Section 9: The Role of Patronage in Artistic Exchange   224

Section 10: Enduring Influences in Modern Art and Design   225

Chapter 17: Legal Systems: Islamic Law and Western Jurisprudence   **226**

Section 1: Foundations of Islamic Law (Sharia)   226

Section 2: Influence of Islamic Jurisprudence on European Legal Thought   227

Section 3: Comparative Study of Legal Principles   229

Section 4: The Concept of Justice in Islam and the West   230

Section 5: Contract Law and Commercial Ethics   232

Section 6: Rights and Responsibilities of Citizens   233

Section 7: Criminal Law: Punishments and Procedures   234

Section 8: The Evolution of International Law   236

Section 9: Contemporary Legal Challenges and Islamic Perspectives   237

Section 10: Legacy of Islamic Law in Modern Legal Systems   239

Chapter 18: Medicine: Islamic Knowledge and European Enlightenment   **240**

Section 1: Islamic Medical Practices and Their Transmission to Europe   240

Section 2: Key Islamic Physicians and Their Contributions   241

Section 3: The Impact of Islamic Texts on European Medicine   243

Section 4: Innovations in Surgery and Pharmacology   244

Section 5: Public Health and Hospital Systems   245

Section 6: Anatomy and Physiology: A Comparative Study   247

Section 7: Medical Ethics in Islamic and Western Traditions   248

Section 8: The Role of Medical Schools and Universities   250

Section 9: Disease and Epidemics: Cross-Cultural Responses   251

Section 10: The Lasting Influence of Islamic Medicine   253

Chapter 19: Gender and Society: Women in Islamic and Western Worlds   **254**

Section 1: Women's Roles in Islamic Societies   254

Section 2: Comparative Analysis of Women's Rights and Status   255

Section 3: Influence of Islamic Feminine Ideals on Europe   257

Section 4: Prominent Women Figures in Islamic History   258

Section 5: The Renaissance and Changing Roles of Women 259
Section 6: Education and Literacy for Women 260
Section 7: Marriage, Family, and Social Norms 262
Section 8: Women in Politics and Leadership 263
Section 9: Feminism and Women's Movements: A Historical Perspective 265
Section 10: Ongoing Challenges and Progress 266
Chapter 20: Misconceptions and Legacy: Islam in Western Consciousness **268**
Section 1: Common Misconceptions About Islam in the West 268
Section 2: Historical Roots of Islamophobia 269
Section 3: The Crusades and Their Long-Term Impact on Perceptions 270
Section 4: Orientalism and Representation in Literature and Art 272
Section 5: Impact of Colonialism on Islamic-Western Relations 273
Section 6: Islam in Contemporary Western Media and Education 274
Section 7: Interfaith Dialogue and Understanding 276
Section 8: Islam's Contribution to Modern Science and Technology 277
Section 9: Contemporary Political Dynamics and Islamic Influence 278
Section 10: Reassessing the Islamic Legacy in Western Civilization 280
Appendices **281**
Appendix A: Timeline of Key Events 281
Appendix B: Biographies of Key Figures 286
Appendix C: Maps and Geographic Overviews 288
Appendix D: Comparative Study of Religious Texts 289
Appendix E: Glossary of Terms 290
Appendix F: Annotated Bibliography 292
Appendix G: Collection of Artistic Works 294
Appendix H: Diplomatic Correspondence and Treaties 295
Appendix I: Scientific and Philosophical Texts 297
Appendix J: Discussion and Study Guide 299
Table of Contents **301**